AUSTRALIA GOES TO WASHINGTON

75 YEARS OF AUSTRALIAN REPRESENTATION IN THE UNITED STATES, 1940–2015

AUSTRALIA GOES TO WASHINGTON

75 YEARS OF AUSTRALIAN REPRESENTATION IN THE UNITED STATES, 1940–2015

EDITED BY DAVID LOWE,
DAVID LEE AND CARL BRIDGE

Australian
National
University

PRESS

ANU
PRESS

Published by ANU Press
The Australian National University
Acton ACT 2601, Australia
Email: anupress@anu.edu.au
This title is also available online at press.anu.edu.au

National Library of Australia Cataloguing-in-Publication entry

Title: Australia goes to Washington : 75 years of Australian
                 representation in the United States,
                 1940-2015 / David Lowe (editor); Carl
                 Bridge (editor); David Lee (editor).

ISBN: 9781760460785 (paperback) 9781760460792 (ebook)

Subjects: Diplomatic and consular service, Australian--United States.
                 Ambassadors--Australia--History.
                 Diplomacy--History.
                 Australia--Foreign relations--United States.
                 United States--Foreign relations--Australia.

Other Creators/Contributors:
                 Lowe, David, 1964- editor.
                 Bridge, Carl, 1950- editor.
                 Lee, David, 1965- editor.

Dewey Number: 327.94073

Cover design and layout by ANU Press.

Cover photograph: US President Richard Nixon (left) with Australian Ambassador
to the United States, Keith Waller, in the White House, Washington, 3 March 1970.
Source: White House, US Government.

Contents

Acknowledgements

The conference and witness seminar facilitating the production of this book enjoyed support from the Contemporary Histories Research Group at Deakin University and the Australian Department of Foreign Affairs and Trade (DFAT). Gina Dow in the department provided support in relation to photographs. In addition, Kings College London and the Australian embassy in Washington provided assistance for which we are grateful; and a special thanks to former DFAT and embassy officer Tanya Smith, whose advice in relation to a number of matters was invaluable.

Several doctoral students at Deakin University also played important roles. In particular, for his assistance in relation to the conference and witness seminar, we thank Chris Speldewinde, and for her help towards the production of this volume, we thank Celeste Thorn. Mathew Turner has provided assistance in generating transcripts of the witness seminar that partners this volume (blogs.deakin.edu.au/contemporary-history-studies/witness-seminars/).

Acronyms

ALP	Australian Labor Party
AMS	Agreement on Maintaining Security
ANSF	Afghan National Security Forces
ANU	The Australian National University
ANZUS	Australia, New Zealand, United States Security Treaty
APEC	Asia-Pacific Economic Cooperation
ASEAN	Association of Southeast Asian Nations
ASIO	Australian Security Intelligence Organisation
AusMin	Australia–United States Ministerial Consultations
AWB	Australian Wheat Board
DEIP	Dairy Export Incentive Program
DFAT	Department of Foreign Affairs and Trade
EAS	East Asia Summit
EASI	East Asia Strategy Initiative
EEC	European Economic Community
EEP	US Export Enhancement Program
FEC	Far Eastern Commission
FTA	Free Trade Agreement
GATT	General Agreement on Tariffs and Trade
GDP	gross domestic product
IMF	International Monetary Fund
INTERFET	International Force for East Timor
MFN	Most Favoured Nation
MX	Missile-eXperimental

NAA	National Archives of Australia
NAFTA	North American Free Trade Agreement
NATO	North Atlantic Treaty Organization
NLA	National Library of Australia
NSC	National Security Council
ONA	Office of National Assessments
PACOM	Pacific Command
PRG	Provisional Revolutionary Government of the Republic of South Vietnam
SEATO	Southeast Asia Treaty Organization
SPNFZ	South Pacific Nuclear Free Zone
TPP	Trans-Pacific Partnership
UN	United Nations
WNG	West New Guinea
WTO	World Trade Organization

1

The Australian embassy in Washington

David Lowe, David Lee and Carl Bridge

The year 2015 marked the 75th anniversary of Australian diplomatic representation in Washington. It also marked the end of one era and the start of a new one for the current embassy building on Massachusetts Avenue on Scott Circle, which is being demolished and rebuilt in order to meet expanded needs. The current embassy building has served Australians since 1969. While the milestone of 75 years of Australian representation in Washington passed quietly, the rich history of prominent Australians, including some of our best-known ambassadors, working at the coalface of Australia–US relations warrants more investigation than there has been to date. This study aims to address this omission.

Without overburdening the construction metaphor, the theme of substantial rebuilding while strengthening Australia's presence and range of diplomatic endeavours sets an appropriate tone for the trajectory of this book. From humble beginnings when RG Casey arrived to found the legation in 1940 (in a large house on Cleveland Avenue) with a modest staff of five, to today, when the embassy boasts more than 250 personnel, marks a spectacular rise in the Australian presence. Yet neither the increased numbers nor an implied sense of steady growth in people-to-people contact between Australians and influential Americans will do by way of telling the full and complex story of Australia's representation.

The legation set up in 1940 laid the foundations for one of Australia's longest functioning posts. Having established an Australian High Commission in London and appointed the first high commissioner (Sir George Reid) at the beginning of 1910, Australian governments waited 30 years before establishing any other overseas posts. Washington was one of three set up in 1940, the others being Ottawa and Tokyo. The period 1940 to 2015 saw extraordinary changes in the modes of communication between nations, the types of personnel who contribute to diplomacy, and the volumes of politicians, visitors and others drawing on embassy resources and time. One of the tasks of this book is to assess the significance of such changes as they played out in relation to particular Australian ambassadors in Washington and particular diplomatic episodes of note.

Similarly, the expectations and performances of different ambassadors over time is a constant thread. Ambassadors work to expectations different from those attached to the leaders of governments. The best-known early 'diplomatic' encounter between Australia and the US, the testy negotiations between Australian Prime Minister William Morris Hughes (best remembered as 'Billy' Hughes) and US President Woodrow Wilson in Paris at the end of World War I, is therefore unhelpful even if it makes for compelling reading. Hughes clashed noisily with Wilson, whose attempts to undermine European control over colonies and inform the peacemaking with liberal internationalist principles met resistance from others in addition to Hughes; but, given Hughes's penchant for colourful metaphor and cutting riposte, it is not surprising that he attracted attention for his behaviour. In the eyes of some observers, Hughes brought something of the Anzac legend to the conduct of Australian diplomacy in 1919, punching above his weight, heedless of recognised forms of authority, and informed by a strident, self-interested brand of nationalism. To others, including members of the Australian delegation, he was more noisy than compelling, and he hardly set a diplomatic standard for US–Australia relations.[1]

If there is such a thing as an 'ideal' Australian Ambassador to the United States, what are the characteristics most needed? Such a question invites consideration of both generic attributes – those that make for an ideal

---

1   See Carl Bridge, *William Hughes: Australia*, Haus Histories, London, 2011.

ambassador abroad – and particular attributes that lend themselves to service in the US. Among the generic qualities listed by Joan Beaumont in her analysis of Australian diplomats serving overseas up to 1969 were:

> integrity, intelligence, negotiating skills. The ability to win the trust of foreign governments and leaders in the wider community, sociability, cultural sensitivity, a willingness to acquire an understanding of the political and historical background of other countries, and of course, diplomacy itself – tact and adroitness in personal relationships.[2]

The qualities of the ideal diplomat have attracted special attention from scholars for the period leading up to our starting point of 1940, on account of diplomats' prominence in the interwar years, but also for their inability to prevent war, and the suggestion that this was the beginning of decline for an elite group that had hitherto successfully managed international relations at some remove from both national leaders and their populaces. World War II then marked a temporary sidelining of professional diplomats as heads of government and their advisers dominated wartime summits; and, beyond 1945, the start of a new era of increased air travel and telecommunications logically meant that postwar governments grew less dependent on ambassadors overseas.

This snapshot of diplomatic change is analysed in rich detail, and through multiple case studies, in two well-known collections of essays led by Gordon Craig, *The Diplomats, 1919–1939*, and *The Diplomats, 1939–1979*.[3] The earlier volume focused on Europe and the US, with one chapter on Japan, and the second volume incorporated more of Asia and the Middle East. Australia, as well as Canada, Africa and Latin America, appeared in neither. Otherwise, the most notable difference between the two volumes was the shift in the second towards political leaders as primary agents. Reviewers generally found the second volume less satisfactory than the first for, to summarise the main lines of criticism, in acknowledging the power shift away from the diplomat in international relations towards political leaders and the democratisation of foreign policy (including a greater role for public opinion), the second volume

2   Joan Beaumont, Christopher Waters, David Lowe, with Garry Woodard, *Ministers, Mandarins and Diplomats: Australian Foreign Policy Making, 1941–1969*, Melbourne University Press, Melbourne, 2003, p. 162.
3   Gordon Craig and Felix Gilbert (eds), *The Diplomats: 1919–1939*, Atheneum, New York, 1963; and Gordon Craig and Francis Loewenheim (eds), *The Diplomats, 1939–1979*, Princeton University Press, Princeton, 1994.

means travelling; ask for advice to keep up with the complex nature of changing policy considerations; treat embassy staff as professionals and recognise their skills; and recognise that Australia's security interests and those of the US may not always be the same.[9]

There are some common themes running through these analyses and recommendations, some of which resemble extensions of those more generic skills identified by Beaumont, Gyngell and Wesley. But between the desirable generic attributes and those especially appropriate for Washington also lie qualities of energy and scale. Being able to manage networks of connection on a scale not seen at most other posts, while hosting a seemingly continuous flow of important Australian visitors and leading a large embassy team, are among the most notable of requirements. Similarly, high levels of intellectual and physical energy are needed in order to keep up with the cascade of information relating to politics and policy considerations and changes in Washington while ensuring, at the same time, that adequate attention is paid to the states beyond the District of Columbia and New York, and that the full diversity of the US is appreciated. And the need to be resolute and possibly even forceful in advancing distinctively Australian interests is the other distinguishing characteristic. Logically, this should go without saying for all heads of overseas missions, but the suggestion by those with the greatest experience is that this is especially needed in Washington, where Australian and US security interests, in particular, can readily be conflated. The chapters that follow pay attention to these 'special' Washington factors of scale, energy, personal relationships leading to influence and the opening of doors, and judicious assertion of Australian interests in their analyses of ambassadors' performances.

While growing in size and reach, it is not the case that Australia's embassy in Washington has remained completely under the public radar. The embassy, along with the High Commission in London, has occasionally been in the public eye for reasons varying from important security and trade issues in Australia's relations with those key countries to speculation and rumours surrounding likely appointees. Australian governments, both Labor and Coalition, have repeatedly rewarded former politicians with the London and Washington posts – but not to the exclusion of senior career diplomats who have increasingly entered

---

9   John McCarthy, 'From One Ambassador to Another: Good luck if you go to Washington, Joe', *The Drum*, 23 September 2015, www.abc.net.au/news/2015-09-23/mccarthy-from-one-ambassador-to-another/6796964.

the tale. Public interest in the people and work of the Washington embassy may in the past have been too often led by gossip columns and fitful in occurrence, so a thorough historical analysis is well overdue. In this context too then, the need for reflection on and analysis of the embassy's work is apparent, and the embassy's 75th anniversary is a suitable occasion on which to perform this task.

With support from the Australian Department of Foreign Affairs and Trade, a group of experts on Australia in world affairs and Australia–US relations gathered at Deakin University's Waterfront campus in Geelong in October 2014 to examine the thickening ties, crises and changing priorities as experienced by Australia's ambassadors and leading diplomats in Washington during this period. Their analyses, bearing the fruits of original research and benefiting from having tested ideas among colleagues, make up this volume. They are organised as chapters, mostly according to an ambassador's term in Washington, but complemented by overviews where incumbents were short-term or to cater for topics of special interest.

From the outset, the chapters that follow had this consolidated volume in mind. They chart several trends in Australia's overseas policy that continue to be debated today. They consider the American security alliance in the context of World War II, the Cold War and in the post-9/11 era; the distinctive social-cultural milieu in which Australians operate in Washington; the rise of the US Congress as a focal point for embassy work; the changing composition of representatives and tasks according to trade, intelligence and defence considerations; the crisis moments caused by Cold War and conflict in Southeast Asia and by independently minded Australian prime ministers such as Whitlam; and the particular interpersonal relationships, positive and otherwise, that shaped ambassadors' tenures.

We do not cover here in detail the 'pre-history' of official representation prior to 1940. This was significant and led by successive trade commissioners from 1918 to 1930, before the Great Depression hit, and then again from 1938 when Lewis Macgregor restored the line by heading the New York office. The role of trade commissioners continued to be important, and their number expanded after 1940, but we are fortunate that Boris Schedvin has provided much of this story in his history of the Australian trade commissioner service.[10] Similarly, a forthcoming illustrated study of the Australian Embassy Residence in Washington by Christine Wallace and others will complement this volume.

The chapters here benefit from the input of past and present Australian representatives who have served in the embassy in Washington. A feature of the gathering in October 2014 was the presence of former Australian diplomats who worked in the embassy between the 1980s and recent times. They agreed to participate in a witness seminar, expertly facilitated by award-winning journalist Jim Middleton, himself a frequenter of Washington in the 1980s and more recently. The witness seminar is a particularly specialised form of oral history, wherein several people associated with a particular set of circumstances or events are invited to meet together to discuss, debate, and even disagree about their reminiscences. Originally developed by the Institute of Contemporary British History in London in the 1980s, this program established that policymakers, both politicians and civil servants, could and should talk to academics on the record and in public. This engagement consequently marked a cultural sea change in the relationship between policymakers and scholars, and helped to consolidate the principle of open government.

The British have led the way in witness seminars, including a series run in conjunction with the Foreign and Commonwealth Office recalling the activities of overseas embassies and high commissions, and particular episodes such as the Falklands War and the fall of the Berlin Wall.[11] The event held at Deakin in 2014 took its cue from this run of successful events in Britain, and also from the publication in 2010 of a history of Australia's High Commissioners in London that drew partly on witness testimony.[12] The first part of the event featured former members of the Australian Department of Foreign Affairs (and Trade from 1987) and former members of the Australian Armed Forces who served in the Washington embassy in conversation with Jim Middleton and each other; and then answering questions from the floor. These recollections

---

10   Boris Schedvin, *Emissaries of Trade: A History of the Australian Trade Commissioner Service*, Austrade and the Australian Department of Foreign Affairs and Trade, Commonwealth Government of Australia, Canberra, 2008, pp. 21–24 and 66–68 for commissioners prior to 1940.

11   See, for example, Michael D Kandiah (ed.), *The History, Role and Functions of the British High Commission in Canberra*, Foreign & Commonwealth Office, London, 2013, issuu.com/fcohistorians/docs/Canberra_witness_seminar/13.

12   Carl Bridge, Frank Bongiorno and David Lee (eds), *The High Commissioners: Australia's Representatives in the United Kingdom, 1910–2010*, WHH Publishing, Canberra, 2010.

and exchanges were recorded and formed the basis of an agreed transcript, now available online to complement this book.[13] And the views expressed in the witness seminar also informed the subsequent academic presentations and chapters making up this volume.

The structure of this book takes its cue from the decisions and events behind the establishment and subsequent growth of Australia's diplomatic representation in Washington. Impending world war in 1939, with its attendant threats in the Pacific, led Joseph Lyons' Government to decide finally, after years of requests from the American side, to establish a diplomatic legation in Washington. In due course, Lyons' successor as prime minister, Robert Menzies, chose a senior Cabinet colleague with diplomatic experience in London, Richard Casey, to be Australia's founding minister to Washington, and Casey presented his credentials to President Roosevelt in February 1940. Casey was succeeded during the war by two other very distinguished Australians, Sir Owen Dixon, a High Court judge, and Sir Frederic Eggleston, long-time Chairman of the Commonwealth Grants Commission, whose experience of diplomacy stretched back to Versailles and who had been Minister to China. As Carl Bridge points out in his chapter, Casey was a model diplomat, establishing Australia and its concerns in the American public mind by means of a successful publicity campaign, while at the same time winning the confidence of Roosevelt and his inner circle, and networking brilliantly among the American military, administration, and in the business and media worlds. Casey actively and most effectively paved the way for Australia's wartime alliance with the US, looking to America strategically well in advance of Prime Minister John Curtin's more famous 'Look' in the wake of the Japanese attack on Pearl Harbor. Dixon, though a more diffident man and lacking Casey's political nous, mastered the intricacies of wartime supply at the height of the Pacific War, and was trusted implicitly by the Americans. Eggleston, arriving at the tail end of the war and literally too immobile for effective diplomacy in that frenetic period, was eclipsed by Minister for External Affairs Dr Herbert Vere Evatt's mercurial brilliance at the San Francisco conference that established the UN, but nevertheless proved a shrewd and energetic analyst of American politics and policy.

---

13   Available at: blogs.deakin.edu.au/contemporary-history-studies/witness-seminars/.

The first Australian to be appointed as an ambassador, marking the postwar upgrade from legation, was Norman Makin, former Labor politician. Makin occupied the post for four-and-a-half years from 1946 to 1951, and worked hard in constrained circumstances to build a solid foundation and reputation among Washington's diplomatic corps. As Frank Bongiorno outlines in his chapter on Makin, some of the constraints he faced were resources – in the aftermath of the war, a dollar shortage and competing needs for the Chifley Government made for very tight circumstances in new embassy. Some of the constraints related to his minister, still Evatt, who would alternate between sharp criticism of embassy staff and extraordinary demands on their time. Another source of constraint was Makin's own reluctance to immerse himself either in the bigger issues of diplomacy joining the Australians and Americans or the whirl of the Washington cocktail circuit, which he despised. Despite what, at first glance, would appear to be very unpropitious set of circumstances for a new ambassador, Bongiorno suggests that Makin was effective in warding off the excesses of a rampaging Evatt, and Makin's integrity, kindness and Methodist values struck a good note with many, both within the embassy and in Washington.

Makin was followed by an ambassador who was almost an exact opposite. Percy Spender, Australia's longest-serving Ambassador to the US, from 1951 to 1958, arrived there without seeming to relinquish his former role as Minister for External Affairs. He determinedly built up the embassy in size and reputation, and thrust himself into most of the big issues of the day, often without waiting for direction from Canberra. These issues included the attempt to expand the remit and consultative and committee activity around the new Australia, New Zealand, United States Security Treaty (ANZUS), and an increasingly testing environment in the UN as more of the decolonising world joined as members. And, in the eyes of many policymakers, the Cold War took root in Asia, with communist-led challenges in Korea and then French Vietnam causing special concern for the US establishment. Spender saw the early to mid-1950s as a pivotal time in which Australia needed to demonstrate its credentials as an alliance partner with the Americans, and he fretted on the consequences of not being in the right circle when some of the biggest strategic decisions would be made. Given that his term saw the successful testing of US and Russian hydrogen bombs, and serious discussion of the use of atomic weapons in Vietnam, his alarm was hardly exaggerated. His attentiveness to big issues and his success in gaining access to high circles also reflected how hard and effectively he worked. But, as David Lowe suggests in his chapter on the Spender period, there was another more psychological-social dimension to Spender's behaviour. This gregarious man who, with his wife Jean, fitted well into the Washington social set and befriended several high-ranking Americans, including the Dulles brothers, feared being 'on the outer' and what that might mean for Australia – to the extent that it coloured his ambassadorship more than has been appreciated.

Spender's successor, another Menzies Government political appointee in Howard Beale, also enjoyed strong relationships with Washington's policymaking elite. In his chapter, Matthew Jordan analyses Beale's six-year tenure from 1958, a period that saw him locked in testing exchanges about the level of Australia's preparedness to act under the Southeast Asia Treaty Organization in defence of Laos against communist-led challenges, and about the remit of the ANZUS Treaty at the time of Indonesia's incorporation of West New Guinea and then Konfrontasi aimed the newly formed Malaysia. Beale worked hard and effectively in representing Canberra's views and in reporting back the messages emerging from his engagements with President Kennedy and leading members of the State and Defense departments. He initially succeeded in encouraging US thinking about the operability of ANZUS in an indirect way that involved Australia's commitments to Malaya/Malaysia: Australian commitments to countering the Cold War struggle against communism in Southeast Asia could be considered in the context of supporting Malaya/Malaysia, and hence an ally of the US was pulling its weight. But this equation was hard to sustain in the face of minimal Australian defence spending and the need for the Americans to think flexibly in order not to push Indonesia's President Sukarno into the communist camp; and, like his colleagues in Canberra, Beale struggled to make a bigger positive mark in the US–Australia security relationship.

In a case study from the early 1960s, Chris Waters invites us to consider the embassy's engagement with policy-making. He analyses the work of the four-power Study Group convened in Washington in 1962 to examine future trends and development in the colonial territories of the South Pacific. The group comprised the United States, Britain, Australia and New Zealand, and arose from both the general quickening of pace in the dismantling of overseas empires and a recommendation from an ANZUS meeting. Comprised of talented diplomats, the Study Group soon roamed beyond its initial fact-gathering and problem-identification towards policy suggestions. As Waters shows, while Minister for

External Affairs Garfield Barwick was happy with its conclusions, and with Australia's allies' interest in the region, the Menzies Cabinet reacted severely to the Study Group's report. Paul Hasluck, Minister for the Territories, led the counter-action, incensed at the suggestion that Cabinet's policy direction could be set by a group of officials meeting in Washington. The Australian Cabinet watered down the significance of the report, but was not successful in marginalising it in bureaucratic circles. Waters argues that the Study Group's main recommendations did, in fact, serve as important guidelines for Australian officials for the remainder of the decade. The episode highlighted the growing role of diplomats as experts who could help shape Australia's foreign policy.

The first career diplomat to be appointed to the Washington embassy, Keith Waller, was renowned for his tact and insight, and was a logical appointee. Despite this, he arrived by default. He was chosen only after Menzies had searched hard among his ministers and had concluded that none were suitable. Waller served in Washington from 1964 to 1970. He spent unusually long hours with President Lyndon B Johnson, mostly by accompanying Ed Clark, Johnson's appointed Ambassador to Australia and an adviser he relied on for counsel, to visit the President. Despite this, as Peter Edwards shows in his chapter, Waller was not able to exercise any particularly decisive influence in Washington beyond dropping into conversation with other American officials his easy access to the White House. Early in his tenure, the issue that had exercised his predecessors, namely the imprecise safeguards that ANZUS might offer in the event of clashes with Indonesia, did not clarify markedly. The Harold Holt–Johnson relationship was a strong one, but too brief, and the escalation of both American and Australian commitments of ground troops in Vietnam enmeshed the fortunes of the two allies, but not with any sense that Canberra would be kept informed of US strategic thinking. When Richard Nixon became President at the beginning of 1969, this lack of consultation grew sharper; but by this time deteriorating relationships within the Coalition Government in Canberra also made life difficult for an Australian Ambassador in Washington, and Waller was glad to leave to become Secretary of the Department of External Affairs.

The election in December 1972 of the first Labor administration since 1949, as Jeremy Hearder demonstrates, ushered in three of the most turbulent years in the history of the Australian–American relationship. Two of Australia's most experienced diplomats helped the Australian

Government to navigate this first ANZUS crisis in the period from December 1972 to November 1975. These were a former Permanent Secretary of the Department of Foreign Affairs, Sir James Plimsoll, and another of Australia's most experienced diplomats, Sir Patrick Shaw.

Shaw had been both Ambassador to Indonesia and Permanent Representative to the UN, New York. Plimsoll's extraordinary standing as a diplomat and the range of his contacts in America helped smooth the substantial rift that developed in Australian–American relations over matters such as US policies on the conflict in Indochina. As the first of David Lee's two chapters shows, Shaw, who took up his posting in Washington in 1974, played a similar role to Plimsoll in robustly representing his government while at the same time seeking to maintain cordial relations with the US. After two years of what must have been one of his most challenging postings, he died of a heart attack in December 1975.

From 1975 to 1983 the Liberal–National Country Party Government led by Malcolm Fraser moved to strengthen the Australia–US relationship, resisting the efforts by US Democrat President Jimmy Carter to demilitarise the Indian Ocean and seeking to widen the scope of the ANZUS alliance to extend to the Indian Ocean. Reflecting the status of the post of Ambassador to the US was that its occupants were former permanent secretaries of the Department of Foreign Affairs: Alan Renouf from 1977 to 1979 and Sir Nicholas Parkinson, who served from 1976 to 1977 and again from 1979 to 1982. The embassy in Washington during this period helped the Fraser Government handle an issue that would loom as extremely divisive in the 1980s: visits to Australia and New Zealand by US naval vessels that might be nuclear-powered or be carrying nuclear weapons.

When in 1982 the leader of the opposition, Bill Hayden, appeared to equivocate on whether a future Labor administration would continue to permit such ship visits, Prime Minister Malcolm Fraser moved to exploit the Australian Labor Party's (ALP) weakness on the Australia–US alliance in the same way as Robert Menzies had done in 1963 over Labor's attitude to the North West Cape naval base. The subject of David Lee's second chapter is the role of the embassy in Washington in helping the Hawke Government deal with two crises in the Australia–US relationship in the 1980s. The first was the crisis within the ANZUS alliance precipitated by the New Zealand Labour Government's implementation in 1984 of its platform to refuse entry to nuclear-armed or nuclear-powered vessels. The second was brought on by the US Government's decision in 1985 to subsidise agricultural exports to the detriment of Australian primary producers.

Leading the Australian embassy in Washington during this time of crisis was one political appointment and one career diplomat. Sir Robert Cotton was the first political appointment to the position since Beale. Cotton was a Liberal senator from New South Wales who had held senior portfolios in the Gorton, McMahon and Fraser governments and then the position of Consul-General in New York. Appointed to Washington by Malcolm Fraser in 1982, Cotton was gladly retained by Labor Prime Minister Bob Hawke. Hawke, in so doing, was anxious to reassure President Ronald Reagan and his Cabinet of the essentially bipartisan character of Australian policy towards the US. In 1983 Hawke and his Minister for Foreign Affairs, Bill Hayden, brokered a compromise by which the government would continue to support US ship visits to Australia while also introducing a package of measures aimed at promoting the reduction of the nuclear arms race and the establishment of a nuclear-free zone in the South Pacific. This *modus vivendi* in the ALP, however, was strained in 1984 with the election of a New Zealand Labour Government. The ANZUS crisis of 1984 and 1985 was more serious than the contretemps between Whitlam and President Nixon between 1972 and 1974 because it led, in the end, to the dissolution of the tripartite ANZUS alliance that had been in place since 1951. The embassy, however, helped the Australian Government to soften the effect of the rupture on Australia by persuading the US to leave the ANZUS Treaty intact as an umbrella to govern the alliance relationship between Australia and the US, including regular bilateral meetings between the two nations that became known as AusMin.

But no sooner had the ANZUS crisis been settled when another major crisis developed over US trade and economic policy, namely the US decision to subsidise agricultural exports as part of its trade war with the European Economic Community. The Ambassador from 1985 to 1989 was the experienced career diplomat, Rawdon Dalrymple. A major focus of the embassy under Dalrymple's leadership was the lobbying of the administration and, increasingly, Congress, to mitigate the effect of US trade and economic policy on efficient Australian exporters. In both the ANZUS crisis from 1984 to 1986 and the economic disputes from 1985 onward, the embassy was an important means of communication between the Australian and the US Government and Congress.

The embassy was, however, not the only mode of communication. The US embassy in Canberra was an important conduit and, increasingly, prime ministers conducted their own diplomacy by telephone – or sometimes by way of special emissary, as Plimsoll had found during the Whitlam years.

James Cotton argues in his chapter that Australia's foreign relations in the 1990s may be viewed as beginning in 1989 with the destruction of the Berlin Wall and the collapse of communism in Eastern Europe, and ending with the terrorist attacks in the US in 2001. The ending of the Cold War coincided with a major focus by the Australian Government on Australia's increasingly important economic relationship with Northeast Asia and its political relationship with Southeast Asia. The Hawke Government's launching of Asia-Pacific Economic Cooperation (APEC) in 1989, Cotton argues, may be seen as being designed to help prepare Australia for a diminishing US economic impact on Australia. But although APEC was at first conceived without the US as a member, an APEC including the US became the centrepiece of Prime Minister Paul Keating's plans for regional enmeshment. Keating's proposal for a conclave of regional heads of government was ably supported by his Ambassador to the US, Don Russell, a former Keating staffer. Cotton shows how Russell followed a tradition, pioneered by Casey, of seeking to address many constituencies in America but focusing on economic issues in contrast with Casey's main priority of encouraging a military alliance with the British Empire and, through it, Australia. This reflected Keating's conviction that Australia's relationship with the US was entering a phase in which trade and economic issues would play as important a role as security issues. The embassy continued to have a full trade and economic agenda following the change of government in 1996. Under the Howard Government, the embassy in Washington would play a critical role in helping it successfully conclude a Free Trade Agreement with the US. But notwithstanding the increasing focus on Asia in the 1990s, security issues remained important. The Hawke Government made a military commitment to the Gulf War in 1991 supported by Russell's predecessor as Ambassador to the US, Michael Cook. After the election of a Coalition Government in 1996, Australian Ambassadors John McCarthy and Andrew Peacock supported the Howard Government's desire to upgrade the security aspects of the relationship. The increasing salience of security issues culminated in 2001 when Peacock's successor, Michael Thawley, was instrumental in advising the Howard Government to invoke the ANZUS Treaty in response to the terrorist attacks on the US in 2001.

The editors decided not to give detailed historical treatment to the last three Ambassadors to the United States, Dennis Richardson (2005–2009), Kim Beazley (2010–2016) and the current head of mission, Joe Hockey (2016–). Beazley, however, has contributed to the volume in the form of reflections by the outgoing Australian Ambassador to the US. More detailed analyses of these last three ambassadorships await the elapse of further time and the opening of primary historical records under the *Archives Act* 1983, which will see records from 2005 and after become available in the period from 2025 onward. The historical records relating to the current Ambassador, Joe Hockey, will be open to the public around the time of the centenary of the establishment of the Australian legation in Washington in 2040.

In lieu of detailed treatment, the next section of the introduction offers a brief analysis of the last three Ambassadors to the United States. They included one career public servant and two political appointees. The career public servant, Dennis James Richardson, was born in Kempsey in 1947 and educated at the University of Sydney. He joined the Department of External Affairs in 1969 as a graduate, becoming a member of a remarkable cohort that included Allan Gyngell, Sandy Hollway, Ric Smith, Bill Farmer and John Dauth. These men and Richardson all went on to become heads of agencies and to occupy senior diplomatic positions.

Richardson was posted to Nairobi between 1969 and 1971 and to Port Moresby from 1975 to 1977. He then served between 1982 and 1985 as Counsellor in the Australian embassy, Jakarta, under Rawdon Dalrymple, who would himself go on to head the embassy in Washington in the second half of the 1980s. After diplomatic service in Indonesia, Richardson was promoted to the position of Assistant Secretary in the Department of Immigration and Multicultural and Ethnic Affairs, where he served in 1986 and 1987. He then transferred to the Department of the Prime Minister and Cabinet and was promoted to head its International Division between 1988 and 1990. Richardson was subsequently principal foreign affairs adviser in the last years of Bob Hawke's prime ministership in 1990 and 1991. After Paul Keating's replacement of Hawke as Prime Minister, Richardson returned as a Deputy Secretary to the Department of Immigration and Multicultural

Affairs from 1993 to 1996. With the change of government in Australia in 1996, Prime Minister John Howard appointed Richardson to head the Australian Security Intelligence Organisation (ASIO), a post he held until he was appointed Ambassador to the US in 2005. By that time, after terrorist attacks on US soil in 2001 and terrorist bombings in Bali in the following year, issues of intelligence and security were an increasingly important part of the Australia–US relationship. These developments made Richardson, with his decade at the head of ASIO as well as his diplomatic experience, an ideal candidate to head the Australian mission in Washington.

Richardson's tenure as head of mission in Washington straddled the last years of the Howard Liberal–National Party Government and the first two years of a Labor administration under Kevin Rudd. Richardson was Ambassador during a time when a number of aspects of Australia–US relations were becoming a source of controversy in Australia. By 2006 the allied occupation of Iraq was going badly, and the abuse and torture of prisoners at Abu Ghraib and Guantánamo Bay becoming a source of increasing public concern.[14] Of particular worry to many Australians was the detention by US authorities of the South Australian, David Hicks, who had been captured by the US military in Afghanistan in 2001 and detained in Guantánamo Bay but was only released into Australian custody in April 2007. The Cole Inquiry hearings conducted in 2006 were also a source of embarrassment to the Australian Government. These hearings established that the Australian Wheat Board had diverted money to the Iraqi regime of Saddam Hussein during the management of the UN oil-for-food program. Richardson and the embassy in Washington helped the Howard Government manage such thorny problems in the bilateral relationship. These issues were leavened, however, by the celebration of an important milestone in the bilateral relationship. Richardson was head of mission during the centenary celebrations of the 1908 visit of the United States Navy (the 'Great White Fleet') to Australia.

Late in 2007 a Labor Government was elected in Australia and in November 2008 the Democrat Barack Obama was elected President of the United States of America. Possessing a broad range of contacts across the political divide in Washington, Richardson smoothly managed

---

14   James Cotton, 'Australia–America 2006–2010: Waiting for Obama', in James Cotton and John Ravenhill (eds), *Middle Power Dreaming: Australia in World Affairs 2006–2010*, Oxford University Press, Melbourne, 2012, p. 54.

the implications of the changes of government in both Australia and the United States. The periods in office of Rudd and Obama from 2009 heralded a new era of policy convergence in the Australia–US relationship. Both Rudd and Obama had opposed the allied invasion of Iraq in 2003; and both were outspoken about the need for international collaboration to address the anthropogenic causes of climate change. Richardson and the embassy coordinated Rudd's first visit to Washington in March 2009 where the two leaders discussed the need for international palliative measures to address the Global Financial Crisis, including Rudd's ambitious reform plans for the G20 group of nations. The Obama Administration also welcomed the Rudd Government's establishment, with Japan, of the International Commission on Nuclear Non-Proliferation and Disarmament, whose brief was to devise measures to strengthen the nuclear non-proliferation regime. The institutionalised, high-level consultations known as Australia–US ministerial consultations took place in Canberra in February 2008 and in Washington in April 2009, the latter meeting assisted by Richardson and the Australian embassy in Washington. Richardson completed a distinguished term as Australian Ambassador to the US in September 2010 before commencing a period as Secretary of the Department of Foreign Affairs and Trade.

Richardson was succeeded by a political appointee, Kim Beazley, who provides an invaluable reflection, including on his own period as Ambassador, in this volume. Kim Christian Beazley was born in Western Australia on 14 December 1948, the son of Kim Edward Beazley, a federal Labor Member of Parliament and Minister for Education between 1972 and 1975. The younger Beazley was educated at the University of Western Australia and then Oxford University. A tutor and then lecturer in social and political theory at Murdoch University in the years after 1976, Beazley was elected to the federal parliament for the seat of Swan in 1980. With the election of the Hawke Government in 1983, he became the Minister for Aviation from 1983 to 1984, assisting the Minister for Defence. He was Minister for Defence between 1984 and 1990 and oversaw major changes in the portfolio following the landmark 1987 Defence White Paper. As Minister for Defence, Beazley was also an important participant in navigating the ANZUS crisis of 1984 to 1986. He was Minister for Transport and Communications from 1990 to 1991, Minister for Finance in 1991, Minister for Employment, Education and Training from 1991 to 1993, and Minister for Finance again from 1993 to 1996. Following the defeat of the Keating Government in 1996, Beazley became leader of the opposition and came within a few seats of defeating the Howard Government in 1998 but lost more decisively in 2001. After an interlude in which Simon Crean and then Mark Latham led the ALP federal Opposition, Beazley once again held that position between January 2005 and December 2006 before being replaced by Rudd, who went on to defeat Howard at the 2007 federal election. After Richardson's appointment as Secretary of the Department of Foreign Affairs and Trade in 2009, Rudd appointed Beazley Ambassador to the United States, a position that Beazley would occupy with great distinction from 2010 to 2016.

Beazley was one of the best-connected of any of Australia's ambassadors when he arrived in Washington. Like Cotton, Beazley's credentials were respected on both sides of politics, as was reflected by the Abbott Government's decision to extend his term. Beazley had excellent contacts on both sides of the political divide in Washington. He knew many of the top Republican leadership from his time in Australian politics in the 1980s and 1990s, and he proved to be a most popular envoy with the Obama Administration. Beazley's longstanding acquaintance with the US, detailed knowledge of American history and his skill as an analyst of international affairs and Australian politics earned him the respect of Obama and his Secretary of State, John Kerry. This was demonstrated on 13 October 2015 when Beazley hosted Kerry among others at a reception in Washington to celebrate 75 years of friendship between Australia and the United States, and by the warmth of Kerry's remarks on Beazley's departure from Washington.[15]

Beazley's retrospective essay in this volume covers the whole period from 1940. He notes that when he commenced in Washington, the embassy was Australia's second-biggest, after Indonesia, and that after the integration of the Department of Foreign Affairs and Trade with AusAID in 2014, it had dropped to third after Jakarta and Port Moresby. It remains, nonetheless, one of Australia's most important overseas missions with its 93 Australia-based and 176 locally engaged staff and a centrally located chancery and Ambassador's Residence that provide an ideal basis for cultural and public diplomacy activities.

---

15 'Kim Beazley's US ambassador stint comes to an end', SBS, 21 January 2016.

Australian ambassadors to the US in the early 21st century understandably do not have the same access to the US Administration that Casey, Makin and Spender had in the much smaller Washington of the 1940s and 1950s. In contrast to a time when ambassadors had readier access to Presidents and Secretaries of State, a critical part of the ambassador's and embassy's work in the 21st century is in supporting and enabling prime ministerial and ministerial visits. But aside from consular activities, an essential part of the embassy's work, Beazley argues, is the vital task of political reporting. The salience of this was marked particularly by the creation in the 1990s of the embassy's Congressional branch. Relations with members of Congress themselves remain with the ambassador, largely because he or she is the only one that senators or members of Congress will agree to see. While formal diplomatic relations between Australia and the US began in the cauldron of World War II and with Australia and the US under threat from Japan, Beazley concludes, nevertheless, that American priorities have never been more important to Australia and that Australia is a more significant ally geographically than at any time since World War II. In this context, Australia's embassy in Washington, after 75 years, remains one of its most important.

In 2016 Joseph Benedict 'Joe' Hockey was appointed to succeed Beazley. Like the first head of mission in Washington, Casey, Hockey was a former federal Treasurer and aspirant to leadership of the Liberal Party. Born in Sydney on 2 August 1965 to an Armenian father and Australian mother, Hockey attended St Aloysius College, Milsons Point, and then the University of Sydney from which he graduated with a Bachelor of Arts and Bachelor of Laws. Elected as a Liberal for the seat of North Sydney in 1996, he was appointed by John Howard as Minister for Financial Services and Regulation from 1998 to 2001 and Minister for Small Business and Tourism from 2001 to 2004, then Minister for Human Services from 2004 to 2007, and Minister for Employment and Workplace Relations in 2007.

During the period of the Labor Government after 2007, Hockey held a number of senior front-bench positions before being elevated to the position of Shadow Treasurer in 2009. In December 2009, Hockey contested the leadership of the Liberal Party with Malcolm Turnbull and Tony Abbott but was eliminated in the first round of voting in the ballot that Abbott won. After the defeat of the Rudd Government in 2013, Hockey was Federal Treasurer in the government led by Tony

Abbott. On Abbott's replacement as prime minister by Malcolm Turnbull, Hockey resigned from parliament in October 2015, and on 8 December of that year it was announced that Hockey would replace Beazley as Ambassador to the US. Hockey's ambassadorship during a time of another hard-fought US election awaits the attention of future historians.

2

Allies of a kind: Three wartime Australian ministers to the United States, 1940–46

Carl Bridge

Australia's first legation in Washington was born amid the gathering storm clouds of World War II, conceived under Prime Minister Joseph Lyons and announced under his successor Robert Menzies. During the war, three ministers served as head of mission: Richard Casey (1940–42); Sir Owen Dixon (1942–44); and Sir Frederic Eggleston (1944–46). Each was appointed a minister in charge of a legation – a rank and mission below that of ambassador and embassy, so as not to break the formal diplomatic unity of the British Empire/Commonwealth. Menzies' intention was that the minister would act in tandem with the British Ambassador (formally in the senior imperial post) and embassy to achieve common, if independent, goals.[1] Of course, this proved almost impossible in practice in a global war with multiple enemies and fronts and finite resources. Unity of a kind was preserved, but the devil was in the details.

---

1   Menzies' instructions to Casey are in Casey to Roosevelt, 5 May 1940, letter, series RG59, item 701.4711/76 United States National Archives (USNA), College Park, Washington DC.

False starts: 1907 to 1939

The prehistory of Australian diplomatic representation to and in the US stretches back to 1907, and the story is one of a succession of false starts until Casey's appointment in late 1939.[2] Alfred Deakin's invitation in 1907 to the US Government to include Sydney and Melbourne as ports of call on the world cruise of their 'Great White Fleet' of 16 battleships was Australia's first official invitation to the Americans. The visit in August 1908 was a huge success but the fleet sailed away again leaving no lasting legacy; though it did help set the scene for Deakin's establishing of the Royal Australian Navy soon afterwards.[3] Many Australians were unimpressed by US neutrality during most of the Great War and by their refusal subsequently to join the new League of Nations. Prime Minister William Morris (Billy) Hughes, following a visit to the US and a meeting with President Woodrow Wilson, appointed a Trade Commissioner in New York in 1918, mostly for purposes of war procurement, and the office lasted just over a decade until it was snuffed out by the Depression; partly because, as one Australian Cabinet Minister, Sir Henry Gullett, complained, it 'encouraged bigger Australian purchases in America, than American purchases in Australia' (though it was quietly re-established in 1938).[4] When asked in 1927 why Australia had not followed Canada, South Africa and Ireland in appointing a diplomat to Washington, Prime Minister Stanley Melbourne Bruce replied loftily: 'Such appointments – when there is no close relationship between the countries or special questions to be dealt with – were mere indications of an inferiority complex.'[5] As Gullett foreshadowed, trade was a major bone of contention, with the US running a four-to-one balance of trade surplus with Australia throughout this period. This was the cause of a unilateral,

---

2   See my 'Relations with the United States' in Carl Bridge and Bernard Attard (eds), *Between Empire and Nation*, Australian Scholarly Publishing, Melbourne, 2000, ch. 5; Ruth Megaw, 'Undiplomatic Channels: Australian Representation in the United States, 1918–39', *Historical Studies*, vol. 15, no. 60, 1973, pp. 610–30; Norman Harper, *A Great and Powerful Friend: A Study of Australian-American Relations Between 1900–1975*, University of Queensland Press, Brisbane, 1987; and Raymond A Esthus, *From Enmity to Alliance: U.S.-Australia Relations 1931–41*, Melbourne University Press, Melbourne, 1964.
3   Still the best authority here is Neville Meaney, *The Search for Security in the Pacific, 1901–14*, Sydney University Press, Sydney, 1976. But see also Russell Parkin and David Lee, *Great White Fleet to Coral Sea*, Department of Foreign Affairs and Trade, Canberra, 2008.
4   Gullett was reported by Jay Pierrepont Moffat, US Consul-General in Sydney: Moffat Diaries, 1 June 1936, Houghton Library, Harvard University, Cambridge, Massachusetts, USA.
5   Cited by Megaw, 'Undiplomatic Channels', p. 618.

short-lived and ill-fated attempt by Australia at 'Trade Diversion' away from the US and Japan and in favour of Britain in 1936–37. When the British negotiated the Anglo-American Trade Treaty of 1938, partly at Australia's expense and mostly for security reasons, Australia remained aloof.[6]

It was, however, the quest for security that finally caused a rethink in Canberra. In May 1937, following personal encouragement from President Franklin Roosevelt, Lyons appointed the Australian diplomat Keith Officer to a middle-ranking position as counsellor in the British embassy in Washington with a brief to report rather than act.[7] Officer did not have direct access to the US Secretary of State, let alone the President. The limitations of this arrangement were soon exposed. After the Marco Polo Bridge incident in July 1937 escalated Japan's war in China and the Munich and Prague crises of 1938 and 1939 respectively brought Britain and France to the brink of war with Germany, it was decided that full diplomatic missions should be set up in Washington, Chungking and Tokyo. The time for mere listening was over.

Willy-nilly, the era of direct Australian diplomacy in the Asia-Pacific had arrived, and arguably somewhat ahead of the bureaucracy supporting it. The three ministers under examination here reported to a young Department of External Affairs (made a separate administrative department in 1935) in Canberra that was finding its way among other, more established departments with remits for overseas relations, such as Trade and Defence, and a Prime Minister's Department to which Australia's High Commissioner in London reported directly. World War II would see the Department of External Affairs grow in personnel, just as Canberra itself grew in bureaucratic size and accumulating centralised powers, as the government responded to the exigencies of war. The Secretary of External Affairs from 1935 to 1944 was the tough but unadventurous former military man, Colonel William Roy Hodgson. From October 1941, Australia's Minister for External Affairs was Dr Herbert Vere Evatt, an intellectually restless, always demanding and partisan-Labor minister who was determined to gather around him the brightest officials who could be recruited. To this end he instigated

---

6   Ruth Megaw, 'Australia and the Anglo-American Trade Agreement, 1938', *Journal of Imperial and Commonwealth History*, vol. 3, no. 2, 1975, pp. 191–211.
7   Alan Fewster, *Trusty and Well Beloved: a Life of Keith Officer*, Miegunyah Press, Melbourne, 2009.

a diplomatic cadetship scheme from 1943, but Australian representation in Washington was in the hands of political appointees and, until later in the decade, the reception of those representatives' views was also largely in the hands of politicians such as Evatt and Prime Ministers Curtin and then Chifley.

Casey: February 1940 to February 1942

At 50 years old, Casey was the youngest of the three wartime ministers to the US. Lyons' former Treasurer and Bruce's former Liaison Officer in the British Cabinet Secretariat in London in the 1920s, he was admirably suited for the job of establishing the legation – well-connected, politically experienced, a man of great independent wealth, trained as an engineer, with a distinguished war record, and dedicated to public service.[8] He began with two other diplomatic staff and ended with six.

When Casey presented his credentials to Roosevelt, the US leader told him that in its relations with Australia 'the element of distance denoted a declining interest on the part of the United States'.[9] The clear message was that Britain and its empire should look to their own defence. Attempting to reverse this situation became the principal objective of Casey's mission. In order to achieve this, Casey decided upon a two-pronged strategy: a propaganda campaign across the US to publicise Australia and its war effort; and a succession of formal diplomatic initiatives aimed at persuading the American Administration of its need to join the war. A third, related aim was to win the confidence of the American military leadership.

First, let us examine propaganda, or strictly speaking information, because in the US at that time war propaganda was illegal. This was isolationist America, shielded behind Neutrality Acts. A contemporary Sydney *Bulletin* cartoon by Norman Lindsay captioned 'Darkest America', and to modern readers blatantly racist, showed Casey in an explorer's pith helmet as a sort of Stanley in the deep jungle meeting a Livingstone figure. This man was a rather Germanic-looking American

---

8   On Casey's background, see William James Hudson, *Casey*, Oxford University Press, Melbourne, 1986; and Casey's own memoirs: *Personal Experience, 1939–46*, Constable, London, 1962, and *Australian Father and Son*, Collins, London, 1966.
9   Casey to Sir Henry Gullett, Minister for External Affairs, 9 March 1940, letter, in Carl Bridge, (ed.), *A Delicate Mission: The Washington Diaries of R.G. Casey, 1940–42*, National Library of Australia, Canberra, 2008, p. 30.

with a book under his arm labelled 'Isolation' and a file of black carriers behind him. The caption read 'Dr Livingalone, I presume?'[10] Ian Clunies Ross, an Australian who was Head of the International Wool Secretariat, advised Casey through Menzies to hire a firm of New York-based public relations consultants, Earl Newsom and Company, to set up a campaign. One can market 'Australia' to the Americans just as one can market 'wool' or 'tea', Clunies Ross wrote.[11] And he was not far wrong.

Casey's family was photogenic. He was conventionally handsome with a clipped military moustache. A dapper dresser, he had a marked resemblance to the pin-up boy of British politics, Sir Anthony Eden, a sort of political George Clooney of the day, and was soon labelled by the American press 'The Anthony Eden of Australia'. He and his wife, Maie, who was a notable artist, designer and art collector, flew their own small aeroplane, and journalists were quick to dub the pair 'The Flying Caseys'. In two years Casey made 70 major speeches in key venues across the country, 16 of them broadcast on radio, three of these coast-to-coast, and all extensively reported in the press. There were also publicity stunts galore, from his teaching Vice-President Henry A Wallace to throw a boomerang and acquiring Australian animals for American zoos to his unsuccessful attempt to get Walt Disney to introduce Australian cartoon characters, a kangaroo and a koala. Maie organised a major touring exhibition of Australian art through the Carnegie Foundation and wore gowns of fine Australian wool.[12] The Caseys dined, entertained and networked prodigiously in their residence-cum-mission, a colonial revival mansion purchased by the Australian Government on their advice. 'White Oaks', with its red bricks, white columns and portico, was built by a speculator in 1928, sat in leafy and dignified Cleveland Avenue (number 3120), and had once been rented by General George S Patton.[13]

10   *Bulletin,* Sydney, 17 January 1940.
11   Menzies to Casey, 19 March 1940, cablegram, series A3300/66, National Archives of Australia (NAA), Canberra.
12   On Maie's role, see Maie Casey, *Tides and Eddies,* Joseph, London, 1966; Diane Langmore, *Glittering Surfaces: A Life of Maie Casey,* Allen & Unwin, Sydney, 1997; and Audrey Tate, *Fair Comment: A Life of Pat Jarrett, 1911–1990,* Melbourne University Press, Melbourne, 1996. Jarrett was Maie's secretary.
13   This aspect is discussed in detail in my 'Introduction' to *A Delicate Mission,* pp. 5–9, and in Bridget Griffen-Foley, '"The Kangaroo is coming into its own": R.G. Casey, Earl Newsom and Public Relations in the 1940s', *Australasian Journal of American Studies,* vol. 23, no. 2, 2004, pp. 1–20.

The propaganda blitz worked well. Casey put himself and Australia on the US map. So successful was it that when Sir Keith Murdoch, in his wartime post as Australia's Director-General of Information, wanted to crank it up even further in August 1940 with a grandiose campaign of paid advertisements in the press, the State Department advised Casey that they thought it would be counterproductive and stir up criticism from the isolationist lobby. More important, they thought, rightly, that his other activities were sufficiently effective. In his speeches, Casey presented Australia as defending democracy in a threatened world, in effect underwriting US freedom. Australia in the Pacific was depicted as a new country, and Australians were egalitarian, easygoing, freewheeling and get-up-and-go, like their American cousins: potentially a Pacific partner, as Australian war correspondent and author George Johnston put it in an ex post facto book published in 1944.[14] The British Empire was fighting Fascist Germany and Italy alone and could do with American help.[15] Privately, in his diary, Casey despaired. While the Battle of Britain raged and France fell, Americans were around him enjoying the sun on holiday in Florida or on the beach at Atlantic City. The British element of the US population, he wrote, was too diluted for them to realise the 'Old Country' needed help.[16]

On the formal diplomatic front, working, as Casey put it, as the 'other blade of the scissors' to Lord Lothian (and later Lord Halifax), the British ambassadors, Casey saw the President regularly – often with the British Ambassador but 11 times on a one-to-one basis. He also met often with the Secretary of State, Cordell Hull, General George Marshall, the military chief, and many others at the top of American politics and administration. He had a good working relationship with Harry Hopkins, Roosevelt's principal aide, and made close friends of Felix Frankfurter, the Supreme Court judge, and Dean Acheson, a senior diplomat. The prominent journalists and columnists Walter Lippmann, George Fielding Eliot and Dorothy Thompson were regular contacts.

There is not space here to tell the detailed story, but Casey, Lothian and Halifax hardly missed a trick. They placed stories in the press about how the Royal Navy guaranteed the US' Monroe Doctrine, which kept

---

14   George H Johnston, *Pacific Partner*, Victor Gollancz, New York, 1944.
15   For example, his speech to the National Press Club, Washington, 12 March 1940; and his broadcast address on the Columbia Broadcasting Service, 22 March 1941, series A981/Australia 221, NAA, Canberra.
16   See, for example, his diary entries for 5 June and 13 July 1940, *A Delicate Mission*.

foreign powers from meddling in the Western Hemisphere; Casey even tried cheekily to insinuate text to this effect into Roosevelt's speeches (March–July 1940). They helped engineer the temporary closure of the Burma Road supply route from India into China (July–September 1940) both to appease the Japanese and at the same time demonstrate the need for US support when the road was reopened. They helped hatch the 'Destroyers-for-Bases' deal (September 1940) and the secret ABC1 strategic talks between the British and US militaries nearly a year before Pearl Harbor, at which an Australian naval observer, Commander Henry Burrell, was present (January–March 1941). They encouraged the passage through Congress of the historic Lend-Lease Act, revolutionising the financing of the British war effort (March 1941), and they were complicit in the drafting of the Atlantic Charter (August 1941). And Casey was careful to inject Australian and Pacific dimensions as he went, for instance by successfully offering the US Army Air Corps the use of Darwin as a southern staging post en route to the Philippines well in advance of Pearl Harbor. All of these were way stations on the road to US full participation in the war.[17]

But it was not propaganda and diplomatic moves that brought the US into the war. It was the march of international events, which showed that the American economy was so dependent on its trade with Britain and the empire, and equally dependent on the empire's fighting that compelled the US to join in. In particular, the German U-Boats' depredations against US's transatlantic trade and increasing German autarky on the European continent began to squeeze the American economy, still fragile in its recovery from the Great Depression, making the US increasingly more dependent on trade with Britain and its empire.[18] Events and the economic pressures of war convinced Japan to act, too, and its attack on Pearl Harbor on 7 December 1941 finally achieved Casey's and Halifax's objective for them.[19]

---

17   For more detail, see my 'Introduction', *A Delicate Mission*, pp. 9–11. For the British perspective on these developments, see David Reynolds, *The Creation of the Anglo-American Alliance*, Europa, London, 1981.

18   Roosevelt pointed out in the 1940 Presidential Election campaign that the war had boosted the 'neutral' US economy by 3.5 million jobs and was a major factor in pulling the country out of the Depression: David M. Kennedy, *Freedom from Fear: The American People in Depression and War, 1929-1945*, Oxford University Press, New York, 1999, p. 464.

19   Kennedy, *Freedom from Fear*; Warren F. Kimball, *The Juggler: Franklin Roosevelt as Wartime Statesman*, Princeton University Press, Princeton, 1994; and *The Most Unsordid Act: Lend-Lease 1939-41*, Princeton University Press, Princeton, 1991.

That great sceptic, Stanley Melbourne Bruce, at the time sitting as Australian High Commissioner in London, pronounced Casey's achievement across the pond to be 'a star performance',[20] and another with an even better ringside seat, Casey's First Secretary at the legation, Alan Watt, would write in his memoirs:

> It has always been my view that Casey's work in Washington and the United States generally has been under-estimated in his own country. It was not easy in advance of Pearl Harbor, to develop a favourable climate of opinion towards Australia. This the Australian Minister undoubtedly did.[21]

The extremely partisan Herbert Evatt, the new Labor Foreign Minister at the time of Pearl Harbor, said privately to a New Zealand counterpart that Australia had 'a swine in Washington named Casey'.[22] It was an awareness of Evatt's hostility, coupled with his sense that his main task had been completed, that persuaded Casey to resign from his post in early 1942, whereupon a grateful Winston Churchill made Casey British Cabinet Minister Resident in the Middle East, based in Cairo. It was another crucial posting for Australia, given that Rommel's Afrika Korps was threatening the main Suez Canal supply route to Australia, and the Australian 9th Division and air and naval elements were serving in that theatre. Despite Evatt's doubts, however, John Curtin, Australia's new Labor Prime Minister, made it quite clear that he would have rather kept Casey in Washington.[23]

Sir Owen Dixon: June 1942 to September 1944

Perhaps in a conscious effort to counter Evatt, Curtin went to the High Court to find Casey's successor. Sir Owen Dixon, aged 56, was at the height of a stellar legal career, and as wartime tasks had been chairing the boards overseeing Australia's shipping, wool and stevedoring interests. An internationally pre-eminent black-letter lawyer, and a man who took

---

20   Bruce to Casey, 17 September 1941, letter, cited in Hudson, *Casey*, p. 122.
21   Alan Watt, *Australian Diplomat: Memoirs of Sir Alan Watt*, Angus and Robertson in association with the Australian Institute of International Affairs, Sydney, 1972, p. 35.
22   Nelson T Johnson, United States Minister to Australia, to Cordell Hull, Secretary of State, 23 April 1942, in Peter Geoffrey Edwards (ed.), *Australia through American Eyes, 1935–1945*, University of Queensland Press, Brisbane, 1979, p. 69.
23   Bridge, 'Introduction', *A Delicate Mission*, pp. 11–13.

infinite pains to achieve complex tasks, Dixon was an ideal choice for the Washington post at this stage of the war. Nevertheless, he was reluctant to go, not wanting to be labelled an 'evacuee' like Evatt, and it was only after considerable pressure from Curtin that he accepted the post as a war task.[24]

With terrier-like but always polite determination, Dixon would ensure the best possible supplies for Australia of aircraft and other war materials. 'How to divide a deficiency is always the question?', he wrote in defining the key business of his mission.[25] He handled with consummate skill the fiendish intricacies of Lend-Lease and Reciprocal Lend-Lease. (Like Thomas Gradgrind, Dixon wanted 'facts, facts, facts' and was averse to and avoided political and bureaucratic spin.)[26] He also firmly and persistently, though unsuccessfully, questioned the 'Beat Hitler First' grand strategy of the Allies, in the Australian Government's interest. On one notable occasion at a meeting of the Pacific War Council in March 1943, Roosevelt instructed Dixon on the basics of grand strategy. The President said colloquially but pointedly: 'The situation was not to be defeated by Hitler before we dealt with the Japs.' And Roosevelt was correct: geopolitical analysis shows that Germany, with over four times the war-making capacity of Japan, had to be first priority, or the Allies would lose the war.[27] Earlier, at the time of Kokoda (July–September 1942), an annoyed Roosevelt had cabled Curtin, through Dixon, refusing him reinforcements on the grounds that after the Battle of Midway the Japanese no longer had the capacity to invade Australia and were fully occupied in the Guadalcanal battles.[28]

It also fell to Dixon to report and help shape the early steps in 1943 towards a new international organisation, via the new United Nations Relief and Rehabilitation Administration. Personally wary of Evatt – whom he knew only too well having sat with him on the High Court bench for 10 years – Dixon had himself appointed as answerable directly

24 Dixon on Evatt, cited in Philip Ayres, *Owen Dixon*, Miegunyah Press, Melbourne, 2007, p. 134; Watt, *Australian Diplomat*, p. 52.
25 Dixon to Sir Frederic Eggleston, Australian Minister to China, letter, 13 July 1942, William James Hudson and Henry James William Stokes (eds), *Documents on Australian Foreign Policy 1937–1949 (DAFP)*, vol. VI, July 1942 – December 1943, Australian Government Publishing Service, Canberra, 1983, doc. 6.
26 Watt, *Australian Diplomat*, p. 53.
27 Dixon's diary, 31 March 1943, cited in Ayres, *Dixon*, p. 163; Paul Kennedy, *The Rise and Fall of the Great Powers: Economic Change and Military Conflict from 1500–2000*, Unwin Hyman, London, 1988, p. 430.
28 Dixon to Curtin, 16 September 1942, cable, *DAFP*, vol. 6, doc. 48.

to the Prime Minister, though this arrangement never quite worked. Dixon first tried to resign in May 1943 while on a mid-term visit to Australia; this was due in no little degree to his fallings out with Evatt, but he was persuaded by Curtin to stay on *ad interim*. Meeting the Curtin War Cabinet during the visit, a disillusioned Dixon confided later to a friend that he found them a 'pusillanimous crew'.[29] Dixon finally returned home in September 1944.

As minister in Washington, Dixon had some difficult hands to play. When the fighting was at its worst on the Kokoda Track, he had to reassure Roosevelt and Marshall that the matter was in hand, despite stories of Australian troops fleeing before the enemy, as some had done earlier that year from the bombing of Darwin. He had to explain why Australia would not send military conscripts into New Guinea but would allow US conscripts to do the job.[30] He had to try to explain the controversial Anzac Pact of January 1944, an act of Evattean bombast in which Australia and New Zealand claimed primacy in the South West Pacific over the US, when the US Administration had a copy of the text of the agreement and he did not. ('Let's just forget it [the Pact]' was Roosevelt's dismissive response to the hapless Dixon.)[31] And he had to explain why Australia was apparently beginning to demobilise its forces in the latter part of 1943 when the US was still fighting full tilt.[32]

All of this Dixon did as effectively as anyone could have done, but it was a less rewarding task than Casey's. Dixon did, however, have two major weaknesses as a diplomat. As a man drilled in the legal profession, he preferred to work alone and master his brief, with one legal assistant to devil for him, Keith Aickin, who was seconded from the court to Washington as Third Secretary. Dixon did not utilise his diplomatic staff as efficiently as he might have done and this infuriated First and Second Secretaries Alan Watt and Peter Heydon.[33] Dixon was also happier with administrators, technicians and the military than he was with politicians. Though he won Marshall's confidence and that of the Lend-Lease people, he did not read the runes of the general political situation

---

29 Paul Hasluck, *Diplomatic Witness: Australian Foreign Affairs, 1941–1947*, Melbourne University Press, Melbourne, 1980, p. 44.

30 Dixon's diary, 12 June, 1, 7 and 8 October 1942, cited in Ayers, *Dixon*, pp. 145, 154–55.

31 Ayers, *Dixon*, p. 173. On the Anzac Pact, see Robin Kay (ed.), *The Australian–New Zealand Agreement 1944*, Historical Publications Branch, Wellington, 1972; and Anthony Burke, *Fear of Security: Australia's Invasion Anxiety*, Cambridge University Press, Melbourne, 2008, p. 78.

32 Dixon's diary, 10 April 1944, cited in Ayers, *Dixon*, p. 172.

33 Watt, *Australian Diplomat*, p. 52; Ayers, *Dixon*, pp. 142, 147.

and report on trends in, for instance, Roosevelt's re-election campaign in 1944.[34] Nor was he close enough to Roosevelt or Halifax to divine the thinking of the 'Big Three' (Roosevelt, Churchill and Stalin) at the Casablanca (January 1943), Quebec (August 1943), Tehran and Cairo (November–December 1943) summits. (Halifax refused to tell him fully about Casablanca and he first learned the outcome of Quebec from the Australian High Commission in Ottawa.)[35] One cannot imagine Casey allowing himself to get so out of touch with the high political game.

Dixon, like Casey, had to attempt to make up for Evatt's failings; for example, on one occasion Evatt criticised the British for their 'selfishness' in a meeting with General Marshall, who stood up and pointed out that he would not hear such disloyalty to his country's 'most important ally'![36] There would have been no need for an Anzac Pact had Evatt and Dixon won more inside influence in Washington. As historian John Robertson described it, from 1944 Australia slipped into the role of 'redundant ally'.[37] This happened on Dixon's watch.

In the end, soon after the great D-Day assault in Normandy in June 1944, and while in the Pacific the assault on the Philippines was brewing, Dixon was happy to go back to Australia and the High Court. His American friends praised him for his intelligence, balance and disinterestedness. One might wonder, however, whether these virtues suffice in the world of a diplomat.

Sir Frederic Eggleston: November 1944 to April 1946

In September 1944, when he was offered the post as minister in Washington, Sir Frederic Eggleston was 69 years old, very overweight, and suffering from chronic gout, neurasthenia and arthritis. He had been minister to China for four years, based in Chungking, during which time he had had to be carried about that hilly city in a perambulator

---

34 This political blind spot and his tendency to equanimity in discussions with the Americans are what Watt was referring to when he wrote to a friend of Dixon being 'not only out of place, but possibly doing Australia unintentionally considerable disservice'. Watt to JD Hood, 7 September 1943, Sir Alan Watt Papers, series MS3788, National Library of Australia, Canberra.
35 Ayers, *Dixon*, pp. 159, 170.
36 Watt, *Australian Diplomat*, p. 52.
37 John Robertson, *Australia at War, 1939–1945*, Heinemann, Melbourne, 1981, ch. 18.

(a sort of open sedan chair) by his Chinese staff. Eggleston had a formidable intellect, had been at Versailles for the peace negotiations in 1919, had had a stint as a Victorian Liberal state politician and minister, and had chaired the Commonwealth Grants Commission successfully throughout the 1930s. He had an intense theoretical and practical interest in international organisation and relished going to Washington to participate in the making of the next equivalent of the Treaty of Versailles and the framing of what became the United Nations Organization.[38]

Eggleston wrote to Evatt that he feared his health would not bear the strain but 'if the Government was willing to take the risk I am'.[39] He anticipated he would last about six months. 'The Egg', as the diplomatic cadets he instructed in the late 1940s would call him, in the words of another senior diplomat Sir Walter Crocker, 'enjoyed thinking as some men enjoy drinking'.[40]

Unfortunately, as Watt sourly noted, Eggleston's immobility was a great hindrance in Washington. The senior Americans did not have the time to call on him and he had only limited energy to call on them. His junior staff could not fully compensate for this as inevitably they only got to see other juniors.[41] At the San Francisco Conference in April–May 1945, where Eggleston should have been in his element, he broke down and was hospitalised for a week, and convalescing, was taken on long, therapeutic car rides by Leslie Finlay (Fin) Crisp, a junior member of the Australian delegation.[42] Evatt, who was de facto head of the Australian team there, preferred to use his own personal staff, principally Paul Hasluck, and did not talk to or use Eggleston. As Hasluck observed in his memoirs, Eggleston was 'left behind in the rush', his carefully written analyses of issues too late to be useful and left unread.[43]

---

38   Warren G. Osmond, *Frederic Eggleston: An Intellectual in Australian Politics*, Allen & Unwin, Sydney, 1985, is an excellent biography.
39   Eggleston to Evatt, 27 September 1944, letter, in William James Hudson (ed.), *DAFP 1944*, vol. 7, Department of Foreign Affairs and Trade, Canberra, 1988, doc. 303.
40   Sir Walter Crocker cited in Osmond, *Eggleston*, p. 301.
41   Watt, *Australian Diplomat*, pp. 60–1.
42   Osmond, *Eggleston*, p. 248.
43   Hasluck, *Diplomatic Witness*, p. 191. See also: Watt, *Australian Diplomat*, p. 67. Watt, who was with the Australian delegation, thought it 'undignified' for Eggleston to remain at San Francisco and thought he should have returned to Washington and his work as head of mission.

Nevertheless, Eggleston did play something of a role, justifying Australia's positions, particularly on trusteeship matters in arguments with Halifax and the British delegation, and over elected membership of the projected UN Security Council. Eggleston has left us with an eloquent analytical summation of Evatt's achievement at San Francisco in a letter to Bruce, still High Commissioner in London:

> As a matter of fact I consider that Evatt performed a great intellectual tour de force at San Francisco … I know all of Evatt's weaknesses and have no admiration for the way in which he works but I have to confess that I believe he played a very constructive part at the conference and that he pointed out the weak points of the main scheme, conducted a fine campaign against them, and that on the question of the Economic and Social Council and the Trusteeship clause, he was very largely responsible for the draft which appeared … You must not take it that Evatt's campaign was merely a small power v[ersus] a great power campaign. It was a campaign against the defective principles of the Charter.[44]

Wars, Eggleston told a meeting of the British delegation when discussing the need for elected members in the Security Council, were caused by great powers, not small ones, and that great power virtue was no guarantee against them.[45] Halifax, whose 'Holy Fox' nickname was well-deserved, refrained from pointing out the obvious to the sanctimonious Eggleston, which was that small power virtue mattered even less.

In 1947, Eggleston wrote a letter to a friend wherein he perceptively identified his own strengths and weaknesses:

> I do not care whether I am at the head of the procession. Where the ego should be I form a sense of humour, and the reason why I like being at the tail … is that I can tell people's character better from their walk and the backs of their heads than their faces, which are of course synthetic.[46]

Eggleston was by temperament an observer and commentator rather than an actor, and, as his acute biographer Warren Osmond remarks, this made him ultimately 'unsuitable for positions of power'.[47]

---

44   Eggleston to Bruce, 9 July 1945, letter, in William James Hudson and Wendy Way (eds), *DAFP 1945*, vol. VIII, Department of Foreign Affairs and Trade, Canberra, 1989, doc. 130.
45   Ibid.
46   Eggleston to Mrs Katrine Ball, 8 September 1947, letter, cited in Osmond, *Eggleston*, p. 252.
47   Osmond, *Eggleston*, p. 252.

Eggleston increasingly found himself out of sympathy with the Americans, and in September 1945, soon after the Peace, wrote to his nephew:

> I am getting rather fed up with the American atmosphere. The Americans are slow to action, dashing when in fight, and intolerable in victory. I have never seen such National Egotism as this outburst. Whether they will get through the reconversion [to peace] I don't know, but all controls are being discontinued. From now until Christmas they will hog themselves into their food while Europe is starving.[48]

While the San Francisco Conference and Japanese Peace Treaty talks diverted him for another six months, he was more than glad in April 1946 to return to Australia 'to sit on a verandah and play with my grandchild'.[49]

Allies of a kind

Three very different Melburnians served Australia to the best of their considerable abilities in Washington during World War II. It was never easy representing a junior ally to the great power leadership in a global war; and even harder trying to involve a great power in a war they were reluctant to enter. If, as the historian Christopher Thorne put it so well, the US and the UK were 'Allies of a Kind', drawn together for a common purpose but with all sorts of contradictory tensions straining below the surface, Australia, dependent on both and with only a limited amount to offer in return, had an even more difficult row to hoe as a dual ally of an even more qualified kind.[50] Casey, the politician, endured the agony of witnessing American neutrality during the fall of France and the Battle of Britain and helped prepare the American people and their administration to join in the war – a process completed by the Japanese attack on Pearl Harbor. Dixon, the luminous High Court judge, handled the complexities of supply for Australia's part of the Pacific War with great skill, but failed in the high political task of discovering and reporting the evolving political and military strategies of the Big Three.

---

48   Cited in Osmond, *Eggleston*, p. 248.
49   Ibid., p. 249.
50   Christopher Thorne, *Allies of a Kind: the United States, Britain and the War Against Japan, 1941–1945*, Hamilton, London, 1979.

Eggleston, the partial invalid and intellectual, was a thoughtful analyst of the crucial events at the San Francisco Conference, but too ill to make a significant contribution to proceedings as they happened. Only Casey possessed all of the necessary skills and the will to successfully execute all aspects of this demanding position. The other two had significant gaps. Casey, the vitally interested politician-cum-diplomat, was best suited to the role and performed the most important task.

3

Norman Makin and postwar diplomacy, 1946–51

Frank Bongiorno

At the farewell gathering held in Melbourne before he departed to take up his post as Australia's first Ambassador to the United States, Norman Makin commented that he saw one of his tasks as to eradicate the popular impression overseas that 'the Australian is an uncouth fellow, with a ribald sense of humour and singularly lacking in appreciation of the finer things of life'.[1] It would be hard to conjure anyone better qualified to do so than this small, bespectacled and tidy man. Makin was a Labor-type more common in Britain than in Australia: an earnest, abstaining, self-improving Methodist layman.

The son of English working-class emigrants, Makin was born in Sydney in 1889 and raised in Melbourne and Broken Hill. Beginning his working life as a 13-year-old parcel-boy, Makin later became a pattern-maker, a skilled tradesman in the engineering industry, the very kind of workingman who had provided much of the Australian labour movement's political and intellectual leadership up to the 1960s. He rose quickly through the ranks of the South Australian Labor Party, entering parliament for the seat of Hindmarsh in 1919 before he had turned 30. He was speaker of the House of Representatives in the short-

---

1 *Morning Bulletin,* Rockhampton, 24 July 1946.

lived Scullin Government, and having shunned the offer of a wartime ministry in social services and repatriation, he took on the navy and munitions.

In 1946 Makin represented Australia in London at the UN General Assembly and the first meeting of the UN Security Council, of which Australia had non-permanent membership. Indeed, because the chairmanship circulated in alphabetical order, as the representative of a country whose name began with an 'A', Makin was the council's first chairman. He later described his efforts to deal with the verbal brawling among the leaders of the great powers – especially that between Ernest Bevin of Britain and Andrey Vyshinsky of the Soviet Union over the presence of British troops in Greece – as 'the most severe test that I have experienced'.[2] A secret session called by Makin one evening was intended to last only minutes but extended into a two-hour session largely given over to mutual abuse between Bevin and Vyshinsky.[3] By his own account, Makin rebuffed an effort by Bevin, the British Foreign Secretary, conveyed by the Australian Resident Minister in London, John Beasley, to have him 'pulled into line'.[4] Paul Hasluck thought that with his experience as a former speaker of the House of Representatives, Makin had 'proved a fair and capable presiding officer, without knowing much about the political issues under discussion or the viewpoints of the debaters'.[5] But the American representative thought Makin's indecisiveness and inexperience as chairman were major factors in prolonging the verbal stoush between Bevin and Vyshinsky.[6]

Having been permitted this rather sour first taste of international diplomacy, Makin became Ambassador to the US in September 1946, the post having been upgraded from a legation to coincide with his appointment.[7] Arriving at Union Station from Australia after a long

2   Norman Makin, *The Memoirs of Norman John Oswald Makin*, H and L Makin, Mt Martha, 1982, p. 171.
3   'Report by the United States Representative at the United Nations: Record of Secret Session, Meeting of the Security Council, 5 February 1946, from 9.10 p.m. until 11 p.m.', United States Department of State, Foreign Relations of the United States (FRUS), 1946. *The Near East and Africa*, vol. 7, pp. 108–12.
4   Makin, *Memoirs*, p. 171.
5   Paul Hasluck, *Diplomatic Witness: Australian Foreign Affairs 1941–1947*, Melbourne University Press, Melbourne, 1980, p. 251.
6   The United States Representative at the United Nations (Stettinius) to the Secretary of State, 6 February 1946, cablegram no. 501.BB/2-646, in FRUS, 1946. *The Near East and Africa*, vol. 7, p. 114.
7   David Lowe, 'Makin, Norman John', in *Australian Dictionary of Biography*, National Centre of Biography, The Australian National University, 2012; William Coleman, Selwyn Cornish and Alf Hagger, *Giblin's Platoon: The Trials and Triumphs of the Economist in Australian Public Life*, ANU E Press, Canberra, 2006, p. 195.

journey by sea and rail with his wife Ruby, son Lloyd – a returned serviceman who joined the embassy staff – and secretary, Miss MV Gordon, Makin would serve in Washington until April 1951.[8] After his return to Australia, Makin re-entered federal politics at the 1954 election, serving in the House of Representatives until 1963. Remaining an active Methodist layman after the end of his political career, he died in 1982.

Posterity has not been entirely unkind to Makin in its judgements about his capacity as Australian representative abroad. Certainly, no one would contradict the view that he lacked knowledge of international affairs. Alan Watt, a public servant and diplomat who worked under him, thought Makin of limited 'intellectual capacity' but with a lot of political experience. He had made his way up in the world 'the hard way' and 'won friends', recalled Watt, 'by his very simplicity and lack of pretentiousness'.[9] Hasluck's memoir largely agrees with this assessment – Hasluck, like his colleague Watt, makes much of Makin's unfailingly courteous and considerate behaviour, as well as his strength of character, adding that '[h]e had a better mind than [Frank] Forde', the Deputy Prime Minister and, later, High Commissioner in Ottawa. That might not be thought the highest compliment, but Hasluck considered it significant that despite his background as a tradesman, 'Makin was more broadly educated and better read' than Forde, a former schoolteacher. Makin, moreover, knew how to take advice from his officials while still making his own contribution.[10]

Others have been similarly ambivalent in their appraisal of Makin's performance. The historian Joan Beaumont draws on reminiscences of Laurence McIntyre and Ralph Harry, two more diplomats who worked under Makin, in her largely negative assessment, which sits in the context of her discussion of failed political appointments to diplomatic posts in the 1940s. McIntyre, reports Beaumont, judged that Makin was 'out of his depth in the Washington environment … But in some ways he didn't do badly'. His strength was public relations and McIntyre recalled a university address delivered in the middle of a football stadium at which Makin, 'uttering his sonorous platitudes, sounded quite impressive and really seemed to make quite an impression on the audience'. But McIntyre believes Makin largely failed to make the most of the opportunities provided by his high office. Harry, however, paid

---

8   Makin, *Memoirs*, p. 184.
9   Alan Watt, *Australian Diplomat: Memoirs of Sir Alan Watt*, Angus and Robertson in Association with the Australian Institute of International Affairs, Sydney, 1972, p. 81.
10   Hasluck, *Diplomatic Witness*, pp. 243–5.

affectionate tribute to Makin's 'excellent feel for "grass roots" opinion', and indicated that Makin and his wife made an 'unaffected and charming host and hostess'. He recalled the amusement occasioned by 'the little mechanical fountain the Makins used as the centre-piece of their dining table, in order to save the expense of flowers'.[11]

There is obviously a fair amount of condescension here even when, as in the case of Watt, Hasluck and Harry, they were going out of their way to pay tribute to a man they clearly liked, and who made a better fist of the job he had been handed than his background suggested likely. But ultimately, the skills required of a diplomat, and certainly of one in a post as senior as Ambassador to the US, are context-dependent. And the context in which Makin was working had characteristics that fitted him rather well for the task at hand. If we are looking for a diplomat who played a significant role in policy formulation, we are clearly not going to find it in Norman Makin. But he was able to play other roles that were arguably more needed in the highly unusual atmosphere of Australian diplomacy in the late 1940s and early 1950s.

Herbert Vere Evatt's dominance of Australian policymaking in the second half of the 1940s is well-known, although it was tempered by Prime Minister Ben Chifley's important role in financial diplomacy and strategic intervention in particular matters, usually bearing on Australia's relationship with Britain and the Commonwealth. Australia emphasised liberal internationalism, gave a cautious endorsement to decolonisation movements, favoured Western support for economic development in Asia, and sought to influence the international order through the UN. But it was also committed to close involvement in the Commonwealth, a strong bilateral relationship with Britain, and an interest in a regional pact that would secure the involvement of the US in Pacific security. The Cold War increasingly encroached on these ambitions. In the meantime, the singular personality of Evatt was a factor in Australian diplomacy, explaining some things, although not the overall thrust of Australian policy. He was a difficult, unpredictable man. The great powers often resented what they saw as his meddling in matters that were not

---

11   Joan Beaumont, 'The Champagne Trail? Australian Diplomats and the Overseas Mission', in Joan Beaumont, Christopher Waters, David Lowe with Garry Woodard (eds), *Ministers, Mandarins and Diplomats: Australian Foreign Policy Making, 1941–1969*, Melbourne University Press, Melbourne, 2003, pp. 159–60.

properly Australia's concern. This formative period in Australian foreign policy history coincided with the development of a nascent foreign service, one in which senior officers were few and far between.[12]

Here was the complex situation in which Makin came to be Ambassador to the US. The first point that needs to be made is that the Department of External Affairs lacked qualified officers for senior roles in this period, a dearth that militated in favour of political appointments. It is also likely that a former minister such as Makin would have enjoyed better access to the higher echelons of politics than a professional diplomat could have managed. But there were still other advantages to political appointments, considerations more particular to the challenges of Australian diplomacy in the 1940s. Above all, an experienced political operative such as Makin was much better equipped to deal with Evatt – his cranky cables and phone calls, and his regular, unwelcome appearances on the spot – than any professional diplomat could have managed. This was true of John Beasley in London;[13] but it was even more marked in the case of Makin who, unlike Beasley, had never been close to Evatt and had no compunction about standing his ground and telling him precisely what he thought of his behaviour; or, if he did not like one of Evatt's tirades delivered over the phone, simply hanging up on him.[14] In December 1946 at the UN General Assembly in New York, after a typical Evatt cable criticising the performance of the delegation, Makin sent a message expressing his concern at:

> your apparent thought that our Delegation has not exerted itself to the utmost in giving effect to your instructions. Every Member of our team has given you loyalty and constant service with marked ability. I am greatly disturbed at your criticism which I can but emphasise in

12   Alan Renouf, *Let Justice Be Done*, University of Queensland Press, St Lucia, 1983; Peter Geoffrey Edwards, *Prime Ministers and Diplomats*, Oxford University Press/AIIA, Melbourne, 1983 and 'The Origins of the Cold War 1947–1949' in Carl Bridge (ed.), *Munich to Vietnam: Australia's Relations with Britain and the United States since the 1930s*, Melbourne University Press, Melbourne, 1991, pp. 70–86; Ken Buckley, Barbara Dale and Wayne Reynolds, *Doc Evatt*, Longman Cheshire, Melbourne, 1994, chs 19–23; Christopher Waters, *The Empire Fractures*, Australian Scholarly Publishing, Melbourne, 1995; David Lee, *Search for Security*, Allen & Unwin, Sydney, 1995; Frank Bongiorno, "British to the Bootstraps": HV Evatt, JB Chifley and Australian Policy on Indian Membership of the Commonwealth, 1947–49', *Australian Historical Studies*, vol. 37, no. 125, 2005, pp. 18–39.
13   Frank Bongiorno, 'John Beasley and the Postwar World', in Carl Bridge, David Lee and Frank Bongiorno (eds), *The High Commissioners: Australia's Representatives in the United Kingdom, 1910–2010*, Department of Foreign Affairs and Trade, Canberra, 2010, pp. 111–26.
14   Makin, *Memoirs*, p. 198.

the strongest possible terms is totally unjustified. Such criticisms are a source of terrific discouragement to men whose abilities and constant endeavours deserve something much different.[15]

Evatt replied in turn that Makin's 'comment' had been 'quite uncalled for' – he said he wanted to speak to Makin on the phone.[16] We can be certain that Makin would have simply poured himself a cup of tea and again stood his ground; he was loyal to his staff. A professional diplomat, on the other hand, might have thought his career in jeopardy. Later, when Evatt was attempting to discredit Paul Hasluck in the press after Hasluck's resignation from his role in leading the Australian UN mission in New York in 1947, Makin rang Evatt up and told him to stop, reminding him that as a hard-working and loyal servant of his minister, Hasluck deserved better. In a difficult situation, Hasluck had received no support from anyone else and was clearly grateful for Makin's intervention.[17] Again, no professional diplomat could have acted in this way.

Makin had nothing to fear from Evatt. It was Chifley who had appointed him and he was a longstanding politician with a strong sense of his own dignity, integrity and purpose. His unpleasant relations with Evatt are a major theme of his memoirs and diaries. An entry for 9 November 1947 remarked:

> The actual date of the Dr's return is now known but there will be no regrets when we wave him good bye. It has been a nerve strain for everybody. He is certainly the most difficult man I have ever had any official communication with. With pleasure we tender him a farewell dinner.[18]

Harry recalled in his memoir that at the conclusion of one General Assembly meeting, Makin and other members of the delegation went to the railway station to bid the minister farewell. Makin called for three cheers for Evatt, as the train pulled out. Then, as it disappeared, Makin said: 'And now, I think, just one more cheer!'[19] Makin got on much better with both Menzies and Spender, who treated him with respect and, once they assumed their roles as his political masters from

---

15   Makin to Evatt, 9 December 1946, cablegram no. UN961, in *DAFP*, vol. X, doc. 298, p. 481.
16   Evatt to Makin, 10 December 1946, cablegram no. 1734, in *DAFP*, vol. X, doc. 306, p. 492.
17   Hasluck, *Diplomatic Witness*, p. 289.
18   Norman Makin's diary, 9 November 1947, Makin Papers, item MS 7325, item 36, box 6, National Library of Australia (NLA), Canberra.
19   Ralph Harry, *No Man is a Hero: Pioneers of Australian Diplomacy*, Arts Management, Sydney, 1997, p. 94.

December 1949, with gratitude. Of Menzies, Makin recalled: 'He was a superb guest, one of the best that we were delighted to have during our stay in Washington.'[20]

Second, Makin provided a very different kind of Australian face to Evatt's in Washington and New York. Hasluck pointed this out in his memoirs: '[Makin] had unfailing courtesy and dignity in his relations with other ministers and diplomats and at that time those two qualities did need to be demonstrated to foreigners as qualities not unknown in Australian Government.'[21] Makin appears to have been well-liked on a Washington and New York diplomatic circuit to which he was temperamentally unsuited. His own total abstention from alcohol was certainly a disadvantage but he and his wife Ruby were thoughtful and generous hosts, whether their guest was high-and-mighty or the Australian bride and children of a former American serviceman. Interestingly, the Australian-born British Ambassador Lord Inverchapel (Archibald Clark Kerr) – the legendary wartime diplomat in China and the Soviet Union whom Makin found a sad and lonely figure in 1946 – was willing to share with the Australian quite intimate domestic details, including of his turbulent marriage. (Divorced at the time he met Makin, Inverchapel remarried his former wife in 1947.) Inverchapel was a grandson of John Robertson, the 19th-century New South Wales Premier, and a Scot with radical leanings; perhaps these things helped his relations with Makin. Inverchapel's basic decency would have appealed to Makin much more than his famously 'earthy sense of humour', although there is no indication that he made any attempt to try out the latter on his devoutly religious Australian counterpart. When Inverchapel found himself short in church when the collection plate appeared, Makin lent him the dollar he needed to save embarrassment.[22]

As a total abstainer himself, Makin:

> did not like to encourage Cocktail parties. I regard them as useless from a democratic standpoint. It is thought that it cultivates friendships and it is at such gatherings you can get local reactions. FIDDLESTICKS.

20 Makin, *Memoirs*, p. 202.
21 Hasluck, *Diplomatic Witness*, p. 245.
22 Makin's diary (typescript), 19 September 1946, 1, 4 October 1946, Makin Papers, item MS 7325, box 6, folder 41, NLA, Canberra; Donald Gillies, *Radical Diplomat: The Life of Archibald Clark Kerr, Lord Inverchapel, 1882–1951,* IB Tauris Publishers, London and New York, 1999, pp. 146, 181.

No Ambassador worth his salt thinks that. It is only an occasion for social would be's, a lot of small talk, and lack of restraint in the indulgence is apparent.[23]

Makin's combination of socialism and Methodism did not dispose him to look kindly on self-indulgence. As he told his father late in 1946:

Everyone here seems to be looking for luxury. In fact, the display of it in shops just appals one, when you bear in mind the great shortage of those who suffered most from the war in the United Kingdom. The people here do not know what sacrifice or suffering means.[24]

For Makin, a good British-Australian, Britain's wartime deprivation set a kind of gold standard for what might be expected of English-speaking peoples everywhere and always. But he was by no means humourless about such matters. He called a White House reception late in 1947 'a brilliant affair although "austerity" was the note respecting hospitality. Music was the principal <u>free</u> item. What there was of the ladies frocking was attractive and revealing. Lady Inverchapel seemed a little perplexed in keeping things above the Plimsoll line'.[25]

A further point that needs to be stated in favour on Makin as Ambassador: he did the job during a period of acute financial strain, when a shortage of US dollars made running the post difficult. 'We endeavoured to maintain the best of standards as the official facade to a keen, discerning, political and diplomatic community', he reflected in his memoirs, 'but behind the scenes we literally "patched and sewed" to make ends meet'.[26] Embassy staffing was also a problem. He had the experienced Alfred Stirling as his minister for a little over a year, but he was soon off to become High Commissioner in South Africa. Senior posts in Washington remained unfilled. Makin was somewhat unimpressed with Laurence McIntyre, appointed his First Secretary, whom he found 'slow-moving and inclined to be a little obstinate' – which might place McIntyre's own assessment of his Ambassador's obduracy in trivial matters in perspective – although he admired

---

23   Ambassador's Papers, ch. 3, Makin Papers, item MS 7325, box 4, folder 22, NLA, Canberra.

24   Norman Makin to JH Makin (father), 8 November 1946, letter, Makin Papers, item MS 7325, box 5, 29, NLA, Canberra.

25   Makin's diary, 2 December 1947, Makin Papers, item MS 7325, box 6, folder 36, NLA, Canberra.

26   Makin, *Memoirs*, p. 186.

McIntyre's political reporting.[27] Makin was also in the potentially embarrassing situation of having as economic counsellor JB Brigden, whose removal as permanent head of munitions he had engineered when he took over that portfolio during the war, having regarded him as unsuitable.[28] The secondment of a future departmental Secretary, Major James Plimsoll, from the Australian Military Mission in Washington to act as an alternate member to the Far Eastern Commission (FEC), relieved some of the burden on Makin's time. But because the FEC was formally responsible for making policy with respect to occupied Japan, a matter of overwhelming importance in Australian postwar diplomacy, Evatt often insisted on Makin being personally present at its meetings.[29] Diplomats such as John Oldham and Harry provided Makin with support in the everyday dealings of the embassy, but staffing problems were also accentuated in the early years by Evatt's apparent preference for ad hoc appointment of representatives to UN meetings.[30] Makin was therefore frequently called to duty in New York during his time as Ambassador, duties which he considered a diversion from his main role, and which also created personal financial pressures for him. 'In New York again', Makin recorded in his diary in March 1947, 'I am not very fond of this city'. He found New York 'expensive and very cheerless' and a much less comfortable fit than Washington, which he came to look on as a home away from home, and San Francisco, another favourite.[31]

In early 1947, to the embarrassment of Makin and the humiliation of Paul Hasluck as head of Australia's permanent UN mission in New York, Makin was appointed over Hasluck's head when the chairmanship of the Security Council again fell to Australia via the usual alphabetical rotation. Typically, Makin did his best to minimise the personal slight to Hasluck in various ways and by ensuring that at the end of his term 'he made generous acknowledgment' of his service.[32] Of Makin's own performance, Sam Atyeo, the artist-turned-diplomat whom Evatt used with a characteristic lack of subtlety as a backdoor source of intelligence

---

27   Makin's diary, 20 September 1946, Makin Papers, item MS 7325, box 6, folder 41, NLA, Canberra.
28   Coleman, Cornish and Hagger, *Giblin's Platoon*, pp. 195–7.
29   Department of External Affairs to Embassy in Washington, Beasley and Mission in Tokyo, 26 May 1947, cablegram nos 601, 186, 242, *DAFP*, vol. XII, doc. 315, p. 531; Makin's diary, 3 October 1946, all in Makin Papers, item MS 7325, box 6, folder 41, NLA, Canberra.
30   Hasluck, *Diplomatic Witness*, pp. 261–2.
31   Makin's diary, 28 March 1947, Makin Papers, item MS 7325, box 6, folder 36, NLA, Canberra.
32   Hasluck, *Diplomatic Witness*, pp. 283–4.

about Australia's diplomats, was complimentary: 'Old Makin & I exchange notes now. Quite old pals. He really is a nice guy & he did a good job in New York.'[33]

By Makin's own account, the only instruction Chifley gave him on appointment was to build a new chancery building, but to ensure that the trees in the grounds of the official residence were not destroyed in doing so.[34] Makin was able to ensure the preservation of the trees, and made arrangements for the construction of a chancery elsewhere on the site. But William Dunk, then Secretary of the Department of External Affairs, soon arrived and took the matter out of Makin's hands. A building at 1700 Massachusetts Avenue that had previously been used by the Australian War Supplies Procurement Mission was, after alteration, to become the new chancery. Makin thought it unsuitable, but his appeals to Canberra were without effect.[35] At any rate, he was able to keep his promise to Chifley. The Prime Minister wrote wistfully in mid-1949:

> I hope all the trees round the Embassy are looking as beautiful as when I was there, and that the one I planted in memory of Dick Keane is making good progress … I shan't easily forget the beauty of the area in which you are situated.[36]

It would be possible, but misleading, to narrate Makin's time in Washington in terms of the major issues affecting Australia–US relations in the period. Much happened in Australia–US relations between September 1946 and April 1951, but it happened around Makin rather than as a result of any initiative or intervention on his part. He represented Australia on the International Bank for Reconstruction and Development and the International Monetary Fund, and he would sign for the Menzies Government's loan of US$100 million in 1950. In mid-1948, however, he had to deliver the less welcome news that the US had placed a ban on the transmission of classified information to the Australians. He was involved in regular discussions of the Indonesian crisis between 1946 and 1949, when violent conflict between

---

33   Atyeo to Evatt, 12 March 1947, letter, *DAFP*, vol. XII, doc. 21, p. 33.
34   Makin, *Memoirs*, p. 178.
35   Makin to Evatt, 7 November 1946, cablegram no. 1540; Makin to Evatt, 13 November 1946, telegram, No. 1562; Makin to Evatt, 14 November 1946, telegram, No. 1568, Makin Papers, item MS 7325, box 5, folder 30, NLA, Canberra.
36   Chifley to Makin, 30 July 1949, letter, Makin Papers, item MS 7325, box 6, folder 30, NLA, Canberra.

the Dutch and Indonesian Republicans emerged as one of the most significant issues in Australia–US relations. Policy on Japan was also the subject of many Australian approaches to US officials, mostly infused during the period of the Labor Government with the conviction that Australia, as a result of her wartime sacrifice and legitimate security interests, should be treated as a party principal in any peace conference. Australia worried that there was a growing tendency on the US's part to settle important matters ahead of any treaty, and on the part of the Supreme Commander for the Allied Powers, General MacArthur, to act in ways that bypassed the FEC, the Washington-based body to which Makin belonged.

Japanese whaling and fishing rights, which the Australian Government saw as having both security and economic implications as well as raising matters of principle and procedure about Australia's right to consultation, seemed to take up a great deal of Makin's time. On one occasion, convinced he would have difficulty with Dean Acheson, Makin arranged a meeting with President Harry S Truman over a matter involving Japanese fishing rights. Makin claimed that he had formed with Truman 'a warm personal friendship'.[37] Certainly, the two men seem to have got along well in their various brief encounters, a simpatico that might have owed something to the dissenting Protestantism that they shared. William Inboden has shown how Truman, who was a Baptist, interpreted the Cold War as a 'grand spiritual drama' in which the mission of the US as a Christian nation in a struggle with atheistic communism was 'to bring the Kingdom of God nearer to this world'.[38] Makin would have found nothing with which to quarrel in such a view of the world, for he, too, thought that it was right to 'build up our strength to safe-guard ourselves against ruthless marauders' while looking 'ultimately to the glorious realization of the "days of heaven upon earth"'.[39] Still, one wonders what Truman, as a man who believed he was leading a godly nation with a divine mandate through some of the most dangerous times in its history, thought about having the matter of Japanese fishing rights brought directly to him by the Australian Ambassador! Perhaps Truman was grateful that it was not something more serious, for he advised Makin to tell his government that the matter would get the personal attention of the President.

---

37   Makin, *Memoirs*, p. 204.
38   William Inboden, *Religion and American Foreign Policy 1945–1960: The Soul of Containment*, Cambridge University Press, Cambridge, 2008, pp. 116, 122, 143.
39   Norman Makin, *The Full Light: A Sermon Preached at Foundry Methodist Church, Washington D.C., on Laymen's Day February 24, 1951*, n.p.

On some of the issues in Australia–US diplomacy in this period, such as the negotiations over the possibility of an American naval and air base on Manus Island, the Washington embassy seems to have been barely involved. On others, where the attention of the embassy was to some extent engaged, its impact was negligible since, as McIntyre put it, Makin 'wanted a quiet life and didn't want to start anything himself'.[40] Makin's role was mainly to convey messages and instructions from Canberra, sometimes to try to smooth over differences between Canberra and Washington, often to deliver complaints from Evatt. But an insistence on the right to be consulted in matters affecting Australia did not dissipate with the demise of Evatt and the Chifley Labor Government, for it was also evident in Makin's communications on behalf of the Menzies Government over the Korean War, which Australia was desperate to avoid escalating, and in the new External Affairs Minister Percy Spender's arguments for a Pacific Pact, which Spender expected would give Australia access to Western security planning.[41] The desirability, from Australia's point of view, of a Pacific Pact was on the agenda for much of Makin's time in Washington, making little progress before 1950 but culminating in the signing of the Australia, New Zealand, United States Security Treaty (ANZUS) in 1951 after strenuous diplomacy by Spender, who succeeded Makin as Ambassador to the US after his resignation as minister.

Makin appears to have carried out this kind of work satisfactorily, although there are plenty of indications that, especially early in his tenure, he lacked confidence in his own grasp of detail and capacity to communicate it in meetings with US officials. In July 1947, at a meeting with US officials on Japanese whaling in the Antarctic, he 'requested that he be allowed to read some notes which he had made in order that he could express more clearly the thought of his government and people in reference to the whaling expedition'.[42] The request does not suggest

---

40   Laurence McIntyre, interview by Mel Pratt, 1975, transcript, p. 1/2/19, ORAL TRC 121/67, NLA, Canberra.

41   'Memorandum of Conversation, by the Deputy Assistant Secretary of State for Far Eastern Affairs (Merchant)', 29 November 1950, in FRUS, 1950. *Korea*, vol. 7, pp. 1257–8; 'Memorandum of Conversation, by Mr. Horace H. Smith, Senate Liaison Officer, Office of the Assistant Secretary of State for Congressional Relations', 14 September 1950, in FRUS, 1950. *East Asia and the Pacific*, vol. 6, pp. 214–17.

42   'Memorandum of Conversation, by the Chief of the Division of North-east Asian Affairs (Borton)', 3 July 1947, in United States Department of State in FRUS, 1947. *The Far East*, vol. 6, p. 247.

a tight grasp of detail on his part. Indeed, the same lack of confidence in dealing with policy complexity appears to be at the heart of an anecdote offered by McIntyre on a meeting with Dean Acheson:

[I]t was a golden opportunity to really have an exploratory discussion, because Dean Acheson agreed to this in a relaxed kind of way and was obviously prepared to discuss a range of topics in addition to the one that we'd gone to see him about. But Norman really gabbled off the message that he was supposed to deliver and then, rather to Dean's surprise, more or less got to his feet and fled out the door ... he really had no conception of seizing opportunities and using them to the best advantage.[43]

There are other clues that when matters became more complicated and called for a grasp of detail, Makin did, as McIntyre has suggested, find himself out of his depth. In January 1948, having delivered the message to an Assistant Secretary of State that Australia thought the Indonesian Republic, and not the Dutch, should receive the foreign exchange from its exports, he was asked whether the Australian Government had in mind only the Indonesian Republic, or the United States of Indonesia (which included territory controlled by the Dutch). 'At this point', says the US record, 'Mr Makin read his telegram of instructions which left no doubt that his government had reference to the Indonesian Republic and not to the United States of Indonesia'.[44] Indeed, an examination of the relevant Australian cablegram indicates that only someone who had either failed to read the document at all, or had given it only the most cursory glance, would have felt the need to consult it again to clarify its meaning at such an embarrassingly late moment.[45]

The US record on Makin's diplomacy particularly in the early years is sometimes unflattering, occasionally shading into sarcasm. In August 1947 Makin and Stirling called on senior State Department officials to discuss the Indonesian situation. 'At considerable length and without understatement', the US record comments, 'Mr. Makin dwelt on the important role of Australia in that area, and in the world, its keen interest in seeing peace in Indonesia, and its fears that continuance of strife would result in a threat to Australia'. Makin went on to refer to

---

43 McIntyre, interview, p. 1:2/14.
44 'Memorandum of Conversation, by the Assistant Secretary of State for Political Affairs (Armour)', 29 January 1948, in FRUS, 1948. *The Far East and Australasia*, vol. 6, p. 85.
45 Department of External Affairs to Embassy in Washington, 27 January 1948, cablegram no. 80, in *DAFP*, vol. XIII, doc. 34, p. 40.

Indonesian accusations that the Dutch had violated a ceasefire agreement, but when Undersecretary of State Robert A Lovett, the author of the report on this meeting, asked the Australian Ambassador if he believed the charges that had been made, '[w]ith some embarrassment he replied that he did not know whether they were true and that he had cited them merely to show continuance of uncertainty'. Lovett then asked why, if the Australian Government 'felt so keenly about the matter, it waited five days' since the US had made its own offer of good offices before suggesting joint mediation in the dispute. 'Mr. Makin replied that he did not know but that Mr. Evatt was somewhere at sea and perhaps it had been difficult to communicate with him.' Then, when asked if he had any reason to believe the Dutch would accept an offer of joint mediation, Makin referred to Australia's wartime assistance to Holland and that he felt sure Dutch 'gratitude' would result in their ready acceptance. Lovett 'said that the experience of the United States has been that gratitude was a rare and short-lived emotion'. After Makin and Stirling had left the meeting, the officials present agreed that 'Australia was motivated largely by Mr. Evatt's desire to play a leading world role and to take the limelight where ever possible' and they resolved to have nothing to do with any proposal for joint mediation. Makin, at least, was sufficiently attuned to their reception of his proposal to recognise this much, for his own report to the department concluded: 'My definite impression was that [Lovett] did not welcome our offer.'[46]

Lovett's record of this meeting indicates a feeling that Makin was long-winded, prone to exaggeration, underprepared, naive and perhaps also a mere mouthpiece for Evatt's personal ambitions.[47] While perhaps unduly harsh, there is testimony from closer to home that confirms some of these impressions of Makin's frailties as a diplomat. Keith Waller, an Australian diplomat who would himself become Ambassador to the US in the 1960s, succeeded McIntyre as First Secretary in 1947. He recalled Makin as 'completely uninterested in foreign affairs' to the extent that he did not even have an office in the chancery building and was rarely to be seen there. On one occasion, Waller recalled some instructions having arrived from Canberra that Makin should go to see General George Marshall, the Secretary of State, about a particular matter. Waller had little success in trying to get some time with the Ambassador to discuss

---

46 Makin to Department of External Affairs, 5 August 1947, no. 1048, in *DAFP*, vol. XI, doc. 250, p. 233.
47 'Memorandum of Conversation, by the Undersecretary of State (Lovett)', 5 August 1947, in FRUS, 1947. *The Far East*, vol. 6, pp. 1013–15.

the matter. Makin – claiming to be too busy – 'refused courteously but quite firmly' and instead asked Waller to prepare a brief that he would read in the car on the way to the meeting. When they went to see Marshall, the American had a large pile of papers in front of him that indicated he had been very well-briefed; so much so, that he was able to point out that Australia had changed its position on the matter at hand:

> Makin was completely flabbergasted by all this and finally he said 'Well perhaps the best thing I can do is to give you this bit of paper', and he then handed over my brief. I was covered in confusion ... and Marshall read it, with his eyebrows going up into his hair, and said 'Thank you very much, Mr. Ambassador' and handed it back and said 'I can assure you that your views will receive very careful consideration', and showed him out. Makin was jubilant, he thought he'd really had a great success. He was a very stupid man.[48]

There is also an incident recounted in Secretary of Defense James Forrestal's diary – published posthumously in 1951 – which suggests that Makin's inclination towards helpfulness might on another occasion, late in 1948, have overwhelmed his representative function. When Lovett 'expressed annoyance' in an interview about Evatt's criticism of the US failure to restrain the Dutch, 'Makin was deeply apologetic and expressed the hope that he might be able to say to his government that we would like them to withdraw their suggestions. Lovett said he would not make such a request – that was up to the Australians themselves'. In his memoirs, Makin denied that he had made the apology attributed to him.[49]

On the whole, we learn little about the major diplomatic issues of the day from Makin's own diaries and memoirs, which in itself possibly tells us something about how he saw his role. He had much more to say in his memoirs about his religious activities – he was a regular preacher at Washington's Foundry Methodist Church where, on Australia Day 1947, he addressed a congregation of 1,200 on 'The Cavalcade of Life' – and his speech-making.[50] An old socialist stump orator who had made his mark battling Billy Hughes's proposals for conscription in 1916,

---

48 Keith Waller, interview with JDB Miller, 1974–1977, ORAL TRC 314, pp. 2:1/14-16, NLA, Canberra. My thanks to Peter Edwards for directing me to this source.
49 Walter Millis, (ed.), *The Forrestal Diaries*, The Viking Press, New York, 1951, p. 541; Makin, *Memoirs*, p. 208.
50 Makin, *Memoirs*, p. 191; Makin's diary, 26 January 1947, Makin Papers, item MS 7325, box 6, folder 36, NLA, Canberra.

he was unimpressed with the American habit of reading formally from a prepared text. Makin was a self-critical public speaker, knowing well when he had hit his mark, as well as when he had missed.[51] He was not an innovator in public relations in the manner of Richard Casey during the war, but was busy and active, using his religious networks effectively in gaining a feel for US public opinion. Makin enhanced a well-earned reputation for political astuteness after predicting, against the weight of expert commentary and opinion polling, that Truman would win the 1948 presidential election. His religious interests also took him to some out-of-the-way places, which it is impossible to imagine any other Australian Ambassador visiting in the late 1940s. On one occasion, he accompanied a visiting Australian Labor parliamentarian, a member of the Salvation Army, to a dilapidated and dimly lit Washington citadel where the two men's arrival caused considerable surprise, since the service was an all-black affair. When they were told that they would probably prefer another nearby citadel – which happened to be a white one – they insisted on staying and were treated with great honour, sitting on raised platforms with the leader, reading bible lessons and giving their own testimonies.[52]

Makin got around the country as well, preaching, speech-making and accepting honours. Soon after he began his ambassadorship, he found himself in – of all the unlikely places – Hollywood. In Los Angeles to attend the christening of the first of four aircraft his government had ordered from the Douglas Aircraft Company, Makin also visited Warner Brothers where he met Jimmy Durante, Kathryn Grayson, Sir Charles Aubrey Smith and Mickey Rooney. While 'not much impressed' by Rooney, he better liked Smith, 'still a great Englishman' who 'likes fostering the great national game of cricket. He himself was an international player, and I noticed that he wore his M.C.C. tie and his Cambridge blazer. Well done, Sir Aubrey!' At an evening reception, he presented silver plaques to more actors – Edward Arnold, Robert Young, Linda Darnell, James Cagney and Laraine Day – for their help in promoting Australian war loan appeals.[53] But the most unlikely image from Makin's time as Ambassador – indeed, it is one of the strangest images in the history of Australian diplomacy – comes from a New York 'Town Hall Meeting' on the question of whether the UN Security

---

51 Makin's diary, 26 January 1947, Makin Papers, item MS 7325, box 6, folder 36, NLA, Canberra.
52 Makin, *Memoirs*, pp. 211–12.
53 Makin's diary, 15, 17 September 1946, Makin Papers, item MS 7325, box 6, folder 41, NLA; Makin, *Memoirs*, pp. 187–8.

Council's veto was a threat to world peace. At the moment when the chairman, acting on a vote of the audience, announced Makin and a colleague as the winning team, he was immediately mobbed by 50 to 60 bobby-soxers, teenage girls more commonly associated with devotion to the young Frank Sinatra. 'The increasing pressure', recalled Makin, 'and their hysterical chant became frightening'. He and his teammate had to be rescued from their young admirers by the chairman and the police.[54] In the volatile, unpredictable postwar world, pious Adelaide Methodists could get themselves into the most peculiar of scrapes.

The day before Makin left Washington in April 1951, he called on President Truman to bid him farewell. 'We seem to have got along quite well. You haven't been at all difficult and it has been good at all times to receive you.'[55] There is something to be said, at times, for people who 'haven't been at all difficult', for an experienced glad-handler skilled in the art of flattering the powerful, but also, when necessary, one able to stand up to the bully, as Makin did with Evatt. In the context of US–Australia diplomacy of the early Cold War, Makin's modesty, kindness and equanimity had much to commend them.

54   Ibid., p. 194.
55   Ibid., p. 218.

4

Percy Spender and Club America in the 1950s

David Lowe

In March 1952, almost one year into his term as Ambassador, Percy Spender wrote a long, concerned letter to Dick Casey, Spender's successor as Australian Minister for External Affairs. Spender was worried that the new Pacific Council, recently born of the Australia, New Zealand, United States Security Treaty (ANZUS) (but not yet having met), was in danger of being marginalised by the amount of strategic planning activity occurring under the umbrella of NATO, supplemented by separate high-level conversations relating to Japan and Germany. Given NATO's dominance and its consideration of the broadest possible range of international security matters, that body inevitably presided on matters that would affect Australia in the Pacific. Spender therefore urged Casey to consider lobbying for some form of formal connection to NATO to avoid being constantly 'on the outer'.[1] This last comment, one that was repeated in similar forms by Spender over the next six years, sets the tone for this chapter.

Prior to his arrival in Washington in May 1951, Spender's story had been one of strong ambition and determination overcoming humble beginnings and enabling him a spectacular rise in Australian social, legal and political circles. Born in 1897, the son of a Sydney locksmith,

---

1   Percy Spender to Richard G. Casey, 18 March 1952, letter, Spender Papers, item MS 4975, box 1, folder 3, National Library of Australia (NLA), Canberra.

he had earned a place at Sydney's Fort Street High School, known for enabling social mobility, and he had subsequently been a night student in arts and law before becoming a successful barrister and then entering federal politics in 1937. He stood then as an independent candidate for the Sydney seat of Warringah, but soon joined the major anti-Labor party, the United Australia Party, which was replaced in the political firmament by the Liberal Party of Australia after World War II. During the first part of World War II Spender had served in Menzies' Cabinets, first as Treasurer and then Minister for the Army, and he remained on the bipartisan Advisory War Council after Labor took office in October 1941. Spender did not play a major role in the formation of the new Liberal Party at the end of the war, but he joined and became Minister for External Affairs in Menzies' Liberal/Country Party Coalition Government elected in December 1949.

As Minister for External Affairs for only 16 months (December 1950 – April 1951), Spender is rightly remembered for his key role in connection with two landmarks in Australia's foreign policy, the Colombo Plan for Co-operative Economic Development in South and Southeast Asia, and the ANZUS Treaty between Australia, New Zealand and the United States. The Colombo Plan, briefly known as the 'Spender Plan', took its final name from a meeting of Commonwealth foreign ministers in Ceylon at the beginning of 1950, and was fleshed out at two further meetings that year. These yielded a permanent organisation comprising regular meetings of participating countries in a consultative committee and a separate group overseeing technical aid. Less a 'plan' than a coordinated series of bilateral agreements, the Colombo Plan became one of the most constructive means by which Australian governments engaged with a decolonising Asia over the next 30 years.

A security pact for the Pacific was one of Spender's publicly stated goals from the moment he took office as Minister for External Affairs. He also declared, in March 1950, that he wanted the Australia–US relationship to become '[s]omewhat the same relationship as exists within the British Commonwealth',[2] a bold declaration given the deep ties between Australia and Britain. During the second half of 1950, after the outbreak of the Korean War on 26 July, American interest in a Pacific security pact grew, as part of a broader vision of an island chain of security running

---

2   *Commonwealth Parliamentary Debates*, House of Representatives, 9 March 1950, vol. 206, pp. 635–6.

from Japan to Australia. US Special Envoy John Foster Dulles visited Australia in February 1951 for talks with Spender and his colleagues that ultimately led to the drafting of the ANZUS Treaty, signed later that year and ratified by all parties by the following year. The backdrop of deepening Cold War tension was crucial in this process towards the conclusion of the tripartite security treaty – when Dulles was in Canberra in February 1951, the South Korean capital Seoul lay in communist hands and Chinese forces had joined North Koreans in a bloody struggle against American-led UN forces there. Whether the treaty would meet Spender's high expectations of access to US global strategic planning in the Cold War remained to be seen.[3]

A new standard

It is well documented that Ambassador Spender's life and work in the US from 1951 to 1958 marked a new high in the assertiveness and effectiveness of an overseas representative.[4] In overview, Spender was a very successful ambassador in a number of ways. First, he drew on every aspect of real and imagined authority that came with a Minister for External Affairs (December 1949 – March 1951) translating to the position of ambassador, rather like Australian high commissioners in London who had drawn on their authority as former prime ministers, and like later ambassadors in Washington – Beale, Peacock, Beazley and Hockey – who drew on their authority as ministers. Spender thus constantly pushed the boundaries of his remit with Canberra. Even if he could not circumvent the supremacy of his Prime Minister, Menzies and also Casey, as makers of foreign policy as much as he would have liked, Spender ensured the continued rise in importance of the American alliance and the rise of the Washington embassy in Canberra minds.

The terms of his appointment marked a new high for Australia's foreign service. He earned an annual salary of AU£3,500, plus travel and child allowances, at a fixed exchange rate of AU£1 to US$4.86. In his final year of service, 1957, the real rate of exchange stood at US$2.25. He also received a lump sum living allowance of AU£14,350, against which, contrary to standard departmental practice, he did not need to

---

3   See David Lowe, 'Percy Spender: Minister and Ambassador' in Joan Beaumont, Christopher Waters, David Lowe with Garry Woodard, *Ministers, Mandarins and Diplomats: Australian Foreign Policy Making 1941–1969*, Melbourne University Press, Melbourne, 2003, pp. 62–74.
4   Ibid., pp. 75–87.

produce receipts for expenditure.[5] Not only were these terms at great variance with the parlous conditions of more junior members of the diplomatic service, they reverberated in ways that shifted the landscape of plum, politically sought-after overseas posts. It was significant, for example, that when Sir Eric Harrison was appointed Australia's High Commissioner to the United Kingdom in 1956, he argued for parity with Spender's conditions rather than any previous standard that had been used for London.[6]

The strong sense of activism and licence that Spender carried with him to Washington was especially evident during the first half of his tenure, through 1954, and was felt and mostly welcomed by other members of the embassy. Alan Renouf, then Second Secretary in the embassy, has recalled the excitement and challenges of making the running on policy without waiting for Canberra's instructions. Spender once told him to draw up a draft of an agreement between Australia and the US on shared information about atomic energy, and when Renouf suggested seeking instructions from Canberra, Spender's reply was: 'Bugger instructions. I don't need instructions on a thing like this. I know better than Canberra.'[7]

Similarly, Spender established and maintained a high profile in Washington and further afield in the US. He did so especially through accepting invitations and undertaking speaking tours offered by community groups such as Rotary and also universities wanting to add variety to their convocation speakers, in the process generating good publicity and goodwill towards Australia. Spender was particularly well-known as a speaker in different cities of the US for the English-Speaking Union of the United States, the mission of which was 'To strengthen the friendly relationship between the peoples of the United States of America and of the British Commonwealth by disseminating knowledge of each to the other, and by inspiring reverence for their common traditions'.[8] Thanks to his wife Jean who accompanied him on

---

5   Casey to Menzies, 10 December 1957, letter, M2576/1 item 39, National Archives of Australia (NAA), Canberra; Spender to Casey, 2 August 1951, letter, Casey Desk Correspondence, Department of Foreign Affairs and Trade (DFAT), Canberra.
6   Casey to Menzies, 14 June 1955, memo, enclosing Menzies to White draft letter (sent 29 June 1955), M2576/1 item 39, NAA, Canberra.
7   Alan Renouf and Michael Wilson, 23 November 1993, interview, TRC-2981/6, 51, NLA, Canberra.
8   English-Speaking Union, New York, *A Chronicle of the English Speaking Union*, New York, 1970.

many of his trips across the States and recorded details in a published memoir, *Ambassador's Wife*, we have a good record of Spender's restless energies playing out well beyond the District of Columbia.[9]

Spender's longevity was a factor in his impact in Washington. Towards the end of his tenure he had become dean of the British Commonwealth ambassadors, and he was not backward in reminding the British embassy of his pre-eminence in protocol for the Royal visit by Queen Elizabeth and the Duke of Edinburgh in 1957.[10] Indeed, Spender struck an effective balance between drawing on the collective strength of the Commonwealth and the enduring prestige of the British (or English-speaking) world, on the one hand, while cultivating a strident sense of Australian diplomatic distinctiveness on the other. In addition to his longevity, the other material factor that helped build his profile was his successful building of embassy numbers during this time. He successfully campaigned for additional personnel attached to Australia's representation at the UN and in the embassy's publicity department. At the same time, he relished his own annual performances leading Australia's delegations to meetings of the General Assembly (after Casey had come for the opening sessions) to the middle of the decade and driving, at local and regional levels, Australia's successful campaign for an elected seat on the Security Council. Bearing out his strength as a former politician, he also ran successful campaigns to hold firm on Article 2(7), the domestic jurisdiction clause of the Charter that kept the UN from hearing domestic matters, unless there was a threat to peace, and in maintaining Western bloc solidarity on several issues relating to the Korean War.[11] So engaged in UN affairs was Spender, and so keen to wield his own influence, that by the time of the successful bid for the Security Council seat in 1955, Canberra was forced to think through and provide greater clarity to the relationship between the head of mission at the UN and the Ambassador in Washington. Both New York and Washington gained in quality and number of Australian diplomats during the 1950s, a product also of the more general rise in diplomacy in New York as more nation-members joined the UN, and of

9   Jean Spender, *Ambassador's Wife*, Angus and Robertson, Sydney, 1968.
10   Ibid., pp. 184–5, 188–9.
11   See especially David Lowe, *Australian Between Empires: the life of Percy Spender*, Pickering & Chatto, London, 2010, and 'Mr Spender Goes to Washington: An Australian Ambassador's Vision of Australian-American Relations, 1951–58', *Journal of Imperial and Commonwealth History*, vol. 24, no. 2, 1996, pp. 278–95.

Casey's enduring faith in the powers of personal diplomacy.[12] Such were the new Australian expectations that one US-based British diplomat remarked in 1954:

> Canberra may be content to be told that discussions are about to begin in Washington on topics of interest to Australia and that Australia will be told in due course afterwards what has happened. The Australian embassy here (whatever the attitude of Canberra) will not accept this.[13]

There is, underpinning this sketch of Spender and his legacy, a strong theme of restless, energetic behaviour; of someone who pushes to the limits the representational brief of the ambassador as he determines to give himself the strongest possible sense of licence and the capacity to be an agent of change. Such activism reflected Spender's personality and was more possible for two powerful considerations: first, for his having made the transition to Washington from the post of Minister for External Affairs; and secondly, for there being too few precedents up to that point in 1951 of Australian ambassadors overseas to have set some boundaries around behaviour. Percy Spender made the most of both these factors.

Networks and members

This chapter now turns to another, less-explored feature of Percy Spender's tenure as Ambassador, namely his anxiety at the prospect of being left out of clubs wherein the best networks operated and the biggest decisions were made. This was evident in his concerned letter to Casey, cited at the beginning of this chapter, about the risk of Australia being left out of a NATO club. Club membership is a metaphor that has broader utility to the history of Australian representation in the US. In Spender's case, it took on particular significance for reasons that go to the sociopolitical dynamics of being in Washington in an era that was distinctive for: the development of the ANZUS Treaty and the hopes that it might constitute an open door to NATO or at least higher level strategic planning with global remit; the sudden growth of

---

12   Casey and Menzies to Spender, 7 June 1955, Casey desk correspondence, DFAT, Canberra; Casey diary entries, 21 September, 7 October 1955, Casey Diaries, MS6150, series 4, box 27, NLA, Canberra.
13   RH Scott (British Embassy, Washington) to WD Allen (UK Foreign Office), 30 December 1954, DO 35/10777, The National Archives, London.

the international diplomatic community through the admission of new nations to the UN Organisation; and the behaviours of the Washington 'set', including the diplomatic corps.

In other words, the undercurrent of much-sought membership of an increasingly important but elusive 'club' wherein the most important decisions affecting the free world were being made has particular resonance with the conditions Spender faced in the 1950s. And, given his recurring sensitivity to being left 'on the outer', we profit from bringing to this picture a stronger sense of what he felt it was to be 'in or out' in Washington. The contemporary observer whose work best targeted this slippery notion of 'clubbish' behaviour among elites in 1950s America was the controversial sociologist, C Wright Mills. Of three books he produced between 1948 and 1956, the best-known and most highly regarded was *The Power Elite*, published in 1956.[14] In this work, Mills argued that the new wielders of power in America were effectively understood from a Weberian more than a Marxist perspective. They depended for their status more on institutional and social standing than on economic power; and they dominated positions in government, the military and the corporate world. A sharp critic of the US national security state, Mills paid special attention to the importance of schooling ('the one deep association that distinguishes the social rich from the merely rich and those below')[15] and the ongoing associations and sensibilities attached to attending the right school. He noted the rise of the military and he argued that families of 'old money' were being marginalised by the new elite. Claiming that a new epoch had dawned, he wrote that:

> a conjunction of historical circumstances has led to the rise of an elite of power; that the men of the circles composing this elite, severally and collectively, now make such key decisions as are made; and that, given the enlargement and the centralization of the means of power now available, the decisions that they make and fail to make carry more consequences for more people than has ever been the case in the world history of mankind.[16]

---

14   Charles Wright Mills, *The Power Elite*, Oxford University Press, New York, 1956. The other two titles were *New Men of Power: America's Labor Leaders*, Harcourt, New York, 1948, and *White Collar: the American Middle Classes*, Oxford University Press, New York, 1956.

15   Mills, *Power Elite*, p. 63.

16   Ibid., p. 28.

The different cities of the US shaped the particular characteristics to what constituted 'society' in different locations, according to Mills. In Detroit, for example, it was who you were in the auto industry; and in Washington the equation was simple: anyone official was society. The power of wealth in the Capitol was, 'overshadowed and out-ranked by official Society, especially by the Embassy Row along Massachusetts Avenue'.[17] There was no cafe society as such in Washington, because the key affairs took place in embassies, private houses and official residences: 'In fact, there is no really firm line-up of Society in Washington, composed as it is of public officials and politicians, of familied hostesses and wealthy climbers, of widows with know-how and ambassadors with unofficial messages to impart.'[18]

Although criticised at the time for featuring more assertion than evidence, Mills' *Power Elite* became an enduring critique of the US Cold War establishment, and, when read with President Eisenhower's parting warning in 1961 about the development of an overly influential 'military-industrial complex', its influence on interpretations of the decade has lingered. Not surprisingly, the sociocultural dynamics of exclusive clubs has also continued to interest commentators. A recent study of membership of US country clubs, for example, stresses the basic qualities of homophily – the act of mixing with people like oneself. Interactions with people like oneself instil and reinforce the unwritten laws of social life and ensure that the next generation is able to assume their rightful place; and such interactions reinforce a group's distinctiveness, divisions between 'them' and 'us'. And US club membership is a means by which you perpetuate group identity by reinforcing networks, liaisons and a shared sense of loyalty to the group.[19]

For many Australian politicians and diplomats of the 1940s and 1950s, club memberships of some form were the norm. In Spender's case, his rise in seniority through Sydney's masonic lodges and through the Royal Empire Society paralleled his rise in Australian politics from the late 1930s. His story was also one of transcending class origins, given his relatively humble background followed by rapid rise in law and then politics. Schooling at Fort Street High, based on excellent results at primary level, was an important platform for later success at the University

---

17   Ibid., pp. 83 and 78.
18   Ibid., p. 83.
19   Jessica Holden Sherwood, *Wealth, Whiteness, and the Matrix of Privilege: The View from the Country Club*, Lexington Books, Lanham, 2012, pp. 15–17 and passim.

of Sydney and at the New South Wales Bar. His career success prior to entering politics in 1937 was matched by upwards residential mobility in Sydney – arriving in Woollahra, via Bellevue Hill and Turramurra.

It is beyond the scope of this chapter to interrogate Australian or US educational and social organisations in any depth, and it can only touch indirectly on privilege and class as recurrent themes in the life and work of Percy Spender (although he remained critical of these at the same time that he sought membership among those blessed by them). More central is the importance he attached to being in the right society or club at the start of what C Wright Mills called a new epoch. This was a time when being 'in' might prove absolutely essential, according to his conception of Australia's interests, given the potential for far-reaching decisions, and at a time when a threatening environment and the arrival of new players made the exclusivity of a well-functioning policymaking club all the more precious. Spender, more than his former Cabinet colleagues in Canberra, saw the early 1950s as a pivotal period in which new international dangers would amplify and the shape of new or refashioned alliances would settle quickly. For Australia, a small-to-middle power in the South Pacific, it would be crucial to be sitting at the right table when this happened.

Cold War collegiality

The strategic environment of Cold War alliance and growing concern with communist advances in Asia provided the greatest alarm, from Spender's sense of Australian security interests, and also the most logical means by which to win goodwill in the inner policymaking circles of Washington. During the early 1950s ANZUS, while ratified by 1952, was very much formative in its accepted implications. Deprived of the North Atlantic Treaty's teeth, wherein an attack on one was deemed an attack on all, ANZUS was a work in progress, and no one could be certain of what organisational machinery – what kind of 'O' in NATO – might sustain it. Spender was acutely aware of the potential for ANZUS to suffer the fate of the advisory councils relating to the Pacific in the Second World. These became exercises in providing information to junior allies such as Australia while keeping them distant from strategic policymaking. While ANZUS, and the early ANZUS Council meetings arising from the Treaty, would never satisfy Spender's high expectations for a foot in the door of higher strategic planning, he was determined that no one should spoil the potential at least that ANZUS constituted. When, for example, he heard of the British inclination to disturb or diminish the standing of ANZUS early in 1953, he wrote to Menzies using choice language:

> if we are to allow anything to interfere with ANZUS, whether on the political or military plane, we will lose the only means we have on any effective entry into U.S.A. political and military thinking at a high level and the intimacy which ANZUS unquestionably affords us. For the first time we have got a toe hold into the council of the U.S.A. which affects the world and its destiny at a high and acknowledged level through ANZUS.[20]

For much of Spender's term, he conveyed a strong message that these were transformed, crucial times: pivotal to the outcome of the free world and to Australia's security, and that there were rare opportunities for Australians to punch above their weight in being heard in the highest policymaking circles in Washington. In the kind of language he deployed, Australia could avoid being on the 'outer' in this era of direction-setting and turn its toehold into something that was an alliance of breadth and depth. But, to persist with the metaphor, the toehold enjoyed by Australia – and by extension, for Percy Spender – was not something that would become a more solid footing without Canberra sharing his view that it was time to seize the moment and bank some serious goodwill with the Americans who mattered.

Achieving this in the context of US strategic policymaking was going to be hard, but Cold War crises threw up opportunities. It is easy now to forget how unsettled US defence thinking was in relation to developments in Southeast Asia in the early to mid-1950s. Public statements by Cabinet members could differ greatly from what State Department and Pentagon officials were saying to members of the Australian embassy. As is well-told elsewhere, some of the volatility in US policy came to the fore in relation to the collapse of the French in Vietnam in 1954.[21] This generated a flurry of meetings contemplating some form of US intervention, possibly backed by an international group

---

20 Spender to Menzies, 29 May 1953, cablegram, item CRS A1838/269 TS686/1 part 3, NAA, Canberra.
21 See especially Gregory J Pemberton, 'Australia, the United States and the Indo-China Crisis of 1954', *Diplomatic History*, vol. 13, no. 1, 1989, pp. 45–66; Hiroyuki Umetsu, 'Australia's Response to the Indochina Crisis of 1954 Amidst Anglo-American Confrontation', *Australian Journal of Politics and History*, vol. 52, no. 3, 2006, pp. 398–416.

of allies including Australia. As a case study, the Indochina crisis of 1954 tested the embassy for its complexity, with Spender and senior diplomats needing to sort through the differing views of the Pentagon, State Department, Presidential Office and Congressional leaders. When US officials sought to clarify willingness of their allies to commit to possible military intervention on behalf of the struggling French, Spender was inclined to keep Australia in the right group – those who would respond when the circumstances demanded: 'One of the primary aims of our policy over recent years', he wrote to External Affairs Minister Casey:

> has been as I understand it to achieve the acceptance by U.S.A. of responsibility in S.E. Asia. It is for consideration whether, if we fail to respond at all to the opportunity now presented what U.S. reactions are likely to be if and when areas closer to Australia are in jeopardy.[22]

On this occasion he ran too far ahead of Casey, Menzies and a more cautious Australian Cabinet, and was disappointed to have to temper his government's support in communications with the US State Department.[23]

In the wake of the crisis, or really several crisis moments between April and July 1954, the Australians joined with others keenly interested in the security of Southeast Asia to sign the Southeast Asia Collective Defense Treaty in September, which formally translated into an organisation, the Southeast Asia Treaty Organization (SEATO), soon afterwards. Such was his investment in mechanisms for thickening the US–Australia relationship that Spender drafted and circulated his own version of SEATO, complete with a robust Council, a Security Bureau designed to boost the region's capacity to combat internal communist subversion, and ambitious measures for atomic energy and economic cooperation within the group. Canberra backed away quickly from most of this, nor did the final version of the treaty reflect these more adventurous ideas.[24] Spender's analysis of US thinking behind the establishment of SEATO was that it was a worrying means by which Washington was creating room to move unburdened of the need to consult allies such as Australia. It was desirable chiefly on account of the freedom of action it would lend

---

22   Spender to Casey, cablegram no. 326, CRS A5462/1 item 2/4/1 part 2, NAA, Canberra, underlining in original.
23   Pemberton, 'Australia, the United States, and the Indo-China Crisis', pp. 45–66.
24   Spender, 'SATO' (Spender's draft defined South Asia generously), draft for consideration, 9 July 1954, Spender papers, item MS 4875, box 8, folder Miscellaneous Papers and Documents, NLA, Canberra.

the Americans to meet contingencies in Southeast Asia as they pleased – 'freedom in terms of internal US politics and opinion, in terms of US constitutional practice, and in terms of international western public opinion'.[25]

Spender feared that the Pentagon would ultimately fall back on an 'island chain' defence mentality, the use of US bases strung throughout islands from Japan to the Philippines, as the most reliable and realistic defence of their interests, rather than contemplating intervention against communist-led forces on the mainland of Southeast Asia. Linked with a seeming preparedness for 'massive retaliation' for decisive, possibly nuclear, strikes from US bases, this made good sense to American defence planners. According to Spender, this might not be disastrous to Australia's interests, given ANZUS and Australia's strategic significance at the end of the chain of islands, but he added that such thinking missed the point. Any apparent abandonment of mainland Southeast Asia would inevitably make Australia's security predicament harder in the long run; reliance on 'massive retaliation', envisaging the possible use of nuclear weapons, offered little alternative if that was suddenly to be abandoned or unsuccessful. And finally, he wrote:

> in this context there would not appear to be a great deal of room for Australia to play an effective part in strategic planning for the area. There would in fact be little strategic planning to be done outside the Pentagon. In other words the U.S. would take general responsibility for planning and policy – either alone or, possibly making some provision for limited co-operation with the U.K and perhaps Australia, in a 'standing group' on NATO lines. There is distinct possibility in my opinion that Australia might be regarded as having given through ... SEATO the equivalent of moral support to whatever actions flows from U.S. planning and policy, but would have little opportunity of influencing either.[26]

It seems that Spender was somewhat deflated by the terms of SEATO and what he observed to be the low regard in which it was held in Washington. He did not give up, however, suggesting to Canberra, in relation to subsequent episodes such as the offshore islands crisis endangering Taiwan in 1955, that an Australian preparedness to state

---

25   Spender to Casey, 8 October 1954, Ministerial Despatch no. 6/54, CRS A 4231/2 WASHINGTON 1954, NAA, Canberra.
26   Ibid.

firmly the conditions under which they would join in US-led military action in Asia might help firm up the quality of American collaboration in security policy.[27]

Complicating internationalism

The growth of the international community constituted a challenge to the exclusiveness of the kind of inner-circle membership Spender sought for Australia. While he was in Washington, and also representing Australia at the UN meetings in New York, he witnessed an explosion in membership of the UN. Indonesia's joining at the end of 1950 was significant, and then 19 further members were added in 1955–56, several of them recently independent or members of the communist bloc. Their opposition to Cold War polarity and the accumulation of nuclear weapons, and their support for rapid dismantling of remaining empires and their lobbying on behalf of countries still colonised, became a feature of the new members' activities in the UN. In May 1955, the collective gathering of 29 representatives from Asian and African nations at the Bandung conference in Indonesia lent further strength to these causes while ushering in the non-alignment movement. Cumulatively, such developments radicalised the international community.

As is well-known, Spender was proactive in response. He was one of the most vociferous in his invoking Article 2(7), the domestic jurisdiction clause of the UN Charter, in efforts to keep Indonesia away from what was then called West New Guinea; and this was matched by a more general determination to defend Australia's record and the record of other enlightened colonial powers. In one of his early skirmishes with the anti-colonial group, in the Assembly at the end of 1952 he signalled his impatience with the groups of members who were amplifying the principle of self-determination to histrionic levels, devoid, in his view, of any sense of a colony's development and readiness for self-government.[28] Referring to some draft resolutions along these lines, Spender said that they:

---

27 Spender to Menzies (from London), 26 January 1955, cablegram, TS No. 82, CRS A5462/1 item 3/13/4 part 5, NAA, Canberra.
28 See David Lowe, 'Australia at the United Nations in the 1950s: The Paradox of Empire', *Australian Journal of International Affairs*, vol. 51, no. 2, 1997, pp. 171–81.

form part of a campaign ... which some countries, I regret exceedingly to have to say, see fit to wage against what they call colonialism. They see in this colonialism everything bad and identified with exploitation. They ignore, or pretend to ignore, all or most of its achievements. Many States now Members of this Organization have been led, by the friendly tutelage of a mandate system and by this self-same colonialism, to the attainment of their complete sovereignty and independence.[29]

Spender's embrace of postwar internationalism was real but heavily qualified by his expectation that it would be some time before conditions in the international community enabled a body such as the UN to fulfil its potential. The hopes of 1945, he thought, had fallen well short due to the lack of great power unanimity. It was a case of being optimistic that some of those hopes of 1945 liberal internationalism might one day move closer to realisation but in the meantime there was a need to be mindful of where power lay. 'The Charter of the United Nations is no substitute for power', he said on the 10th anniversary of the UN's formation, in 1955. 'On the contrary, it assumes the existence of power and seeks to see that it is employed for the defence of liberty and not for the enslavement of free people.'[30]

In particular, the atomic arms race, taking hold in the 1950s and assuming ever deadlier proportions in the size of weapons being tested, meant that great power and responsibility lay in the hands of those who possessed bombs. In speaking to the possibility of apocalyptic nuclear war, at the First Committee in November 1953, he said, '[t]he truth of the matter is that it is not within this organization that any solution will be found'. While disarmament efforts foundered on Soviet intransigence over provisions for inspections, Spender reminded members, 'were it not for the supremacy which the US of America in particular possesses in atomic weapon power, and its awful deterrent to war, the peril to the free world would have been very great indeed'.[31] Taken in conjunction with Spender's concerns that voting patterns in the UN would be harder to control with the increasing assertiveness of the Afro-Asian bloc after

29 *UN General Assembly Official Record*, Seventh Session, 403rd Plenary Meeting, 16 December 1952, p. 372.
30 Spender, speech delivered to Lincoln University, Nebraska, 11 July 1955, Spender Papers, item MS4875, box 4, folder 19, NLA, Canberra.
31 Spender's statement in the UN First Committee, 11 November 1953, Spender Papers, item MS4875, box 3, folder 17, NLA, Canberra.

1955, it was a case of managing this forum rather than expecting it deliver in the interests of Australian security – at least in the foreseeable short-term.

The Washington set

As Mills described with reference to officialdom and diplomats in *The Power Elite*, the Spenders were very much part of 'society' as it took shape in Washington. 'Parties, parties and more parties' was how Jean Spender recalled the city, likening it to a social merry-go-round but one that was also competitive and of 'intense interest to so many people'.[32] Among the private papers of Percy Spender held at the National Library of Australia is a 560-page first draft of what became Jean's published book, *Ambassador's Wife*.[33] Mercifully, the transition to print saw a significant reduction in the relentless number of social encounters described, but the unabridged version remains valuable for its rather literal capture of the contents of formal engagement books that Jean kept. As their teenage sons, Peter and John, settled into school and then university (St Albans for the younger John and Yale for both), she and Percy observed with interest the elaborate etiquette attaching to debutante balls, 21st birthday parties and other rituals accompanying the young elite of Washington.[34] Peter embraced the networking opportunities that came thick and fast. He worked at Westinghouse during the summer of 1953 and graduated with a Bachelor of Arts from Yale in June 1954, and in the same month was married at Georgetown Episcopal Church. His bride, Ann Foster Lynch, was the daughter of Charles Francis Lynch, a US Navy Captain, and grand-daughter of the late Judge Rufus Foster, a former senior judge of the US Appeals Court.[35] Peter's brother John graduated from Yale with a law degree three years later. At one point, in May 1956, John benefited from the comments of his father's friend, US Secretary of State John Foster Dulles, on one of his longer essays. As Dulles noted in passing on his admiring comments to Percy, '[i]f my associates in the State Department knew that I had

---

32   Jean Spender, *Ambassador's Wife*, Angus and Robertson, Sydney, 1968, p. 34.
33   Jean Spender, Unpublished manuscript of Ambassador's Wife, Spender Papers, item MS4875, box 9, p. 350, NLA, Canberra.
34   Ibid., pp. 74–5, 257.
35   *Truth,* 23 May 1954, in Spender Papers, Newscuttings Album, item MS4875/32, NLA, Canberra.

taken the time to read anything so extensive, they would be very jealous because I assure them that I cannot read anything more than about two pages long'.[36]

While awash with social occasions, Washington was also slightly more manageable for the Spenders in the 1950s than later. When they arrived in May 1951 the number of foreign embassies there stood at just over 60; when they left in 1958 there were more than 80, which made the obligatory calls for any new ambassador especially gruelling. And the after-effects of US servicemen passing through Australia during World War II were strong in this period. The Spenders were struck by the number of people who approached them in the wake of a speech or some other publicised activity to pass on their thanks for Australian hospitality that had been extended to one of their men-folk.[37]

Washington suited the Spenders for its opportunities to advance certain causes in both formal and informal settings. Percy and Jean enjoyed developing an understanding of the Washington hostess – in Jean's words, 'apart from offering great enjoyment to their guests, they also offered opportunities for encounters and discussions on neutral ground between many official people'.[38] They made friends readily among senior political and military families, including Admirals Carney, Radford and Burke, Herman Phleger, legal adviser in the State Department and friend of President Eisenhower, and the Dulles brothers, as well as Oscar Hammerstein and his Australian wife and interior decorator Dorothy. By 1954, Australian newspapers were describing the Spenders as 'ornaments of the social scene, not only in the national capital but at the cocktail parties of the UNO set in New York and at the summer colonies of Newport, Southampton and other fashionable centres'.[39]

Gregarious and cheeky, Spender was fond of singing current tunes, and made a habit of ending some parties with a rendition of Hank Fort's popular song, 'Put your shoes on, Lucy'. The Ambassador actually bumped into Fort at some of the Washington parties, and sang with

---

36   Dulles to Spender, 14 May 1956, letter, Spender Papers, MS 4875, box 1, folder 5, NLA, Canberra.
37   Jean Spender, Unpublished manuscript of Ambassador's Wife, p. 40.
38   Ibid.
39   *Telegraph* (Sydney), 7 June 1954, Spender Papers, Newscuttings Album, MS4875/32, NLA, Canberra.

her.[40] There was something apt about Percy's love of a song about a wide-eyed Tennessee girl taking up an invitation to go to Manhattan with her 'highfalutin kin' where she saw all the sights, did some 'flirtin' until her bare feet started 'hurtin', and she had to put her shoes on.[41] On one of the many other occasions Australia's Ambassador broke into song, he joined with Mariana Radford, wife of the then Chairman of the US Joint Chiefs of Staff, in a special-service train on their way back from a Navy versus Army football match.[42]

Percy embraced the distinctive Washington atmosphere of mixing with like-minded officials in different contexts that resembled the characteristics of club membership, blending social occasion with business opportunity. Having already become an Australian Director of Goodyear Tire and Rubber Company in 1944, he relished the trappings of this association and the greater opportunities to connect with Goodyear headquarters in Akron, Ohio. He loved it, for example, when the Goodyear Tire and Rubber Company sent its own plane to fly him to meetings in Akron. In October 1953, the *Akron Beacon Journal* feted him as the company's guest speaker at the 55th anniversary banquet.[43] His own interests and his observations of the interconnectivity of corporate, military and government realms led him to urge other Australians to recognise that there were fewer sharp lines between different spheres of business in the US, and that they should adjust accordingly. Early on in his tenure, in some of his longer, more reflective messages to Casey and Menzies, Spender conveyed a sense of Washington policymakers as different from the British for their inclination to see relationships as a package that should not be unpicked into different policy areas: 'The United States official', wrote Spender, 'is not as inclined as his United Kingdom counterpart to draw a firm line between political and economic co-operation and regard as friendly those countries that co-operate politically even though they will not co-operate economically'.[44]

---

40   *Washington Post*, 1 June 1955, Spender Papers, Newscuttings Album, MS4875/33, NLA, Canberra.
41   Hank Fort, lyrics for 'Put your shoes on, Lucy'.
42   Jean Spender, Unpublished manuscript of Ambassador's Wife, pp. 337–38.
43   *Akron Beacon Journal*, 5 October 1953, p 1.
44   Spender to Menzies, 29 April 1952, letter, Spender Papers, item MS4975, box 1, folder 3, NLA, Canberra.

Insider

Spender used the information gathered from his networks to try to intervene in policy discussions at the most propitious time. His drafting of his own version of what was to become SEATO followed his being tipped off that his friend in the State Department, Herman Phleger, was about to draw up the first US draft of the treaty. Spender handed his copy to Under Secretary of State Walter Bedell Smith, and members of the British, New Zealand and Canadian High Commissions, and only then told Casey what he had done.[45] Timing was, of course, everything, and on this occasion it resulted in Casey's annotating some heavily inked question marks on the letter informing him, post-hoc, of these events. Near this time, Spender also wrote one his most strident pleas for Canberra to fall in behind American defence policy for Southeast Asia, and to internationalise the crisis in Indochina in 1954 in a manner that might lead to military support for the French. As noted above, he argued that to have the US committed in Southeast Asia was a primary goal of Australian foreign policy, and to forego the opportunity to facilitate this was, he implied, madness.[46] Significantly, this message came after some long hours spent down the road at the house of John Foster Dulles.

Arguably, Spender became somewhat seduced by the notion that talking to the right people at the right time could make a huge difference in how Australian interests were advanced. He seemed to live with a feeling that the window for Australian influence was small and usually took the form of unscripted, informal encounters; if you missed your chance then you were destined to be swept to one side as old patterns of behaviour dictated how US foreign policy would unfold. At the height of to-ing and fro-ing with Canberra over American thinking about Indochina after the fall of Dien Bien Phu, Spender set out his expectations thus:

> Whether the question be how any settlement in Indo China is to be effectively guaranteed – or in the absence of any settlement – what can and should we do either by way of assistance to the French, etc. or by way of general security arrangements in South East Asia – these are all questions which must in the end by settled by careful and I fear long consultation between at least ten powers. If we delay such a consultation too long the capacity of Australia – since it is not a party to Indo China

---

45   Spender to Casey, 12 June 1954, letter, Casey Desk Papers, DFAT, Canberra.
46   Spender to Casey, 6 April 1954, cablegram no. 326, CRS A5462/1 item 2/4/1 part 2, NAA, Canberra.

discussions – to influence events which can and will bear seriously upon its destiny will I fear diminish, since US thinking one way or another is likely in the meantime, by however tortuous processes, to crystallize.[47]

He finished this cable to Casey by suggesting that Australians had played a big role in ensuring that the Americans had become fully seized of the security importance of Southeast Asia, and it ill behoved Australians now to let the Americans down by appearing to be unwilling to pull their weight.[48] Any ambassador walks a fine line when they allude to a certain 'insider' status among leading policymakers of the country in which they are based. Spender's references to private meetings with Dulles, to consulting with him in Dulles' home and to having access to 'very private information'[49] seemed to cross a line with Menzies, in particular, who began to find it hard, in Spender's communications, to distinguish between Spender's thoughts and those of Dulles.

It is not suggested here that Spender is best understood by his 'going native', a fate sometimes imagined of long-term overseas representatives. Indeed, Sir Percy Spender derived a lot of his cache and even a little mystique from his hybrid identity as a part of the British world but something more exciting than your general Britisher. And his strident Australian nationalism, often manifest in diplomatic exchanges at the expense of the British, was well-noted. He wanted to be an insider, become a club member, more than going native, and he could not mask this in his communications with Canberra. In the latter half of his tenure he would boast about the 'purely personal basis' upon which he was given information, or upon which US delegates had helped him muster support against the Indonesians in General Assembly voting on West New Guinea.[50] It is not that the personally provided, in-confidence information was something flowing only to Spender. It is very likely that other Australian representatives overseas prided themselves on special connections that gave them privileged insights; but for Spender it took on an elevated importance.

---

47   Spender to Casey, cablegram, TS no. 551, CRS A5462/1 item 2/4/1 part 4, NAA, Canberra.
48   Ibid.
49   Spender to Menzies and Casey, 6 June 1954, cablegram no. 568, CRS A5462/1 item 2/4/1 part 4, NAA, Canberra.
50   Spender to Casey, 14 December 1955, Ministerial Despatch no. 3/55, CRS A4321/2 UN 1955, NAA, Canberra.

Spender was widely seen as fitting into the Washington diplomatic scene very readily. A little over a year after his arrival, British journalist Kenneth Harris wrote that 'Of the 70 or so ambassadors who are stationed in Washington, the one who has made the widest and most agreeable impact upon the American people is Spender'.[51] Another journalist, Australian Peter Hastings, who admired Spender, wrote at the end of 1953 of Spender's popularity in Washington; his more relaxed manner and ready wit being well-attuned to after-dinner speeches, his connections to the Dulles brothers clearly a good thing; and his thirst for hard work much admired.[52]

The Washington 'scene' suited Spender's temperament. He enjoyed the sporting aspects of country clubs, including tennis with his wife and sons at Chevy Chase and at other clubs when visiting outside Washington. The Louisville *Courier-Journal*, for example, reports on a game between the Spenders and Walter Lippmann and his wife in 1955.[53] In her memoir, Jean comments several times on her fascination or intrigue at the formality of summer houses and country clubs, and the wealth and privilege attached to them.[54] She recalled visiting the Lippmanns' retreat in Bar Harbor, Maine, and learning that when a property had come on to the market, neighbours had rushed to ensure it was purchased – for one dollar – by someone suitable, rather than allowing the market to decide. In this case, the Ambassador for Luxembourg was successfully encouraged to buy.[55]

As was suggested in Jean's description, Percy was similarly most likely taken aback at this. He had, in earlier days, decried the closed membership shops of clubs such as the Royal Sydney Yacht Squadron and Royal Sydney Golf Club, but he had also worked hard to ascend in social circles.[56] He loved testing himself against others and remained keen to impress. Washington society, as sketched by both C Wright Mills and more admiring commentators, was the perfect testing ground.

51   Quoted in *Daily Mirror*, 13 October 1952, Spender Papers, Newscuttings Album, MS4875/30, NLA, Canberra.
52   *Sunday Telegraph*, 13 December 1953, CRS A5954/1 item 77/5, NAA, Canberra.
53   *Courier-Journal*, Louisville, 22 July 1955, Spender papers, Newscuttings Album, MS 4875/33, NLA, Canberra.
54   Jean Spender, *Ambassador's Wife*, pp. 41, 60.
55   Ibid, p. 130.
56   Lowe, *Australian Between Empires*, p. 28.

Conclusion

The character of Percy Spender of course adds a special dimension to his wanting to be a member of the most important club – the policymaking elite club – in Washington, and his determination not to be left on the outer. He arrived in Washington saying that this was where the most important decisions affecting the international community would be made, and he set about trying to work his way into the groups of policy influencers who mattered the most. He also arrived with a capacity to shape the parameters of his ambassadorial activities that was unprecedented and has not been matched since. For a growing embassy, his determination not to be left out of clubs and networks that mattered was a boon; for the Ambassador himself, it was a goal destined to produce both good results and some frustration, as the 'power elite' set boundaries around its otherwise warm embrace of a gregarious and sharp Australian. From Canberra's point of view, Spender must have seemed the right man for Cold War diplomacy in a growing, volatile national security state centred on the US capital, even as he reached the limits of his influence both in Washington and in Canberra.

5

'Mr Necessity': Sir Howard Beale, 1958–64[1]

Matthew Jordan

Howard Beale was appointed Ambassador to the United States in 1957 at a critical time in American and indeed world history. The Cold War was well underway and tensions between the US-led West and Soviet Russia made the prospect of a 'hot war' with all its awful consequences a real possibility. Moved mainly by the inherent strategic limitations of 'massive retaliation', the US increasingly focused on winning 'hearts and minds' in former colonial territories in the Middle East, Asia and Africa during the 1950s and thereby stopping the spread of global communism.[2] This broadening of the policy of containment, based on a continuing belief that communism was monolithic, found its most pertinent manifestation for Australia in the signing of the Manila Pact in September 1954. The pact, which established the Southeast Asia Treaty Organization (SEATO), committed the US to the defence of signatory countries in the event of communist aggression or subversion. Taken together with the Australia, New Zealand, United States Security Treaty (ANZUS), signed three years earlier, SEATO reinforced Australia's identification of the US as its primary great power protector.

1   For their comments and suggestions on earlier versions of this chapter, I would like to thank David Lowe, David McLean, Neville Meaney, Colin Milner and especially James Curran, who was kind enough to give me a large number of key documents from the John F Kennedy Library in Boston.
2   See John Lewis Gaddis, *Strategies of Containment: A Critical Appraisal of Postwar American National Security Policy*, Oxford University Press, New York, 1982, chs 6–8.

The expectation of closer, if not indeed intimate, US–Australia ties had been openly articulated by Beale's predecessor, Percy Spender, who said shortly after arriving in Washington in 1951 that 'putting flesh on the bones of ANZUS' was one of his key aims.[3] It was a strategic objective shared by Beale, who worked hard and mostly successfully to forge close and continuous associations with power-brokers in Washington during his six-year tenure in an effort to promote the primary objective of binding Australia's defence needs in the Asia-Pacific with American Cold War priorities. While this led to Australia's steady association with US aims and objectives in Southeast Asia, manifested most importantly in Australian long-term involvement in the war in Vietnam, it did not produce the culture of obligation or close consultation that Canberra so desperately sought from the US. On the contrary, the foremost problem for Australia during Beale's term – Indonesia and its policy of 'Confrontation' in West New Guinea and Malaysia – demonstrated both the limitations of ANZUS as a vehicle for achieving Australian objectives and the unrealistic expectations that both Beale and senior policymakers in Canberra placed on the alliance.

The parson's son: Early life, worldview and political career

Oliver Howard Beale was born on 10 December 1898 in Tamworth, then a relatively large township of 15,000 people at the foot of the New England tablelands in northern New South Wales. The son of a Methodist minister, young Howard moved frequently according to the needs of Joseph Beale's flock. From Tamworth the family moved to Lismore, on the north coast, where they spent three years; from there to Penrith, west of Sydney; from Penrith to Wagga Wagga, a hub town in the Riverina; and from there to Willoughby, in north Sydney. In 1910, when Beale was 11, his father died of pneumonia.[4] This had a terrible effect on the family, perhaps aggravating what Beale referred to as a 'delicate' constitution – but what was later diagnosed as rheumatic fever – and consigning the family to a life of struggle on a Methodist widow's 'very small' pension. They moved to Croydon, then an outer

---

3   David Lowe, *Australian Between Empires: The Life of Percy Spender*, Pickering & Chatto, London, 2010, pp. 145–46.
4   Howard Beale, *This Inch of Time: Memoirs of Politics and Diplomacy*, Melbourne University Press, Melbourne, 1977, pp. 4, 10.

suburb of Sydney, where his mother attempted to rebuild. Knowing that 'we only had ourselves to depend on', as Beale would later recall, she exhorted Howard and his three older brothers to 'work and work'. Following the outbreak of World War I, all three brothers joined the Australian Imperial Force. Howard attempted to enlist in 1918 but was rejected because of complications caused by the rheumatic fever. He went back to Sydney University, completed a law degree and was admitted to the Bar in 1925.[5]

Inspired by the resilience of his mother, who imbued him with a deep respect for the liberal-conservative values of hard work, individual initiative and a sense of social responsibility, Beale nevertheless had 'no regard at all' for the United Australia Party, which he dismissed as 'reactionary'.[6] Nor did the Australian Labor Party (ALP) appeal to him. Though conceding that his family background could easily have taken him into the ALP – 'the traditional party of social reform' – Beale was uncomfortable with its emphasis on the idea of community defined by class. He was especially perturbed when the Labor Government of Ben Chifley moved to not only extend wartime controls but also nationalise private institutions such as banks, the insurance industry and the medical profession. It was a defining moment for Beale, who felt that 'those who wanted a future for Australia along different lines ought to get down into the arena'.[7] So when in 1945 Robert Menzies reorganised the country's anti-Labor forces and established the Australian Liberal Party on a platform of abolishing wartime controls and promoting the values and aspirations of middle Australia – the so-called 'forgotten people' for whom Beale had developed such a strong regard – he gave himself fully to the cause. The retirement in 1946 of Frederick Stewart from the blue-ribbon Liberal electorate of Parramatta, west of Sydney, provided an opening to federal parliament and Beale won the seat later that year.[8]

Almost 50, Beale had no intention of sitting passively on the backbench and was unusually boisterous for a new parliamentary member. As Jo Gullett, the Liberal member for the Victorian seat of Henty, wrote his wife at the time, 'Beale the new member is a tiresome fellow

---

5   Mel Pratt with Sir Howard Beale, interview, 20–21 October 1976, series TRC 121/82, National Library of Australia (NLA), Canberra, p. 8. See also ibid.
6   Pratt with Beale, interview, pp. 17–18.
7   Beale, *Inch of Time*, pp. 23, 25.
8   Ibid., pp. 26–28.

with a colossal opinion of himself'.[9] As well as taking every opportunity to criticise the government's continuation of wartime restrictions and its socialisation program, Beale took a particular interest in the role of Australia in international affairs. This was the subject of his maiden speech, during which he attacked the government for showing an insufficient appreciation of Australia's close, or more precisely, integral association with the British Empire.[10] In March 1947, he again weighed into the parliamentary debate on international affairs, saying that there was no point in Australia relying on the US (let alone the UN) for its security: 'Let us face the facts. The United States of America is not greatly interested in Australia.' Great Britain, on the other hand, 'has always been interested in our wellbeing', and with that in mind, he urged that 'the central point of Australian foreign policy must be a tight and close relationship with the British Empire'. This should be done not 'in a spirit of jingoism or empty patriotism, or with any desire to wave the flag', but rather 'to back up our White Australia policy' and to disseminate 'the great traditional and moral force of the British Commonwealth that has stood for so many years'.[11]

When a couple of months later parliament considered a gift of £25,000,000 to 'our kinsmen in the Old Country', as Beale put it, he castigated the government for a contribution that was 'niggardly and mean'; he felt that 'more should be granted' and hoped that 'this bill will be a forerunner of other measures', not only because 'Britain saved the world' during the war but also because 'if England goes we go with it'.[12] The government's introduction of its Nationality and Citizenship Bill to parliament in November 1948 in response to Canada's demands for a local citizenship produced a sharp rebuke from Beale. For him the measure was completely unnecessary because being Australian and being British were indivisible. The essence of the traditional relationship, he argued, employing a peculiar phrase, was 'unforeignness' – the condition of being independent nation-states but sharing a community of culture and (theoretically) interest that bound them together in the Commonwealth. Though many members of the government

9   Jo Gullett to Lady Gullett, 24 November 1946, cited in Allan William Martin, *Robert Menzies: A Life, vol. 2, 1944–1978*, Melbourne University Press, Melbourne, 1999, p. 61.
10   Howard Beale in *Commonwealth Parliamentary Debates*, House of Representatives, 14 November 1946, vol. 189, pp. 295–99.
11   Howard Beale in *Commonwealth Parliamentary Debates*, House of Representatives, 25 March 1947, vol. 190, pp. 1129, 1131.
12   Howard Beale in *Commonwealth Parliamentary Debates*, House of Representatives, 28 May 1947, vol. 192, pp. 2990–92.

were themselves uncomfortable with the change, prompting Minister for Immigration Arthur Calwell to devise legislation that allowed Australians to be both British subjects and Australian citizens, Beale remained dissatisfied: 'We shall not be exactly aliens, but the essence of "unforeigness" will be lost, and the link with the Crown which binds this country to Great Britain will be greatly weakened.'[13]

Thus when Menzies came to power in the elections of December 1949 and Beale was made Minister for Supply, he welcomed any opportunity to assist Britain in this task. A request from Britain to test its newly developed atomic bomb in Australia received wholehearted support from not only Menzies – who inexplicably instructed that the plans initially be kept from his Supply Minister – but also Beale and a series of tests were subsequently held on the Monte Bello Islands (1952, 1956) and at Emu Field (1953) and Maralinga (1956–57). Beale's reasons for supporting the tests, as he later wrote, were moral, sentimental and strategic – a case of 'Atoms Amongst Englishmen' and Australia 'Playing the Empire Card', as historians Alice Cawte and Wayne Reynolds have put it. He thus argued that Britain's possession of the bomb would 'be a supplement to American nuclear deterrent power'; that it would reinforce the 'intimate partnership between Britain and Australia'; and that any refusal by Australia to meet the request would be 'against our own interest, and brutally ungenerous as well'. Taking up a line that would dominate his thinking in Washington, Beale argued that providing this small assistance to Britain allowed Australia to contribute in its own way to the Cold War objectives of its great power ally: 'There are times when a nation must stand up and be counted; for Australia this was such a time.'[14]

---

13   Howard Beale in *Commonwealth Parliamentary Debates*, House of Representatives, 23 November 1948, vol. 200, pp. 3313–14.
14   Howard Beale, *Inch of Time*, p. 87. See also Alice Cawte, *Atomic Australia*, University of New South Wales Press, Kensington, 1992, ch. 4; and Wayne Reynolds, *Australia's Bid for the Atomic Bomb*, Melbourne University Press, Melbourne, 2000, ch. 6.

'Not grown up': Appointment and early observations of US society, politics and culture

After Beale's appointment as Minister for Supply in 1950, he had refrained from talking at length about international affairs and naturally focused on the manifold responsibilities of running a department. While his position as Supply Minister had brought him into frequent contact with members of the American defence establishment, Beale, unlike Spender, had shown no burning desire to place US–Australia relations on a firmer footing. Thus it came as something of a surprise when in July 1957 Minister for External Affairs Richard Casey offered him the Washington post. After lengthy deliberation, Beale accepted. Paul Hasluck, a Cabinet colleague, reflected that he probably 'felt he had had a good spin out of politics' and that 'the Washington post in succession to Spender was attractive'.[15] And yet, Beale's willingness to abandon a promising political career – he was widely touted to replace outgoing Defence Minister Philip McBride – might suggest that he had other reasons for accepting the Washington post. As he himself often noted, his relations with Menzies were strained. Shortly after winning government, according to Beale, Menzies had taken a noticeable dislike to him; the Prime Minister's decision to keep him out of the loop over British nuclear tests in Australia was perhaps an early indication that Beale would never be a 'teacher's pet' like Eric Harrison or Athol Townley.[16]

The hostility may have stemmed partly from Beale's personality – the 'colossal opinion of himself' referred to by Gullett in 1946. Hasluck, who confessed to liking Beale because he was 'one of the very few colleagues who had read the same books, picked up the same literary and historical allusions and spoke the same words as I did', also noted 'a sort of self-regard' that 'just fell short of self-satisfaction'. This was compounded by a tendency to score points in debates 'with too great a sense of triumph and too evident a pleasure in his own accomplishment'. He was profoundly conscious of rank, 'did things with an air' and was one of the few ministers 'who stood up to Menzies', a characteristic that

---

15   Paul Hasluck (ed. Nicholas Hasluck), *The Chance of Politics*, Text Publishing, Melbourne, 1997, p. 70.
16   Pratt with Beale, interview, p. 50. The reference to 'teacher's pet' is Hasluck's. See Hasluck, *Chance of Politics*, pp. 62, 89.

must have gone down like a lead balloon with the Prime Minister.[17] When in 1957 Beale had openly objected to a piece of draft legislation on divorce law that enjoyed the Prime Minister's support, Menzies told him to back down or he would 'take strips off' him. Unperturbed, Beale replied, 'Well, Bob, when we get into committee I'll be trying to do the same to you'.[18] Though Beale vehemently denied that Menzies sent him to Washington to get rid of him – indeed, he claimed that his relationship with Menzies was improving by this time – the long history of tension between them almost certainly played a role in his decision to accept the offer, and for that matter, in the making of the offer by Cabinet in the first place.

Having accepted Casey's offer, Beale waited several months for Cabinet to give its formal approval. Another couple of months elapsed before Casey made an announcement, in December 1957, and the Beales arrived in Washington in March 1958. The reception they were accorded at Union Station, especially from fellow British Commonwealth countries, was noted by the Acting US Chief of Protocol as 'quite a show'.[19] Equally impressed with this demonstration of Commonwealth solidarity, the *Washington Post* contrasted the spectacle of Beale's arrival with that of the new Norwegian Ambassador, who 'slipped into Washington quietly a few days ago and is awaiting a call from the White House summoning him to present credentials'.[20] Beale, for his part, only had to wait a week to present his credentials to President Dwight D Eisenhower, where the usual pleasantries were exchanged about 'the great and continuing friendship which the people of Australia feel for the people of the United States' (Beale) and 'the close friendship of our countries, born of common service in just causes and sustained by our mutual traditions of freedom and justice' (Eisenhower).[21] Though Beale was pleased to report that Eisenhower was 'cheerful and friendly and, like every other American I have met here, seems to hold Australia in high regard', any suggestion that Australia was a top-drawer US ally was

---

17 Hasluck, *Chance of Politics*, pp. 68–69.
18 Pratt with Beale, interview, p. 62.
19 Cited in *Washington Post*, 19 March 1958.
20 Ibid.
21 Beale, 'Remarks upon the Occasion of the Presentation of his Letters of Credence', n.d., and Eisenhower, 'The President's Reply to the Newly Appointed Ambassador of Australia', n.d., both in series A3092, item 221/4/5/1/1, National Archives of Australia (NAA), Canberra.

soon squashed. Eisenhower, mistaking Beale for Casey, commented to him during the ceremony: 'Let me see, you were here during the war weren't you, and then went to the Middle East?'[22]

Beale spent the first couple of months familiarising himself with the mission and his new responsibilities. In the embassy building he discovered 'a very pleasant home and establishment', reflecting, he added in a letter to Casey, 'great credit on the gentleman who chose it in 1940!' At the same time, it desperately needed a coat of paint, new curtains and carpets and fresh wall paintings, some of which looked as though 'they had been painted at the bottom of a deep well on a rainy day'. Like many representatives before (and after) him, however, Beale was deeply distressed by official procurement procedures. Despite being 'Her Majesty's Australian Ambassador' and an ex-Minister for Supply 'accustomed to authorising millions of pounds of expenditure', he found he could only approve capital works up to the princely sum of £A10 a month! Beale complained persistently about the location of the 'ambassadorial lavatory', which was a great nuisance where it was: 'when one treks downstairs to the little place under the stairs in the entrance lobby, it is disconcerting to be waylaid by visitors and ear-bashers who have just been told you are not in'.[23] Beale soon had an opportunity to rectify this situation. During a visit from Casey, who happened to be suffering from his 'old amoebic dysentery' and found the location of the toilet inconvenient, Beale presented him with a handwritten authorisation for a new one, which Casey obligingly signed. Treasury, furious at these underhanded tactics, reportedly opened a file on the matter unofficially known as 'Beale's shit-house'.[24]

By mid-1958, Beale was in a position to offer some insights on the nature of US society, politics and culture. In a long and lucid letter to Casey in July, he enthused that the American people were 'a fascinating study' and it was easy to understand why 'everybody who comes here wants to write a book about them'. They were 'a vital people', he said, drawing on the image of the frontier pioneer made popular by Frederick Jackson Turner:

> They play hard, they work hard, and they drink hard. I am constantly being surprised by the number of very old men I meet here with sagging wrinkled faces still working, playing, and enjoying life; some

---

22 Beale to unidentified recipients, n.d. (c. April 1958), Sydney, series NA1983/1, item 16, NAA, Canberra; and Beale, *Inch of Time*, p. 119.
23 Beale to Casey, 14 May 1958, Sydney, series NA1983/1, item 16, NAA, Canberra.
24 Beale, *Inch of Time*, p. 121.

of them seem absolutely indestructible. There is a demon of energy in the national character, especially in the north, the east and the west; and it is this demon which has been responsible for the marvellous development of the country.[25]

At the same time, Beale was greatly impressed by the American disposition for 'spontaneous warmth, a throwing open of their homes, and a real eagerness to make you feel at home'. This was considerably magnified in the case of Australians, according to Beale, because of the perceived similarities of experience and outlook between the two countries. ('We're both close to the frontier', as one American friend explained it to Beale.) For this reason, 'the name Australian is an "open sesame" in most parts of the country'. Beyond that, the US possessed a genuine desire to 'do the right thing by the world', a commitment that was essential with the coming of the Cold War. This willingness to 'accept enormous burdens in helping to sustain the free world' was 'a tribute to America's sense of moral responsibility' and 'a genuine national virtue'.[26]

And yet, Beale was quick to disavow certain prominent aspects of American life. There was a tendency to indulge in self-righteousness when approaching foreign policy issues and a failure to understand that international politics was 'the science of the *attainable*' (Beale's emphasis). US leaders too often 'made up their mind in some situation as to what *ought* to be done as a matter of right and wrong' and then allowed their policies to be dictated accordingly, 'irrespective of whether it is practicable, or what devastating consequences may flow from pursuing it', or how much it 'gets them and their friends into trouble'. Citing the US role in the Suez crisis of 1956 as a prime example, Beale speculated that this overly moralistic approach to international affairs was attributable to its inexperience as a world leader. There was, he thus observed:

> a streak of immaturity in their make-up. Hard boiled and tough though they seem to be, and often are, the word[s] 'not grown up' keep coming to the mind in connection with them. They are naive; they want to be liked; they are grateful for recognition of what their country is doing, and bewildered and hurt when their good works are not appreciated.[27]

---

25 Beale to Casey, 7 July 1958, Sydney, series NA1983/1, item 16, NAA, Canberra.
26 Ibid.
27 Ibid.

Americans too often believed their own hype and 'have shouted from the housetops about their greatness, their cleverness, their goodness, their love of freedom (you'd think they invented the damn thing), so that when events don't quite work out as they have come to believe, they get all upset'. He often urged his American friends to 'take a leaf out of Great Britain's book'. In a somewhat teleological vein, he marvelled at the British Empire's success in pursuing its own interests while simultaneously 'creating wealth and health for many nations and people ... keeping the peace for generations, and gradually giving freedom and independence to one colony after another'.[28]

This rather rosy portrayal of the British Empire's record in international affairs was consistent with Beale's pro-British appraisal of the Suez crisis and his quip about the American penchant for claiming the love of freedom as a peculiarly American virtue. At the same time, it demonstrated a typically Australian unwillingness (or inability) to understand US behaviour in the world as a symptom not of inexperience, immaturity or even the nation's puritan foundations – as Beale suggested in a letter to Philip McBride in November 1959 – but rather of a powerful national myth that identified the US as the avatar of liberty with a moral obligation to spread the 'universal' (though, paradoxically, American) principles of freedom and democracy throughout the globe.[29] This accounted for the otherwise inexplicable intensity of the US response to Soviet communism, which presented itself as a rival myth of universal redemption. Beale himself – by no means reticent when it came to flaying the Soviets – was shocked by 'the almost hysterical (and sometimes not "almost") fear of Communism' in the US. A creature of his own culture, Beale not only failed to understand the peculiar nature and dynamics of American nationalism but also expressed the lofty hope that US leaders would ultimately defer to 'a certain Anglo-Saxon reasonableness which, in the last resort, prevents things from being pushed too far'.[30]

Consistent with these cultural prejudices, Beale was deeply critical of the US constitutional system. As he explained it to Casey shortly after arriving in Washington, those who helped the Executive govern were

---

28   Ibid.
29   See especially Michael H Hunt, *Ideology and US Foreign Policy*, Yale University Press, New Haven, 1989; and John Fousek, *To Lead the Free World: American Nationalism and the Cultural Roots of the Cold War*, University of North Carolina Press, Chapel Hill, 2000. See also Beale to McBride, n.d. (c. November 1959), Sydney, series NA1983/1, item 16, NAA, Canberra.
30   Beale to McBride, c. November 1959.

generally drawn from the outside business world and were thus 'ignorant of the processes of popular government and of the needs and aspirations of *people*', while those elected to Congress and therefore responsible for legislating for the people often did so 'without all the facts which the Executive has before it' (Beale's emphasis). This produced 'a sort of rivalry' between the Executive and Congress – 'both sides having great power in their own right' – which often crippled the President's capacity to govern.[31] This perceived systemic weakness was a constant theme of Beale's missives on what he referred to as 'the crazy political system over here'.[32] During the 1960 presidential election campaign between Richard Nixon and John F Kennedy (who Beale hoped 'doesn't win because the Kennedy clan … are too rich and too anti-British'), he kept up this line of criticism, focusing in particular on the new format of live television debates.[33] So appalled was he by this development that he wrote a terse letter to the *New York Times* under the non-de-plume 'Observer', saying that the debates presented viewers with 'tabloid answers', 'no humour' and 'crude and distorting' opinions on international affairs; the whole thing had the appearance of 'a quiz kid show'.[34] He told Menzies that 'we should be on our guard against such "Debates" in Australia'.[35]

Nothing he had seen during the arduous six months of campaigning and saturation of the public with the two candidates had altered his earlier belief that the American political system was 'the craziest in the world'.[36] When Kennedy was elected by the slimmest of margins in November, Beale gradually retreated from his earlier hostility, partly because the new President genuinely liked Australians (he had been rescued by one when his torpedo boat was sunk in the Pacific during World War II)[37] and partly because he was committed to closer relations with Great

---

31 Beale to Casey, 7 July 1958.
32 See Beale to Athol Townley, 3 September 1959, cablegram no. 1863, Canberra, series A6364, item WH1959/08, NAA, Canberra.
33 Beale to Holt, 10 March 1960, Sydney, series A1983/1, item 16, NAA, Canberra.
34 *New York Times*, 25 October 1960.
35 Beale to Menzies, 21 October 1960, cablegram no. 2903, Canberra, series A6364, item WH1960/10, NAA, Canberra.
36 Beale to Menzies, 21 October 1960, cablegram no. 2903, and Beale to Menzies, 'Presidential Elections', 9 November 1960, cablegram no. 3075, Canberra, series A6364, item WH1960/10, NAA, Canberra.
37 For details of Kennedy's rescue by Arthur Reginald ('Reg') Evans, who was reunited with the recently appointed President in a ceremony in Washington in 1961, see *Washington Post*, 2 May 1961.

Britain. At the same time, Beale was struck by the quality of Kennedy's senior advisers, telling Menzies in January 1961 that the President had assembled 'an impressive team' around him:

> Almost all, if not all, of those on the Cabinet and Assistant Secretary level are university graduates, many with high honours, and including four Rhodes Scholars … In one field or another, all of them seem to have had considerable administrative experience.[38]

For Beale, this development was to be welcomed because it brought the US system closer to the British model. As he told Menzies a month later, 'the American system is now showing some slight resemblance to our parliamentary system' while the President was 'looking a little more like a Prime Minister'.[39] Though the analogy was somewhat overstated, Beale's new-found admiration for the Kennedy Administration with its focus on experienced ruling elites – what David Halberstam sardonically referred to as 'the best and the brightest' – again demonstrated the extent of his cultural bias.[40] The Kennedy Administration was now more agreeable not because of the system that had put him there, but on the contrary, because it seemed to circumvent the unbridled populism that many Australian leaders associated with US politics.

'Our first concern': Beale's attitude to ANZUS, Southeast Asian conflicts and 'Confrontation' with Indonesia

Beale's critical observations of the US political and social system were not unusual. Like many Australians, his worldview embodied the accumulated experience and wisdom of the British Commonwealth and his frequently disapproving attitudes towards American society and culture reflected this fundamental orientation. Even Spender, who wore his pro-American colours openly, admitted that his cultural and sentimental views remained firmly wedded to 'the British world'.[41] This perception of the US as culturally and even politically 'foreign' –

---

38   Beale to Menzies, 24 January 1961, cablegram no. 154, Canberra, series A6364, item WH1961/01, NAA, Canberra.

39   Beale to Menzies, 2 February 1961, cablegram no. 227, Canberra, series A6364, item WH1961/01, NAA, Canberra.

40   David Halberstam, *The Best and the Brightest*, Random House, New York, 1972.

41   Lowe, *Australian Between Empires*, pp. 154–55.

or, more precisely in Beale's phrasing, as a country lacking the quality of 'unforeignness' that was characteristic of Australia's relations with Britain – was even more pronounced among policymakers at home. The consummate statesman, Menzies nevertheless felt uncomfortable and indeed anxious in the company of US leaders. During a visit to Washington in the mid-1960s, the Prime Minister showed his sweat-covered palms to the then Australian Ambassador, Keith Waller, and remarked: 'I don't know, Waller, why is it that I should be so much more nervous when I see the President of the United States than when I see the Queen.'[42] For Australians, as David McLean has observed, 'while the US, as the leading Pacific military power and an English-speaking nation, was Australia's natural protector, it was not a "British" society, and Australians therefore could not entertain the same expectations as they had in the case of the United Kingdom'.[43]

And yet, this was not through want of trying. In strictly strategic terms, Australia identified wholly with the US as its great power protector and worked hard to cultivate such a profound sense of obligation that American policymakers would not only act automatically to defend Australia in the event of a crisis but also meet these commitments without asking Australia for anything in return. In 1959, Cabinet rejected a 'Strategic Basis of Australian Defence Policy' paper that proposed a greater Australian capacity to operate independently of allies, preferring instead to fall back on the view that 'ANZUS is the most effective Treaty to which Australia is a partner'. Indeed, Cabinet resolved that any Australian undertaking in Southeast Asia 'would depend … primarily on whether United States forces were committed. The best guarantee we can have that deployment of our forces is judicious is a parallel United States commitment in the area'. This assessment that Australia's interests were best served by close association with the US nevertheless assumed that 'Australian forces available for contribution to a war on the mainland of South East Asia will inevitably be small'. The paper's assessment of Australian action in the event of a crisis between the US and China over Formosa (Taiwan) nicely encapsulated the government's approach to the alliance over the next decade: 'It might

---

42   Cited in David McLean, 'From British Colony to American Satellite? Australia and the USA during the Cold War', *Australian Journal of Policy and History*, vol. 52, no. 1, 2006, p. 73.
43   Ibid., p. 74.

be politically desirable, in the interests of close relationships with the United States and to encourage the preservation of its forward position in Asia and South East Asia, to offer a token force contribution.'[44]

Embracing this position, Beale was quick to push Canberra for a favourable response when in September 1959 the US requested that Australia contribute to a possible military intervention in Laos. Adopting the key tenet of the Strategic Basis paper, he urged that 'we should perhaps consider to what extent it would be against Australia's best interests if the United States were to carry the full military burden'. At the same time, he assured acting External Affairs Minister Sir Garfield Barwick that the actual military contribution expected of Australia would probably be very small: 'For political reasons they will ask for token forces but I would not be surprised if the Military Commanders did not regard these as more of a nuisance than an effective contribution.'[45] A couple of days later, Beale, having received word that the government would await the outcome of negotiations for a UN mission to Laos but was nevertheless prepared to plan for a possible intervention, went on the offensive. In a discussion with Deputy Secretary of State Douglas Dillon, he said all the right things. Notwithstanding the UN mission, SEATO should be brought to 'a state of preparedness' and any military action should be 'a joint SEATO effort'. Having said that, he added cunningly, Australia 'realised of course that [the] United States would have to bear the main military burden of any military intervention'. Pressing for maximum advantage, Beale only asked that Australia 'be given sufficient insight into American intentions to be able to develop their own planning along appropriate lines'.[46]

The intervention never happened, largely because the UN mission resulted in an almost immediate easing of tensions. After a US proposal to 'neutralise' Laos led to a ceasefire there and US attention shifted to the growing communist insurgency in the Republic of Vietnam, Beale was again quick to press Canberra for more assistance. Indeed, he did

---

44 'Strategic Basis of Australian Defence Policy', January 1959, in Stephan Fruhling (ed.), *A History of Australian Strategic Policy since 1945*, Defence Publishing Service, Canberra, 2009, pp. 258, 261, 272.

45 Beale to Garfield Barwick, 'Laos', 9 September 1959, cablegram no. 1918, Canberra, series A11536, item 10, NAA, Canberra. See also Peter Edwards with Gregory Pemberton, *Crises and Commitments: The Politics and Diplomacy of Australia's Involvement in Southeast Asian Conflicts, 1948–1965*, Allen & Unwin, Sydney, 1992, pp. 211–12.

46 Beale to Barwick, 'Laos', 11 September 1959, cablegram no. 1942, Canberra, series A11536, item 10, NAA, Canberra.

not wait for a formal request from the US Administration – sections of which were actually unenthusiastic about bringing foreign military personnel into Vietnam – telling Menzies in December 1961 that something more than verbal support was needed.

> I know it is not possible to do much at present, but I hope that after the elections the Australian Government will decide to increase its assistance to South Vietnam, not merely because additional appropriate aid is desirable, if not essential, for the survival of South Vietnam, but also because demonstrable Australian support would make a very favourable impression on the United States Administration.

As with Laos, he did not think that much would be required – some additional military equipment, 'a few groups of jungle and guerrilla fighting experts' for training purposes – but importantly, he claimed that such a gesture would demonstrate that 'support of Vietnam is not merely an American operation'.[47] When the Pentagon eventually warmed to the idea of introducing foreign advisers, Beale, again anticipating any request from the Americans, urged a pre-emptive commitment on the grounds that it would 'help to make Australia's mark with the United States Administration'.[48]

Beale's urging of Canberra to support US policies in Southeast Asia was founded on classic, if deeply flawed, Australian thinking about the nature and promise of the US alliance. The emphasis here was not on a united Western commitment to 'forward defence' but rather the imperative of maintaining a US presence on the Asian mainland at minimal cost to Australia. By recommending token military contributions to American efforts in Laos and Vietnam, Beale, like policymakers at home, hoped to ingratiate Australia with the US Administration and thereby compel American leaders to underwrite Australian security interests in the Asia-Pacific. This policy of 'defence on the cheap' was perhaps reinforced by the genuinely warm relations between the two countries. But the expectation that the US would blithely act as Australia's great power protector without any kind of qualifying criteria or commensurate benefit to the US was manifestly unrealistic. So, too, was Beale's corresponding belief that if only Australia was willing to meet US expectations in Southeast Asia this would enhance Australia's

---

47   Beale to Menzies, 5 December 1961, cablegram no. 3007, Canberra, series A6364, item WH1961/11, NAA, Canberra.
48   Beale to Barwick, 16 February 1962, cablegram no. 357, Canberra, series A6364, item WH1962/02, NAA, Canberra.

ability to influence Washington. The extent of Australia's profound sense of entitlement to US protection and the shortcomings of this thinking were soon apparent in the contradictory policies of the two countries towards Indonesia. Indeed, this problem not only represented the single greatest challenge to the alliance – or at least Australian expectations of it – since ANZUS was signed in 1951 but also dominated Beale's tenure as Ambassador to the US.

Writing in his memoirs many years later, Beale, after emphasising Australia's overall preoccupation with 'the Near North', went on to observe that within this framework:

> Indonesia was our first concern. In the government we did not say much publicly about the extent of our interest in the new nation and our concern for what might happen there, but these things were never far below the surface.[49]

While Australia–Indonesia relations were excellent to begin with, largely because of the role Australia had played in supporting Indonesian independence from the Netherlands in the late 1940s, tension soon developed over the status of West New Guinea (WNG). Australia was determined to keep the territory out of Indonesian hands, mainly because of the special strategic significance it attached to the whole island where the Japanese advance had been halted during World War II, and throughout the 1950s Canberra not only encouraged the Dutch to remain at all costs but also attempted to enlist guarantees of military assistance from Britain and the US in the event of hostilities with Indonesia.[50] The US, though suspicious of Indonesian President Achmed Sukarno, increasingly accepted the need to prevent Indonesia from being lured into the Soviet camp and so began to reconsider its previous opposition to Indonesian control of WNG.[51] By 1961, as Sukarno moved inexorably towards the use of military force, Kennedy wanted a solution. A State Department plan to establish a UN-backed Indonesian trusteeship for the territory received a hostile reception in Canberra. When Menzies

---

49   Beale, *Inch of Time*, pp. 155–56.
50   See generally Gregory Pemberton, *All the Way: Australia's Road to Vietnam*, Allen & Unwin, Sydney, 1987, pp. 70–106.
51   Ibid., pp. 81–3.

met Kennedy in Washington in February 1961, he thus told him point-blank that any plan of this kind was 'fantastic' and that 'the ideal solution would be continued Dutch administration under a trusteeship'.[52]

Beale, who was present at the discussion, agreed with his Prime Minister. When Kennedy pulled him aside after a meeting at the White House and asked how Australia viewed the prospect of WNG going to Indonesia, Beale insisted that 'the whole Australian nation would view it very gravely indeed'. In pressing this case, he emphasised 'the threat to the rest of New Guinea if a Communist Indonesia became our land neighbour'. Kennedy seemed to be satisfied with Beale's arguments, including the contention that 'the sheet anchor to which we should all cling was the principle of self-determination', and the matter was allowed to lapse.[53] Secretary of State Dean Rusk was equally sympathetic to Australian views. When, in September 1961, the Netherlands unsuccessfully pushed for the territory to be placed under UN administration – a scheme that Australia now supported in the face of Dutch moves to vacate the territory – Beale urged Rusk to submit a US resolution that would ensure that WNG was kept from Indonesia. Pulling out all the stops, he shrewdly appealed to the very aspects of the American national myth of which he had been so dismissive:

> I said that [Australia] would be surprised and very disappointed if United States – whose nationhood was founded on this principle [of self-determination] – could not stand up and be counted on. I said it seemed to me that sometimes ... members of United States Government under-estimated United States influence and moral authority around the world.[54]

Beale's subsequent claim that his meeting with Rusk was the 'determining factor' in the US decision to float its resolution in the UN was no empty boast. According to National Security Council official Bob Johnson, 'the position of the Australians is central to the Secretary of State's thinking', and National Security Advisor McGeorge Bundy concurred, observing that 'most of the specialists in the area believe that

---

52   Record of Meeting between John F Kennedy and Menzies, 24 February 1961, John F. Kennedy Library (hereafter JFKL), National Security Files (hereafter NSF), box 8, folder 1/1/61–3/2/61.
53   Beale to Menzies, 6 April 1961, cablegram no. 825, Canberra, series A11536, NAA, Canberra.
54   Beale to Menzies, 15 November 1961, cablegram no. 2832, Canberra, series A6364, item WH1961/11, NAA, Canberra.

the Secretary's respect for the Australians and dislike of Sukarno has led him to take a position in the UN debate which, if continued, can only help the Communists'.[55]

Any temptation to gloat over Australia's apparent ability to influence the decision-making processes of a great power was soon dispelled when the American resolution was defeated and the US was then forced to vote against an alternative Indian resolution supported by Indonesia. Deeply embarrassed at being forced to take an 'anti-Indonesian' position in the UN, Kennedy and Rusk now surrendered to the arguments of 'the specialists'. Accordingly, in December 1961, Beale was called in to the State Department by Assistant Secretary of State for Far Eastern Affairs, Averell Harriman, to discuss WNG. The absence of Rusk seemed to symbolise the State Department's determination to prevent sentiment from clouding the issue, an objective that was reinforced when Harriman was 'called away' and the grim news was delivered by his deputy, John Steeves. As delicately as he could, Steeves told Beale that with Indonesian threats of force increasing 'it was not now possible to stand still'. While the US sympathised with Australia's position and was committed to its security, it 'was convinced that by force or pressure Sukarno would get Netherlands New Guinea'. When Harriman returned and repeated this line, Beale could only forlornly insist that 'several real choices for the Papuans' be kept open. Too hard-headed to be persuaded by the appeal to principle that had worked so well with Rusk, Harriman replied that any act of self-determination for the Papuans would be a 'farce' and there was no hope of obtaining a real expression of opinion from 'such an ignorant people'.[56]

A couple of days later, after the initial shock of the meeting had sunk in, Beale advised Canberra to develop an exit strategy so as to avoid alienating Australia in the event of a Dutch retreat. Wisely, he urged that the government should 'get prepared, if necessary, to "roll with the punch"', i.e. accept the result with the best possible grace *when the time came, before it was too late*' (Beale's emphasis).[57] But the Australian Government was

---

55 See Robert H Johnson to Kennedy, 'West New Guinea', 30 November 1961, memorandum, and McGeorge Bundy to Kennedy, 'West Irian', 1 December 1961, both in JFKL, NSF, box 205, folder 11/12/61–11/30/61. For Beale's comment, see Beale to Menzies, 17 November 1961, cablegram no. 2854, Canberra, series A6364, item WH1961/11, NAA, Canberra.

56 Beale to Menzies, 'Netherlands New Guinea', 19 December 1961, cablegram no. 3136, Canberra, series A6364, item WH1961/12, NAA, Canberra.

57 Beale to Menzies, 21 December 1961, cablegram no. 3163, Canberra, series A11536, item 13, NAA, Canberra.

unwilling to throw in the towel just yet. After a flurry of cables between Canberra and Washington (and other posts) during the first week of January 1962, Barwick (now External Affairs Minister) instructed Beale to approach the Americans again and reassert the Australian position. Beale dutifully approached Harriman and argued the Australian case before asking directly whether the US would intervene in the event of Indonesia using force. To this Harriman replied that 'in his opinion the answer is *no*', and when Beale pressed him by asking whether the US would help Australia if it provided military assistance to the Dutch, he warned that 'it would be against our best interest to intervene'. The most the US was prepared to do, Beale quoted Harriman as saying, was to 'yell its head off' in the UN.[58] When, in one last throw of the dice, Beale approached Rusk a week later and repeated these arguments, saying that Australia was deeply disillusioned with the US lack of support, the Secretary of State, according to Beale, 'cut back quickly and curtly with a rhetorical question as to whether Australia itself had mobilised, and then went on to say that if I came back again [to say] we had done so it would be more persuasive'.[59]

There was no effective response to such a brutal slap-down and Canberra now accepted the inevitable. As Menzies told Kennedy somewhat ruefully during a visit to the US in June 1962, self-determination for the West Papuans was 'tomorrow's fairy-tale'. Australia, he told Harriman two days later, 'is resigned to having Indonesia as a neighbour'.[60] There was a sense of betrayal in these comments; that when Australia needed its great power protector, the US had been found wanting. It also encouraged the belief that Sukarno, thus emboldened, would now seek to satisfy his expansionist ambitions elsewhere in the region. This fear soon assumed palpable form following a British proposal to bring Malaya, Singapore and the British territories of Sarawak, Brunei and North Borneo together in a Malaysian federation. Though initially open to the idea, Sukarno became positively hostile when an Indonesian-backed rebellion in Brunei was put down by Britain with Australian assistance. In January 1963, Indonesia declared a policy of 'Confrontation'

---

58   Beale to Menzies and Barwick, 8 January 1962, cablegram no. 46, Canberra, series A6364, item WH1962/01, NAA, Canberra.
59   Beale to Barwick, 16 January 1962, cablegram no. 107, Canberra, series A6364, item WH1962/01, NAA, Canberra.
60   Memorandum of Conversation between Kennedy and Menzies, 'West New Guinea', 17 June 1962, JFKL, NSC, box 8, folder 8/1/62–9/6/67; and Memorandum of Conversation between Harriman and Menzies, 'Indonesia', 19 June 1962, JFKL, NSF, box 8, folder 6/17/62–7/3/62.

towards the federation.[61] While Australia discerned a familiar pattern of intimidation, bluff and diplomatic pressure in Indonesian attitudes to Malaysia, the US took a more cautious view. Reprising the main argument advanced during the WNG dispute, Harriman told Beale that every effort should be made to prevent Sukarno from 'taking a false step' and becoming further entangled with the Soviet Union. Indeed, in a thinly veiled dig at Australia, he 'switched suddenly' to WNG and said that 'if a settlement had been reached sooner this debit to [the] USSR would not have been so great and the Indonesian economy would have been in better shape'. There were, he urged, 'lessons to be learnt from West New Guinea'.[62]

But the only lesson that Australia seemed to draw from the WNG dispute was not that it should channel its resources into meeting the potential and apparently imminent threat from an expansionist Indonesia, but rather that it should seek further guarantees of protection from the US. In Washington, Beale, while somewhat perturbed when Harriman told him that the US was only prepared to commit to Malaysia in the event of 'overt aggression', nevertheless urged Australian support on the now familiar grounds that 'the Americans would be surprised and disappointed if we decided otherwise, as they would consider it in our vital interests to do so'.[63] Though the US did subsequently agree to invoke ANZUS in the event of a direct attack on Australian forces in Malaysia, Kennedy himself demanded immediate consultations to clarify expectations on both sides. When in an extraordinary display of defiance Canberra stonewalled the Americans for several months, Kennedy again pulled Beale aside. The Ambassador told him that 'every Australian' believed that in the event of 'some military clash in our part of the world which we can't handle ourselves, then the United States is committed under the treaty and also morally and honourably to come to our aid'. This reading only seemed to reinforce the need from the US perspective for immediate consultations. As Beale humorously told it in his memoirs:

---

61   See generally John Subritzky, *Confronting Sukarno: British, American, Australia and New Zealand Diplomacy in the Malaysian-Indonesian Confrontation, 1961–65*, St Martin's Press, New York, 1999.
62   Beale to Barwick, 'Talks in Washington', 2 February 1963, cablegram no. 332, Canberra, series A6364, item WH1963/01, NAA, Canberra.
63   Beale to Barwick, 13 February 1963, cablegram no. 423, Canberra, series A6364, item WH1963/02, NAA, Canberra.

Someone told me that when Kennedy advanced this view of the matter at one of his National Security Council meetings, General Maxwell Taylor said, 'My God! Does that mean that if some drunken digger in a slouch hat gets his ear shot off by an Indonesian sniper we've got to send down the Seventh Fleet?' – to which President Kennedy responded with a smile, 'Well, that's what Beale says'.[64]

For Kennedy, however, it was no laughing matter. During a meeting with Beale and Australian Treasurer Harold Holt in October 1963, he spoke sternly about the Australian Government's stalling tactics and insisted that the proposed talks 'ought to take place quickly'.[65] More importantly, it became abundantly clear over the course of the conversation that the two countries not only disagreed on how to manage Indonesia but also possessed contrary expectations of the alliance. When Beale urged Kennedy to be 'firm with Sukarno' – a point repeated by Holt, who complained that the Indonesians were 'behaving like juvenile delinquents' – the President bluntly rejected his suggestion that the US should threaten Sukarno with military and economic reprisals:

> The President said that the United States had not said anything like that. We have been working on an entirely different track and with considerable success … We have *not* said 'if you do so and so the result will be war with the United States'. Right now something like that would not, in our opinion, be helpful. He felt that we have done the right thing with Sukarno through persuasion.

But for the Australians this difference of opinion on how to handle Sukarno was the least troubling aspect of the conversation. When it came to the question of US obligations under ANZUS, Beale went for broke. Asked by Kennedy how Australia understood these commitments in Malaysia, the Ambassador blurted out that any attack by Indonesia on Australian forces – even by guerrilla units – would bring ANZUS into play and 'the United States would be automatically engaged'. Though Holt promptly retreated from this position, Kennedy took the opportunity to leave the Australians in no doubt about the limits of US

---

64   Beale, *Inch of Time*, p. 181.
65   Beale to Menzies, 2 October 1963, cablegram no. 2611, Canberra, series A6364, item WH1963/10, NAA, Canberra.

support in Malaysia. 'The Australians felt that if they got themselves involved we would also be obliged to be involved', Kennedy noted, before dropping a bombshell: 'but this was not the United States view'.[66]

This was reinforced a couple of weeks later when Barwick visited Washington and was handed an aide-mémoire containing such strong caveats that any situation that would justify US intervention in Malaysia was virtually inconceivable. Indeed, Kennedy, wanting 'to make sure that the record was straight', told Barwick that the American people 'have forgotten ANZUS and are not at the moment prepared for a situation which would involve the United States' in a war with Indonesia. In response, Barwick could only say in a somewhat wounded tone that 'the United States, through Harriman, had encouraged Australia to support Malaysia'.[67] It was a remarkable exchange, not only because Kennedy felt such a strong urge to give the Australians a reality check on the nature of the alliance but also because the Australian response demonstrated precisely why such a dressing-down was deemed necessary. The admission by Beale, Holt and Barwick that the Australian Government had only agreed to support Malaysia in the belief that the Americans would automatically become involved – even though Australia had a direct strategic interest in the dispute irrespective of US commitments – was consistent with the Australian Ambassador's numerous missives to Canberra on the desirability of contributing to US efforts in Southeast Asia. Although he sometimes showed a more nuanced understanding of the alliance and its limitations – at the peak of the WNG dispute, for example – Beale could never escape the unrealistic expectations of ANZUS that dominated thinking at home and later prompted senior officials to commit ground troops to Vietnam. Beale had left Washington by the time the Vietnam decision was taken, but many years later he justified Australian involvement in the war with the same questionable assumptions about the alliance. Despite the 'lessons' of WNG, Malaysia and Vietnam itself, he still believed in the 1970s that Australian support for US policies would guarantee American protection in all circumstances:

---

66   Memorandum of Conversation between Kennedy, Harold Holt, Beale and Roger Hilsman, 2 October 1963, JFKL, NSF, box 8A, folder 8/14/63–10/3/63.
67   Memorandum of Conversation between Kennedy, Barwick and Beale, 17 October 1963, JFKL, NSF, box 8A, folder 10/18/63–11/16/63.

The Australian government believed … that Australia could not eat its cake and have it too: it could not refuse to give help if called upon in a proper case, and yet expect to be given help when it needed it … In taking this stand the government was not being a puppet, it was being prudent.[68]

Conclusion

In May 1964, Beale had returned to Australia after six years in Washington. Menzies wanted to replace him with Athol Townley, but that plan died with Townley in December 1963. A scramble to find a suitable Cabinet minister to fill the post proved unsuccessful, and Beale on several occasions offered to remain in Washington until someone was chosen. But Menzies spurned these entreaties. When Beale forced the issue by cabling Menzies directly, the Prime Minister instructed him to relinquish the post and return to Australia. This episode proved that, despite Beale's frequent claims to the contrary, tension between the two men remained strong. Indeed, when Menzies visited Washington a few weeks after Beale's departure, Alan Renouf, who was acting head of mission, asked him why he had refused Beale's offer to stay. Menzies replied by saying:

'You know my nickname for Howard Beale?' and I said no. 'Mr Necessity'. And I looked at him and I said, 'What do you mean?' And he said, 'Necessity knows no law'.[69]

It was a comment that reflected the depth of contempt Menzies still felt for Beale. The remark probably got back to Beale, but far from stewing over it, he turned the insult into a compliment by encapsulating his time in Washington with a phrase by Winston Churchill: 'Ambassadors are not sent abroad as compliments, but as necessities for daily use.'[70]

Embracing this role for himself, 'Mr Necessity' dutifully served the Australian Government and people by not only assuming the representative and advocacy roles required of the position but also fulfilling the first rule of diplomacy, namely, keeping the home

---

68 Beale, *Inch of Time*, p. 167.
69 Michael Wilson interview with Alan Renouf, 23 November 1993, Canberra, series TRC 2981/6, NLA, Canberra, pp. 76–77.
70 The section of Beale's memoirs concerned with his time in the US was thus titled 'Necessities for Daily Use'. Beale, *Inch of Time*, p. 113.

government comprehensively apprised of political, strategic and foreign policy developments in the host country. Though not as independently minded or as forceful as his predecessor, Beale by virtue of a gregarious personality probably enjoyed even greater and more continuous access to the highest levels of policymaking in Washington than Spender. One of the striking features of Beale's reporting was the regularity with which he received audiences with the most senior US officials. The intimacy of these personal contacts was confirmed by the US record of conversation between Kennedy, Holt and Beale in October 1963, which ended by noting: 'As is his custom, Sir Howard Beale arranged to speak to the President privately after the Minister had left the room.'[71] Availing himself of this undeniable advantage, Beale worked hard to convey the views of the Australian Government to the US Administration and, conversely, to provide advice to policymakers in Canberra when the current was running against them. Thus he argued fiercely for the Australian position over Indonesian 'Confrontation' in WNG and Malaysia, sometimes with limited success, but advised Canberra to 'roll with the punch' once US policies shifted.

While Australia undoubtedly became more strategically integrated with the US during Beale's tenure, there is no reason to believe that this necessarily entailed a 'switch from British sycophant to American lickspittle', as historian Humphrey McQueen colourfully put it.[72] Like many Australians of the time, Beale certainly felt some sentimental attachment for the US as an English-speaking, culturally similar country, but his worldview remained an essentially British one. He was deeply critical of the American brand of democracy, only warming to the Kennedy Administration when it seemingly took on Anglo characteristics. He questioned the competence of the US to lead the 'free world', believing that it was not sufficiently 'grown up' and urging his American friends to follow the example set by Britain as a world power. At the same time, Beale's reasons for promoting closer strategic ties with the US showed an acute appreciation of Australian interests and a commitment to using the alliance for Australian purposes. He persistently encouraged Australian policymakers to contribute to US efforts in Southeast Asia not because he possessed feelings of servility

---

71 Memorandum of Conversation between Kennedy, Holt, Beale and Hilsman, 2 October 1963.
72 Cited in McLean, 'British Colony to American Satellite?', p. 67. This is a common theme of many books that deal with the US–Australia alliance. For a critical appraisal of this literature, see David McLean, 'Australia in the Cold War: A Historiographical Review', *International History Review*, vol. 23, no. 2, 2001, pp. 299–321.

for America, but on the contrary, because he believed that such support would 'make Australia's mark' with the US Administration and thereby enlarge the American sense of obligation to protecting Australia. The hard-headed nature of this advice was reflected in Beale's frequent assurances that such support would not require a large sacrifice on Australia's part; the US would bear the main burden of any commitment, while Australia's contribution would consist of 'token' military personnel.

This thinking, which reflected rather than influenced attitudes at home, demonstrated the unrealistic expectations that Beale and other Australian leaders attached to ANZUS. It not only overestimated the willingness of the US to do all the heavy lifting in Southeast Asia while Australia sat pat, but also underestimated how fundamental differences of interpretation could subvert Australian hopes for the alliance. They thus expected the US to set aside its own assessment of the strategic priorities in Indonesia, namely, preventing Sukarno from drifting further towards the communist bloc, and provide an open-ended commitment to Australian security in the event of a war with Jakarta over 'Confrontation' in WNG and Malaysia. The most surprising aspect of these disputes was that the US went as far as it did to meet Australian expectations, not only accommodating Australia over WNG until it was no longer possible to reconcile these expectations with American priorities, but also promising to support Australia in the event that its forces were overtly attacked in Malaysia. In the end, this policy of 'guilting' the Americans into supporting Australia's regional security had only limited success. But it did not prompt a fundamental shift in thinking on Australia's part. Beale continued to argue the case for a minimal commitment to Vietnam in the unreal expectation of absolute US loyalty. The decision to commit combat troops to Vietnam came long after his departure, but it reflected the same flawed assumptions. It bred an undue dependence on ANZUS that lasted until the 1970s, preventing Australia from taking a more constructive role in the alliance and embracing a deeper engagement with the countries of its own region.

6

Official influence in the making of foreign policy: The Washington Study Group on the South Pacific, 1962

Christopher Waters

This chapter is an exploration of the role of embassy and departmental officials in the making of Australian foreign policy. Do embassy staff and departmental officials working in overseas posts such as Washington ever determine foreign policy? Or are their functions restricted to other tasks, such as reporting on developments in the host nation, maintaining good relations with host countries and implementing policy through actions and exchanges with host governments? This chapter takes as its case study the establishment in 1962 of a four-power Study Group in Washington to examine future trends in the political, social and economic development of the colonial territories in the South Pacific. It examines the impact of the Study Group's recommendations in Canberra with a concentration on the Menzies Cabinet's response to their proposals.

While there are obvious dangers of trying to draw any general answer to these broad questions from one historical example, this case study does suggest some interesting, if tentative, answers, at least for the early 1960s. This is an especially important case study as the Study Group's report sparked a full-blown Cabinet discussion about the role of ministers, as opposed to officials, in the making of foreign policy. The episode also suggests that developments in the history of government practices, especially the use of expert study groups, in the early 1960s were challenging the traditional Westminster principles of government, including ministerial responsibility for policy decisions. It provides insights into the growing potential for the embassy officials in Washington to play a more important role in policy development and thereby sheds more light on the history of Australia's representation in the US.

One of Australia's most distinguished ambassadors of the era of the 1950s and 1960s, Sir Walter Crocker, wrote in his book *Australian Ambassador: International Relations at First Hand* that in his 18 years as an ambassador or high commissioner, 'I had no effect on Australian foreign policy: I had been naive in thinking that I could have'.[1] Here is a definitive statement made by one of the heads of mission in this era most qualified to have made a significant impact on Australian foreign policy. Such a firm negative declaration makes the historian pause for thought before he/she starts the search for a significant role in policymaking for heads of mission, let alone for lower ranked officials in embassies and high commissions. Despite Crocker's blanket denial of influence, these questions are worth pursuing especially in the course of a book exploring the history of Australian representation in the most important capital in the world by the 1960s: Washington.

Without doubt, Crocker was correct in his assessment that he could not change the broad foundations of Australia's international policies in the 1950s, such as the White Australia Policy, the seeking of security through close relations with 'great and powerful friends', the policy of opposing the nonaligned bloc, foreign economic policy such as the 1957 trade agreement with Japan, and the general Australian anti-communist policies during the Cold War. Such broad policy directions cannot be changed by individual heads of mission or their officials. The foundations of foreign policy are determined by the government and are often backed by deep and enduring public opinion that make them difficult to change.[2] Yet international historians can all point to specific policy decisions down through the decades where we can trace

---

1   Walter Crocker, *Australian Ambassador: International Relations at First Hand*, Melbourne University Press, Melbourne, 1971, p. 1.
2   For a study on the making of Australian foreign policy see Gary Smith, Dave Cox and Scott Burchill, *Australia in the World: An Introduction to Australia's Foreign Relations*, Oxford University Press, Melbourne, 1996.

some degree of influence by ambassadors, especially powerful figures such as Percy Spender, Australian Ambassador to the US in the 1950s, or senior officials who were close to their minister, such as John Burton, Secretary of the Department of External Affairs, in the late 1940s; not all policymaking remains the preserve of the Cabinet.[3]

The focus of this chapter is not on the role of such very high-profile officials, but rather on the diplomats in overseas posts, and those within the department who travel from Canberra on specific missions. These are Australian officials who participate in international consultations or study groups that lay out the groundwork for policy, develop expert understanding of issues and formulate policy options through their own work and official exchanges with the diplomats of other nations that later become recommendations for future Australian policy. While the final decision remains with the Cabinet, the spadework in terms of foreign policymaking has been done by the officials both at home and abroad. Where does the line fall?

The case study is of a four-power Study Group that met in Washington in 1962. This group of officials produced a report on future political, economic and security trends in the South Pacific region and suggested guidelines for future policy as the colonial territories moved towards independence. This first major examination of the future of the South Pacific in the 1960s by the Australian Government was driven by the activist External Affairs Minister, Garfield Barwick. He was an interventionist minister who followed in the tradition of Herbert Vere Evatt and Percy Spender.[4] A Cold War warrior, Barwick's concern over the threat of communism drove his foreign policy.

By early 1962, a number of international developments led Barwick to focus on the South Pacific. These included what Barwick perceived was a growing communist threat to the region, the change of policy by the US, Britain and Australia over West New Guinea that cleared the way for an Indonesian takeover, and the accelerating progress towards decolonisation in other parts of the world, especially Africa.[5]

---

3   David Lowe, *Australian Between Empires: The Life of Percy Spender*, Pickering & Chatto, London, 2010, ch. 7; Joan Beaumont, Christopher Waters, David Lowe with Garry Woodard, *Ministers, Mandarins and Diplomats: Australian Foreign Policy Making 1941–1969*, Melbourne University Publishing, Melbourne, 2003, pp. 53–4.
4   Beaumont, et al., *Ministers, Mandarins and Diplomats*, chs 3–4.
5   See the papers in CRS A1838, item 277/2 part 2, National Archives of Australia (NAA), Canberra.

The Australian Government's broad aims for the South Pacific were, firstly, to keep the area out of communist control and, secondly, to bring about the establishment of 'politically and economically stable Governments well disposed towards Australia'.[6] Barwick was determined to develop, with Australia's allies, a broad and detailed policy towards the decolonisation of the region.

The need to concentrate on the future of the South Pacific was crystallised at the 1962 ANZUS (the Australia, New Zealand, United States Security Treaty) meeting held in Canberra; Barwick represented Australia; Keith Holyoake, Prime Minister, represented New Zealand; and Dean Rusk, the American Secretary of State, represented the US. They agreed to establish a Study Group on the South Pacific made up of officials of the three ANZUS nations, with Britain and France also to be invited to attend.[7] The initial New Zealand suggestion, for occasional meetings of officials in Wellington to 'discuss and co-ordinate policies', was accepted at the Canberra meeting.[8] Rusk subsequently proposed a Study Group based in Washington, made up of official representatives from the US, Britain, Australia, New Zealand and France to 'explore possibility of developing a cohesive plan for the future'.[9] These officials were, in the words of one New Zealand memorandum, to be experts on the region.[10]

Rusk's proposal was accepted with alacrity by Australia, New Zealand and Britain. The Study Group's purpose was to consider the future of the South Pacific. It was great power politics that drove this renewed interest. As Dean Rusk said privately after the ANZUS meeting, the US was determined that 'not one wave of the Pacific should fall under Communist influence'.[11] He argued that something needed to be done to protect the colonial territories from subversion and give them some sort of economic and political security. The American Secretary of State understood that the problems were complex – for example, the racial

---

6   'Prospective Developments in the South Pacific', Australian briefing paper for 1962 ANZUS meeting, n.d., CRS A1838 item 277/2 part 2, p. 193, NAA, Canberra.

7   Cabinet Submission No. 590, 8 March 1963, CRS A1838 item 277/2 part 5; and papers in CRS A1838 item 277/2 part 4, NAA, Canberra.

8   New Zealand Ministry of External Affairs to New Zealand Embassy, Washington, 18 May 1960, cablegram no. 275, CRS A1838 item 277/2 part 2, NAA, Canberra.

9   Ibid.

10   New Zealand Memorandum, 'Washington Talks on the Future of the Pacific Territories', 23 November 1962, CRS A1838 item 277/2 part 5, NAA, Canberra.

11   Beale to Barwick, 14 May 1962, cablegram no. 1239, CRS A1838, item 277/2 part 2, NAA, Canberra.

issue in Fiji and the scattered nature of some of the other island groups – but he was prepared to allocate resources and money to a detailed policy program that was designed to solve them. Rusk believed that Australia and, to a lesser extent, New Zealand should play important roles in securing the region and moulding the decolonisation of the region.[12]

Barwick was delighted by the heightened American interest in the South Pacific. A major aim of his foreign policy had been to draw the US more closely into the region and bind it more tightly into the security of Australia. Indeed, that was a key motivation for the Australian Government in participating in the four-power Study Group. The Study Group met in Washington throughout the latter months of 1962, culminating in a formal three-day conference in late November.[13] After attending the initial organisational meetings France withdrew, apparently out of the suspicion of what 'they thought would be predominantly Anglo-Saxon discussions'.[14] The series of meetings led the expert officials from the four nations to prepare position papers on various issues, discuss and debate them at considerable length and reach some shared conclusions on guidelines of future policy. Australia was represented by BG Dexter and AD Campbell from the Australian embassy in Washington and Keith Douglas-Scott, the Australian Consul in Noumea, who flew in for the November conference. The detailed discussion papers and minutes of the meetings enable the historian to follow these discussions closely.

The discussion papers prepared by each nation were based on their expertise and knowledge of their own Pacific territories. The New Zealand Department of External Affairs, for example, authored a significant paper entitled 'The United Nations and the South Pacific'.[15] The paper drew heavily on their recent experience of bringing Western Samoa to independence.[16] It noted that the United Nations' interest in the South Pacific had been so far 'spasmodic and relatively mild', but considered this was likely to change in the near future.[17] This change

---

12 Ibid.
13 Record of meetings of the Pacific Working Group, 26–28 November 1962, CRS A1838 item 277/2 part 4, NAA, Canberra.
14 Cabinet Submission No. 590, 8 March 1963, CRS A1838 item 277/2 part 5, NAA, Canberra.
15 Paper, 'The United Nations and the South Pacific', 3 October 1962, CRS A1838 item 277/2 part 4, NAA, Canberra.
16 See James Wightman Davidson, *Samoa mo Samoa: The Emergence of the Independent State of Western Samoa*, Oxford University Press, Melbourne, 1967.
17 Paper, 'The United Nations and the South Pacific', 3 October 1962, CRS A1838 item 277/2 part 4, p. 1, NAA, Canberra.

would be driven by the anti-colonialist sentiment of the new members of the UN, mainly in Africa and Asia, which had recently decolonised. As a result New Zealand proposed a positive, not an obstructive, policy response to the likely growing interest by the anti-colonial bloc of nations in the UN. Such a response would include policies of economic, social and political development in the colonial territories themselves and a welcoming attitude to UN visiting missions to the region. While it recognised there would be strong criticisms and difficulties, it argued a positive approach by the four powers would be the best policy in the long run.[18]

As another example of the expertise brought to the Study Group's deliberations, Britain produced a paper entitled 'Sino-Soviet bloc interest in the Pacific' about likely communist bloc interest in the region in the future. The British paper identified the UN as the major forum through which the Soviet Union took an interest in the colonial territories of the South Pacific. It predicted that the Sino-Soviet bloc would use the continued colonial control by the Western powers of the South Pacific as a situation to exploit for their own ends. Even the smallest territory could become a target of their criticism, which might complicate the task for the colonial powers in finding long-term political solutions for these tiny entities. The direct involvement by the Soviet Union, mainly in the form of the ship visits, was limited to Fiji. The British paper also drew attention to the activity of Australian and New Zealand trade unions and local communist parties in supporting strikes and workers' campaigns in Fiji. The local Chinese communities were also seen as potential fronts for Chinese communist penetration of the region. Yet the conclusion of the paper was that communism was 'unlikely to gain a real foothold at present'.[19] Again there was a concerted effort at an official level to bring together the evidence of communist activities in the region so that countermeasures could be developed.

Specific papers on each colonial territory were drawn up by each colonial power and circulated to each member of the Study Group for discussion. These papers set out the geographic, historical, demographic, economic, social and political profiles of each of the territories. The problems each territory faced were identified and potential solutions were presented. Papers were authored on, for example, the Gilbert and Ellice Colony,

---

18 Ibid.
19 Paper (UK), 'Sino-Soviet bloc interest in the Pacific', n.d., CRS A1838 item 277/2 part 4, NAA, Canberra.

the British Solomon Islands Protectorate, the Fiji Colony, and the New Hebrides Condominium.[20] A careful process had been initiated of gathering the facts, identifying both existing and future problems and canvassing possible political and economic solutions, including different forms of continuing relationships between the colonial territories and their respective colonial powers. It was a case of drawing together expertise and knowledge on the island territories in order to come up with viable long-term solutions.

In the preliminary meetings in October and November 1962, there were some frank and revealing exchanges on the interests and policies of the four governments. On the future of Micronesia, for example, the American representatives explained that their political plans envisaged representation by a non-voting member in the US on the Puerto Rican pattern, but not full independence, even in the long term.[21] In its initial meetings, as another example, the Study Group agreed that the future of Melanesia, indeed for much of the Pacific, would be 'greatly influenced, if not determined by developments in Papua-New Guinea'.[22] The Study Group was touching upon delicate ground in discussing future political and economic developments in Australia's colonial territories as there was no representation from the Australian Department of Territories, which was responsible for the administration of both New Guinea and Papua. There were also discussions regarding the 'possibility of a Melanesian Association of Australian and British territories'. The Australian position was that while this would ultimately be a question for the Melanesians to decide for themselves in the future, their decision would obviously be influenced by Australian and British actions and policies.[23] There was general agreement that it was important that 'progress in the Australian and British territories were kept roughly in line'.[24] It was clear that the Study Group was already going well beyond the task of gathering facts on which policy decisions could be taken to floating policy ideas that might be taken up by their respective governments in the future.

20   See the collection of papers in CRS A1838 item 277/2 part 4, NAA, Canberra.
21   Australian Embassy, Washington to Canberra, 11 October 1962, cablegram no. SAV.1057, CRS A1838 item 277/2 part 4, NAA, Canberra.
22   Ibid.
23   Ibid.
24   Ibid.

The formal four-power conference that was held in Washington commenced on 26 November 1962 and lasted three days.[25] It enjoyed a high-powered membership. The US was represented by five Department of State officials, the US Commissioner from the South Pacific Commission, one official from the Department of the Interior and two officials from the Department of Defence. The British sent four officials from their Washington embassy and one senior official from the Colonial Office in London. Australia was represented by one official from the Department of External Affairs in Canberra and two officials from its embassy. New Zealand's representation was one official from the Department of External Affairs in Wellington, one from its delegation to the UN in New York and two officials from its embassy.[26]

As in the previous meetings, there were full and frank exchanges on key issues and discussion centred on the future direction of policy for all their colonial territories and for regional organisations such as the South Pacific Commission and the South Pacific Council. The discussions covered the political problems faced by each of the Pacific colonial powers in their territories, possible constitutional settlements and the methods to be adopted to meet the increasing interest of the UN in the region. In particular, the Study Group considered what forms of constitutional arrangement with the respective colonial powers, short of full independence, might be achieved that would be acceptable to the local peoples and to world opinion. The level of future interest from Asian and African nations and by the communist powers was also assessed. The three Australian officials played a full part in the discussions, including an outline of Australian policy in Papua and New Guinea and on the future of Nauru. The minutes of the meeting indicate that, at times, the meeting was more like an academic conference than a gathering of government officials. The Study Group inevitably continued to go beyond a fact-gathering and problem-identifying exercise to a consideration of policy alternatives for the future.[27]

Out of the whole process came a paper of agreed conclusions by the Study Group. The conclusions were a series of judgements and principles drawn up to be guidelines for future policy on the South Pacific.

---

25 For the full record see Minutes, 'Pacific Working Group: Record of a Meeting held in Washington, D.C.: 26–28 November 1962', n.d., CRS A1838 item 277/2 part 4, NAA, Canberra.
26 Minutes 'Pacific Working Group: Record of a Meeting held in Washington, D.C.: 26–28 November 1962', CRS A1838 item 277/2 part 4, NAA, Canberra.
27 Ibid.

The conclusions reached included assessments of the viability of the colonial territories for future independence, the possible timing of decolonisation for the different territories in the region, alternatives to full independence for some of the colonial territories, the diplomatic strategy needed at the UN to defuse the criticism by the anti-colonial nations, and policy ideas for maintaining the Western hegemony over the South Pacific. The Study Group considered that only three of the island territories were candidates for full independence: Fiji, Tonga and Papua and New Guinea. Their logic was that Fiji would be viable as an independent nation if the internal issues could be resolved, Tonga could not be denied on historical grounds and the precedent of Western Samoa, while Papua and New Guinea, with the British Solomon Islands Protectorate possibly included, also had the size and population required.[28]

For the other island territories the Study Group concluded that, as they could never be viable independent nations, solutions short of full independence would be required, such as integration or association with the colonial power or some form of federation. It was recognised that any such solutions would need the consent of the local peoples. The Study Group recommended that practical cooperation between the island territories that may come together should be encouraged, but 'artificial groupings should not be pursued for their own sake'.[29] The meeting suggested that all possible steps should be taken to anticipate and avoid outside pressure pushing island territories into independence where that outcome was not desired by the inhabitants. These steps should include action at the UN to deflect such pressure and garner support from UN members for solutions short of full independence. They urged long-term planning to establish frameworks of self-government within which the ambitions of the islanders could be fully realised and which were defensible at the UN. The Study Group recommended that the four powers take pre-emptive action at the UN to gain the 'maximum acceptance by members of solutions short of independence'.[30] The meeting also found that the greatest care should be taken to ensure that after any transfer of power the security of the region was not placed in any jeopardy. In other words, where independence was to be granted, the governments must be of a nature that they will align the new nations

---

28 Memorandum, 'General Conclusions of the meeting' in ibid.
29 Ibid.
30 Ibid.

to the West and not the communist bloc. Additionally, the meeting concluded that Japanese economic penetration of the South Pacific should be watched, any Indonesian influence should be discouraged and, while there was as yet little evidence of communist activity in the region, 'a close watch should be kept for signs of it'. The Study Group noted that France could probably not be dissuaded from conducting nuclear testing in the South Pacific, but recognised such action would bring unwelcome international attention to the region.[31]

In summary, the conference of officials in Washington from the four powers had concluded that only three of the South Pacific colonial territories had the potential to become viable nations. The remainder of the territories were too small or too scattered. The alternative policy strategies recommended by the officials for these smaller territories included their reorganisation into larger bodies with limited, but permanent, self-government, which would stand alongside continuing links to their colonial power. The Study Group also considered it desirable that international powers, outside of the four members of the Study Group and France, be kept out of the region. Its view was that the UN's intervention in the region would be counterproductive and should be minimised. Underlying the thinking of many of the officials at the meeting was the imperative of the Cold War and the future potential threat of communism to the region. The Study Group had proposed that the process of decolonisation should be gradual and carefully controlled with any timetable not to be influenced by actions in other parts of the world or pressure from outside the region.[32] In effect, the Study Group had laid out a detailed blueprint as to constitutional and political development in the region, as to policy at the UN, as to future cooperation between the four powers and as to their continuing hegemonic control over the South Pacific. The officials from the four nations were, in effect, actively formulating policy proposals for each of the governments.

Barwick was very pleased by the results of the Study Group's meeting in Washington. Heartened by the increased American interest in and commitment to the South Pacific, the Minister for External Affairs was also very positive about the Study Group's blueprint for the future political development of the region. While acknowledging there was

---

31 Ibid.
32 Christopher Waters, "'Against the tide'": Australian Government Attitudes to Decolonisation in the South Pacific, 1962-1972', *The Journal of Pacific History*, vol. 48, no. 2, 2013, pp. 194–208.

something of 'a lowest common denominator' about the conclusions, he felt they were a sound basis for future discussions and policy.[33] Barwick incorporated the conclusions into a paper he took to the Cabinet in April 1963 for endorsement by ministers as broad guidelines for Australian policy towards the South Pacific.[34] In the Cabinet submission the Minister for External Affairs reported that the Kennedy Administration was using the Study Group's conclusions to formulate, for the first time, 'a general policy for the Pacific'.[35] He stressed the importance of continuing to encourage the 'new-found American interest' in the region and the need to continue discussions with the other colonial powers on future policy directions.[36] Barwick's Cabinet paper became the occasion for a lengthy and detailed discussion by ministers over not only the specific conclusions of the Study Group, but more importantly over the role of Cabinet as opposed to officials in the development and determination of policy. The Cabinet notebook makes for fascinating reading.[37]

In introducing the paper to Cabinet, Barwick stated that the establishment of the Study Group had achieved two objectives. The first was that it had induced American interest in the region – a key goal of Barwick's foreign policy – and Washington had adopted the Study Group's conclusions as US policy. The second objective had been to provide the Australian Government with guidelines for future policy in the South Pacific. Accordingly, Barwick requested that Cabinet endorse the Study Group's conclusions. Nothing in the paper, Barwick assured the Cabinet, involved an intrusion into Australia's own colonial territories. Yet this proposal stirred up a hornet's nest. Not surprisingly, Paul Hasluck, the Minister for Territories, was first to launch an attack. While he acknowledged that it was important to get the Americans involved in the region, Hasluck argued that some of the issues and actions outlined in the guidelines were matters for Cabinet to decide and not some group of officials working internationally. As an example, he stated that Australian policy towards Japanese activity in the South Pacific was for Cabinet to decide, not public servants. He asked the Minister for External Affairs what endorsement of the conclusions in the paper would actually mean. Specifically, Hasluck was concerned that

---

33   Cabinet Submission No. 590, 8 March 1963, CRS A1838 item 277/2 part 5, NAA, Canberra.
34   Ibid.
35   Ibid.
36   Ibid.
37   Cabinet notebook, 30 April 1963, CRS A11099 item 1/60, NAA, Canberra.

the paper pre-judged matters of individual interest to ministers that had not yet been put to Cabinet. He was also worried that, if the Study Group continued along the same lines, it would get closer and closer to issues that fell within his own portfolio of Territories. He warned that officials would go too far and 'present Govts [sic] with so little elbow room as to be meaningless'. For Hasluck, the key questions were what endorsement of the paper meant to the Cabinet, and what it meant to the Americans.[38]

Menzies too waded in vigorously, querying what Barwick meant by endorsement of the report. The Prime Minister said he assumed it meant acceptance of a line of policy. He did not know this had been the purpose of the Study Group, which the Prime Minister thought had been simply 'to study and exhibit a problem'. Menzies continued that, if the Study Group was to make recommendations, it was badly constituted; for example, there was no representation from the Department of Territories. Declaring that if Cabinet endorsed the report and made these principles Australian policy, this would be a 'major decision', Menzies questioned whether the Cabinet took decisions on that basis. He accepted the need to stay in touch with other governments, but he did 'quarrel with accepting policy the ultimate implications of which we don't yet foresee'. Realising he was losing the battle, Barwick defended his approach. He countered by saying that on the fate of West New Guinea, Australia had not acted soon enough in supporting the US. There was, he declared, no 'meeting of minds' on that issue until it was almost too late. Barwick said this was an opportunity, under ANZUS, to think clearly about Oceania and line up our views with the Americans with the aim of keeping Chinese or communist influence out of the region. This Australian initiative, he stated, was designed to get the other powers involved and safeguard the future of the region. It was not, he continued, foreclosing on policy for Territories. He defiantly concluded, '[t]his [is] a sensible not to say necessary look ahead'. Menzies was not persuaded. He challenged Barwick to state what authority attached to these points: 'What does endorsement mean?' he repeated.[39]

Recognising he was losing the argument in Cabinet, Barwick retreated a little. Stating that 'guidelines' may have been the wrong word, he said he should have put forward the views expressed in the report as his ideas

---

38   Ibid.
39   Ibid.

as minister, which he added they were. Barwick also noted that in the future the Study Group would only do what the government asked it to do and nothing more. Sensing victory, Hasluck suggested that he would accept the word 'note' rather than 'endorse'. Other ministers supported Menzies and Hasluck. Shane Paltridge, for example, said that the Cabinet should not delegate to the Study Group the capacity to go forward with new policy issues. It should continue its study and report to member governments the results. He concluded that it had 'beyond that no power whatever'. William McMahon said the Study Group had been a worthwhile exercise. He generally agreed with Barwick on the contents of the report, but he too could not accept the conclusions as 'guidelines for policy'. Menzies did acknowledge that the Study Group had given Australia access to American thinking as its policy was developing. He described Barwick's historical point about events in West New Guinea as 'powerful'. But Hasluck was not prepared to concede even this point. He saw the process of establishing the Study Group as a 'bad method' of developing sympathetic American interest in the region. Barwick attempted to save something from the wreck. He suggested that the form of the recommendations had created the trouble for Cabinet. Barwick said he too did not want the Study Group to have any status beyond that of a Study Group. He suggested an alternative form of words: that the Cabinet notes the broad lines of the minister's thinking and with certain exceptions, sees no objection to the minister using his stated lines of thought as a basis for further discussion with the other three powers, and that he be allowed to continue to participate in the Study Group as a Study Group. Ministers did not even like this watered-down version.[40]

Bringing the discussion to a conclusion, Menzies declared that he did not like Barwick's amended proposal because it implied that Cabinet endorsed the conclusions of the Study Group. This would, he continued, only encourage the Study Group to make more recommendations. Menzies noted that in substance there was much in the report that seemed right and that could be supported, but these were matters for Cabinet decision. He concluded, '[f]or myself I would say we note the document, but point out it might be embarrassing to the Governments to have these as policy lines. The Study Group to be a Study Group with

---

40   Ibid.

limits excluding policy-making or policy recording'. With this clear, Menzies said they should record in their own words their judgement on some of the propositions. The Prime Minister continued:

> The central thing is that this brings the US for the first time in a rational and sophisticated way. This is a major matter. But policy must always be for us. Not direct or indirect approval of Study Group proposals. Not in any way cede our policy responsibilities.[41]

Minsters agreed with this statement, but the Cabinet notebooks do record one last Hasluck barb delivered against Barwick. The Minister for Territories said he liked Paltridge's 'view of getting decisions on particular cases – not manifestos'.[42]

Anyone who worked for the Minister for Territories would have understood that Hasluck was an absolute stickler for the Westminster practice of ministers, not officials, being absolutely responsible for policy.[43] Sometimes he went to extraordinary lengths in implementing that practice in his own department and his stand should have come as no surprise to Barwick. Indeed, Hasluck had already advised Barwick of his objections to the form of his proposals and the procedure he had adopted prior to the Cabinet meeting.[44] Menzies too was firmly in the camp that required the principles and practices of the Westminster system of government to be strictly followed, although he was the dominant personality in his cabinets and always welcomed the advice of his senior public servants.[45] He shared the suspicions of ministers such as Hasluck over the use and value of study groups and experts in general, except as a means to provide the facts on any given situation. It seems strange that Barwick, by then an experienced minister, so badly misjudged his Cabinet colleagues and brought forward the proposals in the format that he did. This was especially surprising as the conclusions did not just represent the ideas of Australian officials, but also the shared conclusions of officials from three other nations.

---

41   Ibid.
42   Ibid. After this lengthy exchange on process there was little actual discussion of the substance of the Study Group report and no decisions were taken on its conclusions at this meeting.
43   See Robert Porter, *Paul Hasluck: A Political Biography*, University of Western Australia Press, Perth, 1993, especially pp. 83–6, 276–7.
44   Paul Hasluck, Minister for Territories to Garfield Barwick, Minister for External Affairs, 27 January 1963, letter, CRS A1838 item 277/2 part 5, NAA, Canberra.
45   David Lee, 'Cabinet' in Scott Prasser, John Raymond Nethercote and John Warhurst (eds) *The Menzies Era: A Reappraisal of Government, Politics and Policy*, Hale & Iremonger, Sydney, 1995, pp. 123–36.

Cabinet had asserted its ultimate authority over the bureaucracy and its officials in Australia and in Washington. The Westminster system and principles had been given renewed authority under the Menzies Government with ministers being the sole arbiter of both the general thrust and the detail of foreign policy. It would seem that the diplomats in the Australian embassy in Washington, in the Department of External Affairs in Canberra and Garfield Barwick had been sent a strong message that officials do not make foreign policy.

Yet that is not quite the end of the story. The Study Group conclusions do provide an important insight into how Barwick and his officials viewed the future decolonisation of the Pacific in early 1963. Moreover, Menzies and the Cabinet did recognise the merit of much of the Study Group's report.[46] Such reports sit in departments as a digest of reflections, views and potential actions. As such they both summarise the existing international situation, but also contain the assumptions, detailed information and world views that can be drawn upon and shape future Cabinet submissions, briefing papers for ministers and guidance notes for heads of missions.

In these ways the conclusions of the Study Group were reflected in much of Australian ministerial and official thinking and action towards the South Pacific for the remainder of the 1960s. While not every recommended action was carried out, the Study Group's report did stand as a blueprint for Australian policy towards the South Pacific. The Australian governments throughout the 1960s continued to doubt whether the colonial island territories in the South Pacific could ever make viable nation-states. They continued to work at the UN to deflect criticism by anti-colonial members at the slow rate of change. They continued to support only gradual constitutional and economic development in Australia's own colonies.[47] It is arguable that Australian governments followed the Study Group's broad guidelines until the early 1970s when events such as the independence of Nauru in 1968 and Fiji in 1970 led to an acceleration of the decolonisation of the rest of the South Pacific, with the exception of the French colonies, and forced a re-evaluation of Australian policy. In this way, despite Cabinet's best efforts, detailed studies by officials in overseas posts and at home can define the boundaries of policy choices, can become the guidelines on

---

46   Cabinet Decision No. 992, 30 April 1963, CRS A1838 item 277/2 part 5, NAA, Canberra.
47   See Waters, 'Against the tide', pp. 194–208.

which policy is based and can provide the precedent for detailed policy decisions. As Hasluck feared, study groups and expert reports can sometimes leave governments with 'little elbow room'.[48]

The tension over responsibility for policymaking that led to the lively and lengthy discussion between ministers in April 1963 also suggests that in this era something important was evolving within state institutions as to the principles and processes of policy development. The clash between Barwick on one side and Menzies and Hasluck on the other is evidence that the procedures and principles of foreign policy formulation were starting to change by the early 1960s.[49] The case study of the Washington Study Group from the early 1960s does illuminate new developments in both the history of foreign policy development and government practice, but also in the history of the social sciences and their relationship to the government.[50] The increasing application of the methods of the social sciences and indeed the expertise of these disciplines to the art of government was a feature of 20th-century history. World War II saw this development reach a new height with economists, anthropologists, philosophers, and historians, among many other experts, deployed to use their expertise to 'win the war'.[51]

By the early 1960s, the US Government had taken this use of social science expertise and methodology in the formulation of government policy to a much higher level. The research activities of the RAND Corporation and the approach to government of President Kennedy's Secretary of Defense, Robert McNamara, spring to mind as important examples of the belief in and use of experts, their techniques and their knowledge in government.[52] The belief had developed in some government circles that if you get all the relevant information into a policymaking machine manned by experts, the right decision would come out of the other end of the process.

---

48   Cabinet notebook, 30 April 1963, CRS A11099 item 1/60, NAA, Canberra.

49   On Cabinet government in Australia see Sol Encel, *Cabinet Government in Australia*, Melbourne University Press, Melbourne, 1974 (second edition); and Patrick Weller, *Cabinet Government in Australia, 1901–2006*, University of New South Wales Press, Sydney, 2007.

50   See Stuart Macintyre, *The Poor Relation: A History of Social Sciences in Australia*, Melbourne University Press, Melbourne, 2010.

51   Geoffrey Gray, Doug Munro and Christine Winter (eds) *Scholars at War: Australasian Social Scientists 1939–1945*, ANU E Press, Canberra, 2012.

52   Alex Abella, *Soldiers of Reason: The RAND Corporation and the Rise of the American Empire*, Harcourt, Orlando, Florida, 2008; Robert S. McNamara, *In Retrospect: The Tragedy and Lessons of Vietnam*, Vintage Books, New York, 1996.

Now, the Australian Government had not gone as far down this road as the best and the brightest of the Kennedy Administration, but under Arthur Tange, Secretary of External Affairs for nearly a decade after 1954, there had been some growth of institutional capacity, in the department and in overseas posts, to address long-term developments in world affairs and to generate long-term thinking and more specialist expertise on policy issues.[53] For example, regular meetings of regional heads of missions had been instituted in the second half of the 1950s to discuss broader policy issues.[54] The small policy planning section was established within the department in 1962 to produce planning papers on key long-term international developments.[55]

The Washington Study Group, gathering together officials with expertise on the region to decipher long-term trends and suggest possible policy guidelines, was another such example of this general trend in government practice and procedure. Clearly by the early 1960s the Australian embassy in Washington was developing its capacity to play an active role in international study groups and other forms of consultation. These initiatives were all giving officials both in Canberra and overseas more of an opportunity to contribute to long-term planning away from the hectic pace of day-to-day diplomacy. Like his counterparts in Washington, Rusk and McNamara, Barwick was a supporter of this new approach to government. By his actions in this episode, Barwick seems to have favoured this American model of using experts and officials to formulate policy proposals for government endorsement.

The impact of these developments on Australian foreign policymaking should not be exaggerated. Historians should not underestimate the suspicion and objections of Menzies, Hasluck and other ministers to these intrusions on the prerogatives of Cabinet. But the 1962 Washington Study Group case study is an example of the growing capacity in the

---

53   On the Kennedy Administration, see David Halberstam, *The Best and the Brightest*, Barrie and Jenkins, London, 1972. For Arthur Tange as an administrative reformer, see Peter Edwards, *Arthur Tange, Last of the Mandarins*, Allen & Unwin, Sydney, 2006, ch. 5. For the institutional development of the Department of External Affairs during the Cold War, see Adam Henry Hughes, 'Manufacturing Australian foreign Policy 1950–1966', PhD thesis, The Australian National University, 2012.
54   For examples of these meetings of regional heads of mission see CRS A1838 TS3004/11/36 (Southeast Asia) and CRS A1838 80/1/3/4 parts 2 and 3 (Europe), NAA, Canberra.
55   For the establishment of the Policy Planning section see departmental papers in CRS A1838 625/2, NAA, Canberra.

Department of External Affairs and its officials in overseas missions such as the Washington embassy to contribute meaningfully to the foreign policymaking process.

In conclusion, this case study suggests that a complete picture of the history of Australian representation in the US requires not only study of the work and impact of individual ambassadors, but also of the work of those whose analyses informed their work: the diplomats, the military attachés, the intelligence liaison officers, those officials responsible for economic issues, scientific exchanges. These officials came together in working groups, liaison committees and other international bodies. By charting the activities in which they participated, especially in study groups and other committees, by exploring the place of experts and their expertise within the embassy and changes in government procedures and systems at home, historians will develop a more nuanced and deeper understanding of the role of embassies and their staff in the formulation of Australian foreign policy and how it has evolved from era to era.

Australian Prime Minister John Curtin with US Secretary of State
Cordell Hull, Washington DC, 1944 (Elsie Curtin in background)
Source: National Archives of Australia, M1218, 10

Australian Prime Minister Robert Menzies being welcomed by New York City Council Chairman Newbold Morris at La Guardia Marine Terminal, New York, 1941, before the outbreak of the Pacific War. From left: Newbold Morris, Menzies, Richard Casey, Australian Minister to the United States, and FG Shedden, Secretary of the Department of Defence and Secretary to the War Cabinet

Source: National Archives of Australia, A5954, 1299/2 PHOTO 7423

Australian Prime Minister Edward Gough Whitlam and
US President Richard Nixon, Washington DC, 30 July 1973
Source: National Archives of Australia, M151, 51

Australian Treasurer Harold Holt with US President John F Kennedy,
5 July 1963
Source: National Archives of Australia, M4294, 6

NJO Makin, first Australian Head of Mission in Washington with rank of Ambassador, at his desk in 1946

First ANZUS Council meeting held outside Washington, in Canberra, May 8 1962. From left: Head of Department of External Affairs Arthur Tange, Minister Sir Garfield Barwick, Chief of Air Staff Sir William Scherger, US Embassy Deputy Chief of Mission Mr William Belton, US Secretary of State Dean Rusk

Source: National Archives of Australia, A1200, L41450

Australian Prime Minister John Gorton (fourth from left) with US President Richard Nixon (opposite) at the White House, Washington DC, 1969

Source: National Archives of Australia, A1200, L80843

Percy Spender, Australian Minister for External Affairs, in 1949,
two years before being appointed Ambassador to the United States

Source: National Archives of Australia, A1200, L12797

Alan Renouf, Secretary, Department of Foreign Affairs, talking with Australian Minister for Foreign Affairs Andrew Peacock in January 1976, a year before Renouf's appointment as Ambassador to the United States

Australian Minister for External Affairs Paul Hasluck and US Secretary
of State Dean Rusk break ground for the new Australian Chancery
in Washington, 1967
Source: National Archives of Australia, A1200, L63186

Australian Ambassador to the United States Howard Beale
signing the Antarctic Treaty, 1959
Source: National Archives of Australia, M4619, 216

US President Ronald Reagan and Australian Prime Minister Bob Hawke at the White House, during Hawke's visit to the USA in 1986

From left: US President Jimmy Carter, Australian Prime Minister
Malcolm Fraser and Australian Minister for Foreign Affairs
Andrew Peacock (fifth from left) at the White House, 1980

Source: National Archives of Australia, A6180, 18/3/80/6

Australian Prime Minister Bob Hawke speaks at a press conference
in Washington DC, in 1985, watched by US Secretary of State
George Shultz

Source: National Archives of Australia, A8756, KN18/2/85/41

From left: Australian Ambassador to the United States, Keith Waller, US Secretary of State Dean Rusk and Australian Minister for External Affairs Paul Hasluck at the breaking of ground ceremony for the Australian Chancery in Washington, 1967

Source: National Archives of Australia, A1200, L63189

Rawdon Dalrymple, Australian Ambassador to the United States from 1985 to 1989, speaking in 1993

Source: National Archives of Australia, A6135, K8/6/93/18

Australian Prime Minister Paul Keating and US President Bill Clinton in 1993

Source: National Archives of Australia, A8746, KN29/9/93/173

US Secretary of State Dean Acheson signing the ANZUS Treaty in San Francisco, 1 September 1951, watched by John Foster Dulles (left), who would succeed Acheson from 1953 to 1959

Source: National Archives of Australia, A13307, 50/1

Australian Ambassador to the United States Keith Waller (left) talking with US President Lyndon B Johnson, 1965

Source: National Archives of Australia, A1200, L50722

Australian Ambassador to the United States Michael Cook in 1989

Sir Patrick Shaw, Australian Ambassador to the United States from 1974 to 1975, pictured in 1960

Sir James Plimsoll, Australian Ambassador to the United States
from 1970 to 1973, pictured in 1965

Source: National Archives of Australia, A1200, L52866

7

The Ambassador during the Vietnam War: Keith Waller, 1964–70

Peter Edwards

The tenure of Keith (from 1968, Sir Keith) Waller as Australian Ambassador in Washington was notable for three principal reasons, each of which had an element of paradox. The first arose from his being the first career diplomat to hold the position; the second concerned questions of access and influence; and the third revolved around his involvement with Australian–American diplomacy during the Vietnam War.

The career appointee

In 1964 Keith Waller was chosen as the first career diplomat to be appointed as Australian Ambassador in Washington. At the time, much was made of this development, which was greeted as a major breakthrough for the youthful diplomatic service.[1] It certainly was a pioneering step, but it only happened by default. Waller recalled being told by the Minister for External Affairs, Sir Garfield Barwick, presumably in early 1964, that, having spoken with the Prime Minister, Sir Robert Menzies, Barwick was about to propose Waller for the embassy. Barwick later

---

1   See, for example, Alan Watt, 'Australia and the Ambassadorial Issue', *Australian Quarterly*, vol. 36, no. 4, December 1964, pp. 11–18.

said that Waller turned 'as white as a sheet and then a bit green', and that it was the only time Barwick saw Waller lose his composure. Waller heard nothing more for some time, while the Canberra rumour-mill linked the names of several ministers, including Menzies himself, to the appointment. Then, soon after Paul Hasluck replaced Barwick in April 1964, Waller's appointment was confirmed.[2]

It was no secret that Menzies had wanted to appoint a Cabinet minister rather than a career diplomat, but had been frustrated by the absence of a suitable appointee. In his interview before departure, Menzies said to Waller: 'I'll tell you quite frankly that this is a position in which I would prefer to have a Cabinet Minister, but the ones I consider suitable I can't spare and the ones I can spare are not suitable.'[3]

In fact, Menzies evidently appraised even ministers he did not consider very suitable. According to Barwick's memoirs (which are not always totally reliable on detail), Menzies asked him if he had considered offering the post to John Gorton. Barwick said that he had rejected the idea, because Gorton had shown, as Assistant Minister for External Affairs, that he was inclined to 'freelance'. He would have to insist that Gorton adhered to the policies laid down by the government and the minister, and Gorton would probably rebel against any such instruction. Menzies told Barwick that he could offer the post to Gorton, safe in the knowledge that he would refuse – not because he would object to strict instructions not to 'freelance', but because he wanted to keep open the possibility of becoming prime minister. Menzies clearly thought this unduly ambitious. Gorton's promotion under Menzies had been much slower than others who had been elected to parliament in 1949. In 1964 he was still in the outer ministry – his promotion to Cabinet only came when Harold Holt succeeded Menzies in 1966. Barwick made the offer, and Gorton rejected it, just as Menzies had predicted.[4] Gorton's estimate of his prospects proved more accurate than Menzies'. By January 1968

2   Keith Waller, *A Diplomatic Life: Some Memories*, edited by Hugh Dunn, Australians in Asia Series no. 6, Centre for the Study of Australia-Asia Relations, Griffith University, 1990, p. 35. This monograph is based on the transcript of oral history interviews given by Waller to Professor John Donald Bruce Miller of The Australian National University, the transcripts of which are held in the National Library of Australia.
3   Waller, *A Diplomatic Life*, p. 35.
4   Garfield Barwick, *A Radical Tory: Reflections and Recollections*, Federation Press, Sydney, 1996, pp. 206–7.

Menzies had retired, his successor Harold Holt had drowned, and Gorton had become prime minister, where he remained for the second half of Waller's term.

So how did Waller come to be the first career diplomat appointed to the Australian embassy, albeit by default? John Keith Waller, born in 1914, was one of the bright young men – there were very few women, in the days of the public service marriage bar – recruited to the newly revived Department of External Affairs in the late 1930s and early 1940s.[5] The best of that cohort, including Arthur Tange, James Plimsoll, Patrick Shaw, Keith Shann, Laurence McIntyre, Tom Critchley and Ralph Harry, advanced quickly to senior positions in the 1950s, as the department and its overseas missions grew rapidly and without a generation of older officials ahead of them. Although his application to join External Affairs in 1935 was rejected, Waller transferred there within months of an appointment to the Prime Minister's Department. He rapidly earned a reputation as 'one of the few consummate Australian diplomatists our Foreign Service has known',[6] renowned for his calm efficiency even under the most trying conditions.

His diplomatic skills were displayed as much in dealing with fellow Australians as with foreign interlocutors. He survived for a remarkably long time as private secretary to the notoriously irascible William Morris (Billy) Hughes. In 1943 he was sent to Chungking as Second Secretary to open Australia's first mission to China and then to support Sir Frederic Eggleston, the intellectually powerful but severely arthritic appointee, as head of mission. In 1945 Waller was appointed secretary to the Australian delegation to the San Francisco Conference at which the Charter of the United Nations Organization was drafted. The delegation was notoriously divided into two rival teams of officials and advisers. One, designated by Prime Minister John Curtin and led by the Deputy Prime Minister Frank Forde, had their offices and bedrooms mostly on the 11th floor of the Sir Francis Drake Hotel; the other, chosen and led by the hyperactive Minister for External Affairs, Herbert Vere Evatt,

---

5   See Peter Geoffrey Edwards, *Prime Ministers and Diplomats: The Making of Australian Foreign Policy 1901–1949*, Oxford University Press, Melbourne, 1983, chs 4 and 5.
6   'Editor's Note' (presumably Hugh Dunn), *A Diplomatic Life*, unnumbered page.

had theirs on the 17th floor. Waller, with his office on the 11th floor and his bedroom on the 17th, proved an impartially efficient secretary, winning the confidence of all.[7]

The opinion of one member of the Evatt team would prove especially important in Waller's later career. Paul Hasluck, a temporary appointee to External Affairs, recorded his admiration for Waller's 'unruffled diplomatic finesse in making awkward situations turn out right. If ever Waller dropped a slice of toast, I feel sure that he could arrange that it would not fall with the buttered side down'. Hasluck was critical of many of the young diplomats in External Affairs, but he expressed great respect for Waller's political insight and wise counsel, which, as Hasluck noted pointedly, was delivered 'moderately and succinctly'.[8]

Access and influence

As flagged earlier in this volume, one standard measure of an ambassador's success is their ability to identify the key policymakers in the host government and to gain the best possible access to, and thus influence on, them. In the complex and ever-changing interagency process that shapes policymaking in Washington, that is no easy matter, but crucially important. The paradox here is that Waller had something extraordinarily rare, hundreds of hours of personal contact with the President himself; and yet the circumstances were such that that this 'face time' did not translate into opportunities to exert any significant influence on American policy.

President Johnson in 1965 appointed Ed Clark as his ambassador in Canberra. Clark was often portrayed in the Australian media as something of a buffoon, a good ol' boy with a fondness for *The Yellow Rose of Texas*. In fact, as Robert Caro's multi-volume biography of Lyndon B Johnson makes clear, Clark was, from very early in Johnson's political career, an extremely important adviser, supporter and fundraiser.[9] As Johnson's political fortunes deteriorated, he would summon Clark, who would have to make the arduous trip back to Washington so that

---

7   Edwards, *Prime Ministers and Diplomats*, pp. 162–9; Paul Hasluck, *Diplomatic Witness: Australian Foreign Affairs 1941–1947*, Melbourne University Press, Melbourne, 1980, chs 15, 18–20.
8   Hasluck, *Diplomatic Witness*, p. 203.
9   See, for example, Robert A Caro, *The Years of Lyndon Johnson,* vol. 2, *Means of Ascent,* Random House, New York, 1990, p. 102.

Johnson could speak to him for a couple of hours. It became the custom for Keith and Alison Waller to accompany Clark. They thus got to know Johnson and his wife well. Waller saw that Johnson had a genuine, rather romantic, affection for Australia (which he had visited on leave from Congress during World War II), and a deep appreciation for Harold Holt. His reaction to Holt's death was deep and genuine, leading to his decision to attend the memorial service. But Waller concluded that Johnson was a difficult man to talk to, and that he never had a real conversation despite spending many hours in his company.[10]

For Waller, therefore, the significance of the access to Johnson was not the direct contact, but the ability to drop his name when dealing with people in Commerce or State causing difficulties over trade matters. In his own recollection:

> One had to be very careful about how to exploit the Johnson euphoria for Australia … But from time to time, when a difficult person in Commerce or in State was being tough and unreasonable about access for Australian products, one would shake one's head and say 'Well, I hope I don't have to take this to the White House'. And that would act like a charm.[11]

Confrontation and Vietnam

It would be natural to assume that Waller's term as Ambassador was dominated by the Vietnam War. His time in Washington, from August 1964 to March 1970, included the escalation of the American and Australian commitments, the peak years of the war, the Tet offensive of early 1968, increasingly strong protests against the war, Johnson's decision not to stand for re-election, the victory of Richard Nixon in the 1968 election, and the first withdrawals of American forces under the rubric of 'Vietnamisation'. These events, and the worldwide social and political turbulence associated with the late 1960s, certainly established the climate of his years in Washington; but that is not to say that he played a major role in shaping policy decisions. To explain this third paradox requires reference to his last departmental post before going to Washington.

---

10   Waller, *A Diplomatic Life*, p. 38.
11   Ibid., p. 39.

From 1961 to 1963 Waller was first assistant secretary (at that time, before the creation of a deputy secretary, the level immediately below the head of department) in charge of the division responsible for policy towards Southeast Asia, then the most critical area of Australian foreign policy. In that role, Waller played a major role in policymaking towards 'Konfrontasi', Indonesia's Confrontation of the new federation of Malaysia. Australia opposed Indonesia's stance, but handled the crisis with a skilful and nuanced display of statecraft that Garry Woodard has christened, with understandable pride, 'best practice' in diplomacy.[12] Notwithstanding pressure from across the political spectrum to adopt a stronger military stance, the Australian Government exercised vigorous and independent diplomacy, especially in regional capitals, combined with effective but restrained military actions, shaping and executing a policy designed to allow Malaysia to come into being, but handled with caution in order to minimise damage to long-term relationships with Indonesia and other regional neighbours.

The policy was based on Australian interests and, as the diplomats liked to say, 'refined but not defined' by alliance considerations. But Australian policy was based on close association with both Britain and the US in Southeast Asia. There was no US section within the Department of External Affairs, so Waller was at the heart of Australia's relationship with the US.

External Affairs had a major influence on the policy on Confrontation. The principal policymakers were Barwick as Minister, Tange as departmental Secretary, Waller as division head, and Gordon Jockel as head of the Indonesia-Malaysia desk, together with two highly effective heads of mission, Keith Shann in Jakarta and Tom Critchley in Kuala Lumpur. The Confrontation policy was central to the confidence of the diplomats that, under Barwick, they formed a very effective team. Good personal relations between minister and officials helped – Barwick even borrowed Waller's dinner jacket on occasions. But this relationship did not continue when Hasluck succeeded Barwick in April 1964. Hasluck's relations with departmental officials were generally frosty or worse. Some of the diplomats saw Hasluck as uncommunicative, withdrawn,

---

12   Garry Woodard, 'Best Practice in Australian Foreign Policy: "Konfrontasi" (1963–66)', *Australian Journal of Political Science*, vol. 33, no. 1, March 1998, pp. 83–93. See also Peter Edwards (with Gregory Pemberton), *Crises and Commitments: The Politics and Diplomacy of Australia's Involvement in Southeast Asian Conflicts 1948–1965*, Allen & Unwin in association with the Australian War Memorial, Sydney, 1992, chs 14–17.

and excessively dependent on Menzies; while he regarded them as excessively self-confident and misguided on relations with the US and Southeast Asia.[13] But, as already noted, Hasluck exempted Waller from this critique. A mark of his skill was his ability to retain the confidence of both Hasluck and his departmental colleagues; he was fortunate to be in Washington in the later 1960s, well away from the intradepartmental tensions in Canberra.

Between 1961 and 1964, the department's success in shaping policy towards Confrontation was not emulated in the other developing crisis in Southeast Asia: the growing insurgency in South Vietnam. There is some evidence that the department sought to encourage a similarly restrained policy there, but in this case Menzies dominated policymaking, with the support of a small group of senior ministers including the Deputy Prime Minister, John McEwen.[14] They sought Washington's assurance that American support could be expected if Indonesia escalated its Confrontation of Malaysia, perhaps taking action across the almost indefensible border between Indonesia's West New Guinea and the Australian-administered territories on the eastern half of the island. American reluctance to give any such assurance was obvious; moreover, it was linked to Australian support for the American role in Vietnam. The Australian Government was faced with a huge dilemma. It sought to keep both 'great and powerful friends', the UK and the US, engaged in Southeast Asia, but the British saw Indonesian expansionism as the major threat while seeking to stay out of Vietnam, while the Americans regarded Vietnam as the critical theatre and urged restraint in dealing with Indonesia.

Waller later claimed that he had major reservations about involvement in Vietnam from the outset, including opposing the commitment of the Australian Army Training Team in 1962.[15] This occurred while Waller was still Ambassador in Moscow, but it is consistent with Barwick's initial comment to reporters, after the idea of Australian advisers had been raised in talks with the Americans, that Australia might send 'a handful', perhaps 'three or four men', in non-combat roles. A couple

13   Peter Edwards, *Arthur Tange: Last of the Mandarins*, Allen & Unwin, Sydney, 2006, chs 7–8.
14   See Garry Woodard, *Asian Alternatives: Australia's Vietnam Decision and Lessons on Going to War*, Melbourne University Press, Melbourne, 2004; Edwards, *Crises and Commitments*, chs 16, 18; Peter Edwards, *Australia and the Vietnam War*, NewSouth Publishing, Sydney, 2014, chs 4, 5.
15   Waller, *A Diplomatic Life*, pp. 36–7.

of weeks later, after further discussions with the Americans, Cabinet decided to send a team of 30 advisers. (The Training Team in later years was augmented to 83, then 100, and eventually 200.)

Whatever his reservations, Waller seems to have kept them largely to himself when, as ambassador-designate to Washington, he accompanied Hasluck on a tour of Southeast Asia in June 1964. This was an important stage in the development of Australian policy, for Hasluck formed the view that the situation in Vietnam and Laos was more critical and dangerous than Confrontation, reversing the priorities of most Australians at the time.[16]

Waller's role in Washington, especially in the first two years, was largely an extension of his former role in Canberra. At this time the principal channel of diplomatic communications between Canberra and Washington ran from Hasluck through Waller to William Bundy, the Assistant Secretary of State for Far Eastern Affairs, and Secretary of State Dean Rusk. All four were experienced practitioners, with a good deal of mutual confidence.[17] But this is not to say that the four men had a great deal of impact in shaping policy decisions. Policy on Vietnam, in both Washington and Canberra, was made by the heads of government and their closest advisers. For the most part, Waller and Bundy were conduits, conveying the views of their political masters rather than shaping them significantly. Even Hasluck and Rusk were not always central to their respective government's major decisions. Waller thought that William Bundy was not a great Assistant Secretary, and that his successor in the State Department, Marshall Green, had little influence. He had some success in developing contact with Johnson's national security advisers, McGeorge Bundy (William Bundy's more influential brother) and Walt Rostow.[18]

Within his first weeks in Washington, Waller was reporting American concerns that Britain might be pursuing an unduly provocative policy towards Indonesia. American policymakers also made it clear that Australia should be cautious in its military support for British policy in Confrontation. The Australians were put on notice that Washington would not 'bail us out' in the event of an escalated conflict with

---

16 Edwards, *Crises and Commitments*, pp. 300–1.
17 Ibid., p. 285.
18 Waller, *A Diplomatic Life*, p. 39.

Indonesia.[19] This was the start of a recurring theme of Waller's tenure. Australian ministers constantly sought reassurance of American support under the Australia, New Zealand, United States Security Treaty, either in general terms or with particular reference to Indonesia (at least until Confrontation was declared over in 1966).

Another theme was the constant pressure from the US for Australia to increase its own military capacity and to contribute significantly to the joint effort in Southeast Asia, especially in Indochina. Under the Kennedy and Johnson administrations, well before Richard Nixon enunciated what became known as 'the Guam doctrine' or 'the Nixon doctrine', American policymakers clearly indicated that they expected their allies to share more of the military burden. Washington was becoming weary of allies who seemed willing to 'fight to the last American'. The Menzies Government was well aware of this view, and its importance in any decision about American commitments to Vietnam and elsewhere in the region. Waller was able to report in November 1964 that Rusk expressed particular pleasure over the Menzies Government's introduction of a selective system of conscription, which would produce a greater number of combat-ready forces.[20]

In the period from late 1964 to mid-1965, Australians were concerned both about a critical stage in Confrontation and the worldwide speculation over the future of American policy in Vietnam. It was increasingly likely that South Vietnam would fall to the communist insurgency unless the US and its allies intervened with massive force. In Washington, 'hawks' and 'doves' argued for or against American intervention.

In December 1964 McGeorge Bundy briefed Waller and his New Zealand counterpart, George Laking, on the Johnson Administration's decisions to escalate the war. The principal measure was an increase in the bombing campaign over North Vietnam, but Bundy referred to the possibility of committing US Marines, together with 'such ground forces as Australia and New Zealand might be able to provide'. When Waller sought clarification, Bundy suggested a further 200 advisers (in addition to the 83 already serving with the Training Team).[21]

---

19   Edwards, *Crises and Commitments*, p. 319.
20   Ibid., p. 329.
21   Ibid., pp. 336–7.

In the following months Waller, on instructions from Canberra, repeatedly pressed for more information on American intentions and proposed strategy. It was clear that there was no clear political or military strategy, and that debate was intense within the 'interagency process' in Washington. Waller was the channel through whom Menzies and his senior ministers sided with the hawks, giving every possible encouragement to Johnson to stand firm, to commit American forces, and not to enter the negotiations proposed by the British Government and many others around the world. For example, it was through Waller that Menzies sent Johnson the text of his robust defence of American policy in Vietnam, in response to a group of Anglican bishops who had challenged its wisdom.[22]

When a crucial meeting on military strategy was held in Honolulu in late March, Australia was represented by the Chairman of the Chiefs of Staff Committee, Air Chief Marshal Sir Frederick Scherger, without any adviser from either the embassy in Washington or External Affairs in Canberra. At this time the Australians effectively pressed a battalion on to the Americans, even though American military strategy was still unclear and the Americans had not asked for such a commitment. After delays prompted by the need to secure a formal request from the South Vietnamese Government, Waller conveyed the formal offer of the Australian battalion to Rusk on 13 April.[23]

In subsequent years, Waller was a witness to the positive and negative manifestations of the Australian–American relationship, amid the tensions raised by the increasingly unpopular war. The relationship between governments was increasingly focused on the personal meetings between heads of government.

Waller was present when Harold Holt made his famous statement that Australia was 'all the way with LBJ' on the South Lawn of the White House in June 1966, but he had had no part in shaping it. His role was simply to record how welcome this support had been for the Johnson Administration, especially in contrast to the criticism from the British Government. But the American requests for more support continued, especially as the Indonesian–Malaysian Confrontation wound down. Johnson put pressure on the visiting Australian Treasurer, William

---

22 Ibid., pp. 355–6, 365.
23 Ibid., p. 364.

McMahon, over a further increase to the Australian commitment. This led to the announcement of a decision already taken to add a third battalion to the Australian taskforce.[24]

The personal rapport between Johnson and Holt was not maintained by their respective successors. The Tet offensive, in which the Vietnamese communist forces failed militarily but gained a strategic victory through the impact on American public opinion, occurred soon after Gorton's accession to the prime ministership. At the height of the offensive, Gorton stated publicly that there would be no further increases in the Australian commitment. This was no more than making public what the Holt Government had decided the previous year, but it was a clear sign of the new Prime Minister's distress over the Vietnam commitment. Gorton clearly felt locked into a commitment for which he had never shared the initial enthusiasm of Menzies and Holt, but he could not see a way out. His manifest disdain for the officials in External Affairs and Defence also extended to ambassadors.

When Johnson startled the world in March 1968 with the announcement that he would not be standing for re-election, Gorton vented his anger at the lack of consultation with his Australian ally. Waller could hardly be blamed for that: even many of Johnson's closest associates knew nothing of his decision until it was publicly announced. Soon afterwards, Gorton made his first visit to the White House as prime minister. Waller later recorded that 'a more uncomfortable first meeting between two men I have never seen'. Gorton seemed torn between wanting a demonstration of presidential fellowship, akin to that enjoyed by Holt, and resenting the sense that he was being 'annexed' or 'captured' by the honours and attention that Johnson bestowed upon him.[25]

Nor would matters improve when Nixon was elected in November, to take office in January 1969. Soon after the election, Waller reported that he had no idea what to expect from the new regime. In the Nixon Administration's first year it introduced the policy of 'Vietnamisation', under which more of the fighting would be carried out by the South Vietnamese forces, allowing the Americans to withdraw some of their men. The American withdrawals further added to the tension in

---

24 Peter Edwards, *A Nation at War: Australian Politics, Society and Diplomacy during the Vietnam War 1965–1975*, Allen & Unwin in association with the Australian War Memorial, Sydney, 1997, pp. 154–5.
25 James Curran, *Unholy Fury: Whitlam and Nixon at War*, Melbourne University Press, 2015, pp. 90–2.

the Washington–Canberra relationship. The Australians came under domestic public pressure to begin a similar graduated withdrawal, but the Americans pressed their allies to maintain their much smaller commitments. Gorton was repeatedly embarrassed by announcements of American withdrawals on which it was obvious that Australia had not been consulted. Again Waller had to bear some of his anger, but Nixon and his National Security Adviser, Henry Kissinger, kept their decisions extremely close. Waller found access to the Nixon White House extremely difficult, and thought that William Bundy's successor in the State Department, Marshall Green, had limited influence.[26]

Moreover, an ambassador's effectiveness depends not only on the willingness of the host government to share information and ideas, but also on the ability of the government they represent to give clear directions in executing a coherent strategy. Particularly in the second half of his term, Waller had the misfortune to be the envoy of a tired and increasingly dysfunctional government, which was wracked by intense personal rivalries and dissolving into policy paralysis. Any government would have found it difficult to shape effective foreign and defence policies, especially to seek an honourable exit from the increasingly unpopular Vietnam commitment without prejudicing the American relationship, but it was out of the question for a government torn by the bitter rivalries between Prime Minister Gorton, Foreign Minister McMahon, and the young and ambitious Defence Minister, Malcolm Fraser.

So, despite his professional skill, Waller was a frequently uncomfortable witness to, rather than an active participant in, decision-making on the Vietnam War. Both in the escalation of the war and the beginning of the withdrawal, much of Waller's role consisted of fruitless attempts to find out what the President, first Johnson and then Nixon, had in mind. His lack of success should not be held against him; even the respective presidents' closest advisers and most senior officials were often no better informed.

---

26 Waller, *A Diplomatic Life*, p. 39.

Conclusion

Having formed the view that his predecessor, Howard Beale, had been too long in Washington, Waller himself was glad to leave in 1970. His contemporary and former departmental head, Arthur Tange, was designated to succeed him. Although *agrément* had not been sought, the Tanges and the Wallers exchanged detailed correspondence about the transition. Then, in circumstances worthy of an episode of *Yes, Minister,* Tange was offered both his old job as Secretary of External Affairs and another headship, Secretary of Defence. The outcome of a flurry of communications was that Tange went to Defence, James Plimsoll to Washington and Waller to be Secretary of External Affairs – probably the most important appointments for each of these three outstanding public servants.[27] In that sense, Waller's term in Washington was not, as one might have expected, the pinnacle of his career, but an important step towards the position that was.

Waller's term was significant, but not quite in the ways that one might have expected. He was the first career diplomat appointed to Washington, but only by default. Nevertheless, he did well enough to ensure that he was certainly not the last. Waller had a remarkably large amount of face-to-face time with Johnson, but in circumstances that meant that he had no special influence. He was there for the peak years of the Vietnam War, but he was largely a bystander as far as the major policy decisions were concerned. He was a channel for communications between those who actually made policy, often frustrated by severe limits on the consultation or even information that the Americans offered to their Australian ally. He was also a witness to the tensions in the personal relationships between Gorton and both Johnson and Nixon. Waller was the consummate Australian diplomatist, but the nature of politics and diplomacy at the time were such that his skills were not deployed as effectively or influentially as one might have expected.

---

27   Edwards, *Arthur Tange*, pp. 171–2.

8

'A precious vase':
Sir James Plimsoll

Jeremy Hearder

Sir James Plimsoll proceeded to Washington in 1970 after serving for five years as Secretary of the Department of External Affairs in Canberra. Washington was a typical posting in Plimsoll's career: he went where he was told, he did distinguished work, and he hated leaving.[1] What made it different was his extensive knowledge and experience of the US; his standing among key Americans; and that he departed somewhat embittered because of the circumstances of his leaving. When Plimsoll presented credentials as Ambassador, President Richard Nixon told him: 'You yourself are no stranger to our shores, your accomplishments have been many.'[2] Plimsoll was, indeed, unusually qualified, and well-known in Washington. Since his first visit to the US as an army captain in 1945, he had worked there for more than eight years. In Plimsoll's two periods in Canberra, relations with the US had been a major focus. Ever since his work during the Korean War, Americans had regarded him as one of Australia's most respected diplomats.

---

1 An expanded version of this chapter appears in the author's book: *Jim Plim Ambassador Extraordinary: A Biography of Sir James Plimsoll*, Connor Court Publishing, Ballarat, 2015.
2 President Richard Nixon in reply to Plimsoll's presentation of credentials as Ambassador, speech, I.3417 of 11.6.70, Plimsoll Papers, MS 8048/3, National Library of Australia (NLA), Canberra.

During Plimsoll's time in Washington (1970–74) he faced a number of difficulties. At head of government level, relations were no longer as close personally as had been the case with Robert Menzies and then Harold Holt. Further, for foreign ambassadors, the White House was virtually closed, while the State Department was excluded from involvement in major foreign policy decisions. Australia, a close ally, would receive only short notice of major US announcements. It was partly a reflection of personality. Nixon was 'not an open person. He didn't much like meetings, and preferred to study the papers and decide'.[3] For Australia, this relationship between two close but unequal partners and allies always required careful management. It was not as important to the US as to Australia. As Plimsoll put it, 'A super power looks at things differently from a country the size of Australia'.[4]

Political volatility and social unrest marked the period of Plimsoll's ambassadorship. There were unprecedented demonstrations and riots in major US cities and university campuses in opposition to the Vietnam War and the draft. From 1973, the Watergate scandal reflected an unfolding crisis of governance. Meanwhile, in Canberra also there was unusual political turbulence: during the three-and-a-half years Plimsoll served four foreign ministers, and three prime ministers. Each prime minister insisted on the importance of the US relationship but did little about it. John Gorton, and then his successor, William McMahon, were concentrating on political survival, while the advent of the Whitlam Government brought about a minor crisis in the relationship.

McMahon

Circumstances for the Australian embassy in Washington in 1970 were made difficult by the continuing rivalry between Gorton and McMahon.[5] In 1970 Sir Keith Waller, Plimsoll's successor as Secretary, once mentioned to Plimsoll that letters from Nixon to Gorton as Prime

---

3   Lieutenant-General Brent Scowcroft, personal communication, 4 April 2008. And see generally James Curran, *Unholy Fury: Whitlam and Nixon at War*, Melbourne University Press, Melbourne, 2015.

4   Jim Plimsoll, 30 November 1972, memorandum (unnumbered), series A1838, item 683(72)57, National Archives of Australia (NAA), Canberra.

5   'Both were intensely political but in ways that inevitably brought them into conflict. Neither man had a strong commitment to the party.' Otherwise they 'had very little in common apart from ambition and mutual dislike'. Graeme Starr, *Carrick: Principles, Politics and Policy*, Connor Court Publishing, Ballarat, 2012, p. 190.

Minister, of legitimate interest to the foreign minister, were not being passed to McMahon. Plimsoll understood the department's problem, but also Gorton's reluctance to share sensitive material with a notorious leaker.[6]

Plimsoll's opinion of McMahon, formed in Canberra, did not improve, especially in the wake of an incident prompting physical intervention by the Ambassador. McMahon, as Foreign Minister, visited Washington for the Australia, New Zealand, United States Security Treaty (ANZUS) Council talks in September 1970. At a dinner in McMahon's honour at the Residence, guests included William Rogers, Secretary of State, and Richard Helms, Director of the CIA. After dessert, while guests were still at table, McMahon quietly left. Plimsoll followed him out. He said to Plimsoll that he was tired and was going to bed. Plimsoll reminded him that the guests included a number of important, busy people who had come to meet him. McMahon replied: 'Some other time.' He had turned to go up the stairs when Plimsoll seized him by the back of his coat. 'All right I'll stay', McMahon agreed.[7]

In March 1971, Plimsoll was informed that McMahon had challenged Gorton and was now prime minister. Plimsoll replied: 'Well, that's the end of the Coalition Government, because they won't last with him.'[8] At first, however, Plimsoll was worried that McMahon might replace him with some minister whom he wanted to be rid of.[9]

Plimsoll travelled extensively around the US and his talents in public speaking and handling the media were invaluable attributes. He not only promoted Australia and its policies, but he was the only ambassador representing US allies in Vietnam who travelled so frequently, speaking to local media. As a result, Nixon learned of Plimsoll's public defence of allied policy, and he was pleased. This brought special access to the White House.[10]

---

6   Plimsoll to Keith Waller, 25 June 1970, letter, Jim Plimsoll Papers, MS 8048/3, NAA, Canberra.
7   Arthur Tange, personal communication, 6 January 1998; David Sadleir, 29 January 2000, letter. Tange heard this from Plimsoll and Sadleir heard this from Richard Woolcott, who was also present.
8   *Reminiscential Conversations Between Hon. Clyde Cameron and Sir James Plimsoll*, 1984, TRC 1967, vol. ii, p. 177, NLA, Canberra; Jim Plimsoll, diary, 9, 10 March 1971, Plimsoll Papers, MS 8048/3, NLA, Canberra.
9   JE Ryan, 16 March 1971, diary (unpublished), privately held. Ryan was Number 2 in the embassy.
10   RR Fernandez, personal communication, 19 March 1997. Kissinger told Plimsoll things on the condition that he not tell 'those S.O.B's in State'. Fernandez succeeded Ryan as deputy at the embassy.

In the early 1970s, the Australian Residence had established a reputation for entertaining well, a matter in which there was intense competition among embassies.[11] Plimsoll's strategy was small groups of 'people of some consequence who would get something out of the dinner and let us get something out of the dinner'.[12] Plimsoll was a very active host, and vastly overspent out of his own pocket, perhaps by as much as A$15,000 per year.[13] Plimsoll's contact with the highest officials in the State Department partly reflected previous acquaintance, and partly his unusual standing. His closest contact was with Marshall Green, Assistant Secretary for East Asia, whose responsibilities included Vietnam and China. In a rare opportunity provided to an Australian Ambassador, Green would invite Plimsoll's comments on draft US policy submissions.[14]

During the crisis of the Yom Kippur War in the Middle East in October 1973, although not directly involved, the Australian Government was concerned about possible widening of the conflict. Australia, moreover, was presiding at the UN Security Council, which was heavily involved. In any case, Canberra expected to be treated as 'an ally': to be perceived as being kept well-informed, and as having some dialogue.[15] Plimsoll arranged this with Joseph Sisco, Assistant Secretary of State responsible for the Middle East. Given Sisco's preoccupations, Plimsoll would see him for only 10 minutes at a time, but the arrangement worked effectively to meet an ambassador's need for frequent consultation and sharing of information.[16]

---

11   Peter Costigan (from Washington), *Herald* (Melbourne), 1970–74; Hearder, *Jim Plim*, p. 256; *Reminiscential Conversations* (quoted by Cameron), vol. ii, p. 337: 'Although they rarely made the social columns of the *Washington Post*, the dinners and lunches hosted by Sir James became a legend among the top officials in State, the Pentagon, the White House and the Congress.'

12   *Reminiscential Conversations*, vol. ii, p. 337.

13   Marjorie Knight (Ambassador's Social Secretary), personal communication, 30 May 1997. Plimsoll worked the Residence staff very hard. He had to be reminded about the need for some days off for the staff.

14   Mack Williams, personal communication, 2 July 1998. This illustrated Green's high regard for Plimsoll's knowledge and judgement, not to mention his memory for detail. This often later led to phone calls from the State Department to Counsellors at the Embassy: 'What's this about the Soviet position in the UN First Committee in 1952?'

15   MJ Hughes, personal communication, July 2000.

16   Joseph Sisco, personal communication, 20 August 1996. Sisco, for his part, recalled that he had had no hesitation in doing this for 'one of the best diplomats I dealt with during my entire career'.

Vietnam and China

With regard to the Vietnam War, a most important task for the embassy was to try to predict what the Americans would do next. If US service personnel in Vietnam increased, a request for more from Australia could follow. If numbers decreased there could be domestic pressure in Australia to do likewise.[17] Washington was the 'imperial capital of an empire at war, and at war at home'.[18] With public demonstrations, the National Guard was sometimes deployed in the streets. In May 1971 Plimsoll decided to sleep on his office couch one Sunday night, concerned that a planned demonstration might prevent him reaching the embassy next morning.[19]

For the McMahon Government, the question of diplomatic relations with China was one in which domestic political considerations weighed heavily, frustrating senior officials in the department.[20] Waller gave high priority to having the Coalition Government achieve recognition, but without success.[21] Plimsoll, however, remained more cautious about China.[22] On the evening of 15 July 1971, Secretary Rogers phoned to give one hour's advance notice of Nixon's announcement that Henry Kissinger had visited China from 9 to 11 July, and that Nixon himself would visit there by May 1972. Plimsoll estimated that he managed to have his message in Canberra about 20 minutes before McMahon was due to go into the House for Question Time.[23]

---

17 Williams, personal communication 2 July 1998.
18 Sam Lipski (Washington correspondent for *The Australian*), personal communication, 28 August 1997.
19 Plimsoll's diary, 2 May 1971, Plimsoll Papers, MS8048/3, NLA, Canberra. In the event, the main demonstrations were held elsewhere in the city.
20 HD Anderson, 2 October 1970, note, series A1838/2, item 3107/38/20, part 1, NAA, Canberra. One who penned some thoughts on China policy doubted that 'in the prevailing political climate here' his ideas would 'get far in the immediate future'.
21 Keith Waller, *A Diplomatic Life, Some Memories*, Centre for the Study of Australia–Asia Relations, Griffith University, Brisbane, 1990, p. 44.
22 John Lavett, personal communication, 29 August 2002. During discussions with a counsellor at the embassy, Plimsoll referred to China as 'the enemy'.
23 Sadleir, personal communication, 15 January 2002; Plimsoll's diary, 15 July 1971, Plimsoll Papers, MS8048/3, NLA, Canberra.

The announcement evoked some strong reactions in Canberra about the secrecy with which the US had changed policy.[24] Plimsoll tended to downplay the significance of the China development. Basic differences between the US and China remained 'and are likely to continue for a long time to come'. Both countries were 'still in the exploratory stage of relations', and relations with Japan would be 'more important for the indefinite future'. Plimsoll even expressed some sympathy for the degree of US secrecy. It was 'dangerous' that relevant US officials were not involved and unable to offer advice; Nixon, however, had no alternative. 'Once he had begun consultation with even the closest of US allies, the risks of leakage would have become unbearably high.'[25] Doubtless Plimsoll's unspoken thought was of the current Australian prime minister. As for Nixon's own administration, there had been significant leaks, notably publication of the Pentagon Papers.

Crisis on the Indian subcontinent

The year 1971 also saw troubles in Pakistan, leading to eventual emergence of the new nation of Bangladesh. The US approach was influenced firstly by its relationship with Pakistan as an ally, and an often troubled relationship with India; and, secondly, by its relationship with the Soviet Union. The US was uneasy that the Soviets seemed to be getting closer to India. Kissinger commented: 'We can't allow a friend of ours and China's to get screwed in a conflict with a friend of Russia's.'[26] The situation produced a 'watershed' in the relationship of the superpowers;[27] and the crisis also brought Plimsoll to the attention of US policymakers, such was his reputation for sound counsel in relation to South and East Asian affairs.

---

24 Although a Foreign Affairs policy planning paper had warned that, as a great power, the US would act in its own interests and could change policies quickly. See David Goldsworthy (ed.), *Facing North: A Century of Australian Engagement with Asia, vol. 1: 1901 to the 1970s*, Department of Foreign Affairs and Trade, Canberra, 2001, p. 332.
25 Plimsoll to Canberra, 17 August 1971, memorandum, series A1838, item 625/14/23, NAA, Canberra.
26 Kissinger, quoted in Richard M. Nixon, *RN: The Memoirs of Richard Nixon*, Arrow Books, London, 1979, p. 527.
27 'A Watershed in our Relationship', in *Soviet–American Relations: The Détente Years 1969–1972*, Department of State Publications 11438, Washington DC, 2007, 15 November 1971 – 31 December 1971.

By December the US was concerned that Indian forces, having overcome Pakistani forces in East Pakistan, would invade and conquer West Pakistan. The US, which felt it had no influence in New Delhi, looked to the Soviet Union to 'restrain the Indians'. On 9 December Nixon warned Vorontsov, the Soviet Chargé in Washington, that 'if India moves forces against West Pakistan, the US cannot stand by. We must inevitably look towards a confrontation between the USSR and the US'. The next day Vorontsov told Moscow, after talking with Kissinger, that the US was 'only interested in the situation on the western border between India and Pakistan', and the US 'are turning a blind eye' to East Pakistan (Bangladesh), where India had won.[28]

Plimsoll's sympathy for India was well-known.[29] Similarly, Waller shared Plimsoll's determination to improve relations with India, 'which had never been given the importance which I thought they merited'.[30] Unusually, besides instructions from Canberra, Plimsoll received a personal message from the Prime Minister of India, Indira Gandhi, asking him to intercede with Kissinger, so that Kissinger would have a more balanced view of the Indian position.[31] Plimsoll later recalled that he thought the US, in their support for Pakistan, were 'behaving in a very dangerous way'. He saw Rogers and other officials, 'to try to hold them back from any violent support of Pakistan'. But he was less certain whether his message was getting through to the White House.

Two years later, however, at a White House dinner, Nixon greeted the Australian Ambassador and then turned to the guest of honour and said of Plimsoll: 'He knows a great deal about the Far East, and he was of immense value to us in recent troubles in India and Bangladesh.' Two months later, Nixon saw Plimsoll at another function and repeated the sentiment: 'I will never forget what you did for us on Pakistan, India and Bangladesh. I will always be grateful. We owe you a great debt.' Plimsoll felt that, on hearing it a second time, it was 'not just polite persiflage'. But he was unsure what the President was referring to. Perhaps the US had been contemplating some sort of military intervention, probably naval, in support of Pakistan, and that 'what I had

---

28 Ibid.
29 Lavett, personal communication, 25 March 2002. Plimsoll 'even had meetings in his office with emerging Bangladeshis – at that time no doubt regarded as dissident Pakistanis – to give them advice and encouragement'.
30 Waller, *Diplomatic Life*, p. 45.
31 Williams, personal communication, 2 July 1998. The message to Plimsoll came in such a way that the Indian Ambassador was unaware of it.

been saying to people may have held them back'.[32] Plimsoll saw the emergence of Bangladesh as inevitable. He later noted that the situation had been 'the only issue on which Australian and US policies have diverged markedly'.[33]

In a 1972 article comparing career and non-career ambassadors in the diplomatic corps in Washington, the *Christian Science Monitor* reported that Plimsoll and the Ambassador for Japan, Nobuhiko Ushiba, were 'among the most respected career men'.[34] At the same time Plimsoll was, according to another observer, probably the worst-dressed ambassador.[35]

Watergate

The year 1973 proved a difficult one with the unfolding crisis of governance in Washington, as well as a crisis in Australia's relations with the US. The Vice President, Spiro Agnew, resigned mid-year. The Watergate affair intensified with resignations and subsequent indictments of senior White House figures, the resignation of Attorney-General Elliot Richardson, and the President's firing of the Special Watergate Prosecutor, Archibald Cox.

Plimsoll later recalled realising that there had been a 'diseased atmosphere' detectable in the White House after Nixon's re-election in November 1972, before Watergate 'gathered steam'. A lawyer who had attended a meeting with White House officials told Plimsoll that, when the constitutionality of a proposed measure was discussed, the response was, '[i]f the President wants it, it's constitutional'. Plimsoll, by no means an avid television watcher, found himself often glued to the one television set in the embassy as key witnesses testified before Congressional Watergate hearings. The country became divided, and the conduct of normal business, especially in the White House, became

---

32   *Reminiscential Conversations*, vol. ii, pp. 313–15; Washington to Canberra, 15 December 1971, cablegram no. I.127272, series A1838/272, item 169/11/148, part 51, NAA, Canberra.
33   Post-annual review, 1971–72, series A1838/346 TS, item 693/3, part 14, NAA, Canberra.
34   'Mr Ambassador – Flags, Pomp and A Changing Role', *Christian Science Monitor*, 26 May 1972; Plimsoll Papers, item 8048/16/3, NLA, Canberra.
35   Marjorie Knight, personal communication, 30 May 1997.

increasingly difficult.[36] Nixon seemed to be 'isolating himself' and 'a lot of small but important decisions appear to have been left aside', not least in international affairs.[37]

Plimsoll later recalled finding it hard to believe that Nixon could have been 'that stupid' to be personally involved in the Watergate burglary. If Nixon had admitted involvement early on, 'he would probably have got away with it'. Many members of Congress had their own skeletons in cupboards, and at first they were not 'inclined to pursue him too far'.[38] In reports to Canberra about Watergate, Plimsoll took a cautious approach.[39] As Ambassador, Plimsoll had contact with senior White House figures as well as members of the administration. He knew Maurice Stans and Elliott Richardson, who in different ways both suffered over Watergate. Another he knew was Alexander Butterfield, who later revealed the existence of the tapes of Nixon's conversations. Any leakage of embassy comment on Watergate would have been disastrous for maintaining White House contact, and for achieving what became a major problem: a Whitlam visit to the White House.

The Whitlam Government

On 2 December 1972 the Labor Party, under the leadership of Gough Whitlam, won the election. Plimsoll decided to decline the offer of a job at The Australian National University from the Vice-Chancellor, Sir John Crawford.[40] Plimsoll hoped to establish a good working relationship with Whitlam. He had known Whitlam and his wife Margaret for many years, as well as Whitlam's father, a former Commonwealth Crown solicitor. Whitlam had visited Plimsoll in New York, and in Delhi. In Washington, the Whitlams stayed with him at the Residence in 1970 and 1972.[41] Plimsoll and Whitlam were of a similar age and height, and with similar elephantine memories and enthusiasm

---

36   *Reminiscential Conversations*, vol. ii, pp. 166–8; Plimsoll's diary, 14 June 1973, 25 June 1973, 23 October 1973, Plimsoll Papers, MS8048/3, NLA, Canberra.
37   Washington to Canberra, 19 July 1973, cablegram no. 3834, Plimsoll Papers, Department of Foreign Affairs and Trade (DFAT), Canberra; Washington to Canberra, 21 October 1973, cablegram no. 5805, Plimsoll Papers, DFAT, Canberra.
38   *Reminiscential Conversations*, vol. ii, p. 166.
39   PG Timmins, personal communication, 21 December 1999.
40   Plimsoll's diary, 4 December 1972, Plimsoll Papers, MS8048/3, NLA, Canberra.
41   Ibid., 15–19 July 1970, 26–29 January 1972.

for the arts and literature.[42] Plimsoll had seen Whitlam in Canberra during his consultations in August 1972.[43] On 20 December, Plimsoll returned again briefly for consultations.

This was the beginning of an unusually testing time for Plimsoll and embassy staff. The new Australian Labor Government was raw and inexperienced after 23 years out of office. Whitlam, also foreign minister for the first year, wanted to keep tight control of foreign policy but did not keep his colleagues informed. In his haste to use his new power to change Australian foreign policy towards a 'more independent' stance, he tended to take the US for granted. Nixon, hypersensitive in the wake of the problems of Watergate, was deeply upset by Australia.

Before returning to Canberra, Plimsoll had conveyed Whitlam's personal message to Nixon strongly opposing the renewal of bombing of North Vietnam. Read today, the message seems balanced if intense, 'but Nixon was very annoyed by it because he had never been rebuked by an Australian'.[44] Whitlam had expressed his 'deep concern'. Nixon's reaction was: 'Doesn't he think I'm concerned?'[45] Unaware of Whitlam's message, three of his ministers – Cairns, Cameron and Uren – each issued statements that 'intruded with mounting stridency about murderers and maniacs in the White House'. Nixon's anger 'turned to fury'.[46] All of this 'took some explaining to the Americans, because they had never been subjected to public criticism by Australia; we had always been at great pains to keep our differences in private'.[47]

---

42   Gough Whitlam, personal communication, August 1996; Plimsoll's diary, 16 May 1972, Plimsoll Papers, MS8048/3, NLA, Canberra. Whitlam had been impressed that in 1972 Plimsoll had had James Mollison, Director of the National Gallery of Australia (NGA), to dinner in Washington, along with directors of the major galleries in Washington. Whitlam believed that Australia had never had a gallery director who knew anything about US art. Plimsoll was introducing Mollison to a new world. One outcome was the purchase for the NGA in 1973 of Jackson Pollock's *Blue Poles* painting. Plimsoll held a similar lunch for Mollison again on 25 October 1973: Plimsoll's diary, 25 October 1973, Plimsoll Papers, MS8048/3, NLA, Canberra.

43   *Reminiscential Conversations*, vol. ii, p. 308. Whitlam had mentioned that Kim Beazley (Senior) would like Foreign Affairs, but Whitlam ruled this out on account of his Moral Rearmament background: 'He would never lie – a Minister for Foreign Affairs has to be prepared to lie sometimes.'

44   Waller, *Diplomatic Life*, p. 48.

45   Marshall Green, *Pacific Encounters, Recollections and Humor*, DACOR-BACON Press, Bethesda, Maryland, 1997, p. 135.

46   Edward Gough Whitlam, *The Whitlam Government*, Penguin, Melbourne, 1985, p. 43.

47   Waller, *Diplomatic Life*, pp. 47–8.

On 27 December 1972, Australia announced cancellation of all military aid to South Vietnam, and abandoned a plan to train Cambodian troops in Australia.[48] On 28 December, in Sydney, Plimsoll had a wide-ranging discussion with the new Prime Minister/Foreign Minister. Whitlam was critical of US policies on Vietnam. He took issue with Plimsoll's analysis of US attempts to get out of the war, but apart from the 'intractable question' of Vietnam, he saw no other problems with the US. For his part, Plimsoll was concerned at Whitlam's apparent lack of interest in the possible economic consequences of 'reckless' measures he was considering in relation to French nuclear testing in the South Pacific.[49] Whitlam had earlier denounced French nuclear testing in the region and had pledged to take the matter to the International Court of Justice. Plimsoll's home consultations were shortened as Whitlam asked him to return to represent the government at the funeral of former US President Harry Truman.

Upon becoming Prime Minister, Whitlam signalled a desire for 'a more independent Australian stance in foreign affairs'.[50] Earlier, in 1971, Plimsoll had warned about the dangers of such an 'emotionally attractive' concept, as seen from Washington. He doubted that Australia would 'achieve anything by announcing important decisions without first having genuine consultation with the United States'. Although Australia and the US had 'different roles to play', wrote Plimsoll, their 'basic interests' were the same. Australia needed to work 'in the greatest intimacy. Australia has a bigger interest in that than the US has'.[51] But early 1973 was a heady time in Canberra for the first Labor Government in 23 years. Changes in foreign policy by what Plimsoll called 'dramatic gestures'[52] were easier to achieve than in domestic policies, and there was more to come. Since his return from Canberra to Washington, Plimsoll had 'not looked very happy'.[53] But Plimsoll steeled himself for being 'the meat in the sandwich between an irate White House and the tempestuous new Labor Government in Australia'.[54]

---

48   Peter Edwards, *A Nation at War: Australian Politics, Society and Diplomacy During the Vietnam War*, Allen & Unwin and AWM, Sydney, 1997, p. 324.
49   *Reminiscential Conversations*, vol. i, p. 436.
50   Richard Woolcott, *The Hot Seat: Reflections on Diplomacy from Stalin's Death to the Bali Bombings*, HarperCollins Publishers, Sydney, 2003, p. 112. Text of Whitlam's statement is in *Australian Foreign Affairs Record*, vol. 43, December 1972, p. 619.
51   Plimsoll, Washington, to Canberra, 17 August 1971, memorandum, Plimsoll Papers, DFAT.
52   *Reminiscential Conversations*, vol. ii, pp. 301–2.
53   Fernandez, personal communication, 19 March 1997.
54   Roy Macartney (Washington correspondent), *Age*, 5 February 1974.

He saw Rogers on 8 January 1973, while in Australia, maritime trade unions were boycotting US shipping in response to renewed US bombing of Hanoi.[55] Plimsoll reported to Canberra that 'the dominating question [from Rogers] was: where are Australian–American relations going?', given the statements by the three Australian ministers, and the trade union boycott. Rogers had told him that the statements had 'caused great resentment in the White House and in the Administration generally'.[56] Plimsoll and Rogers, who knew each other well, had a 'reasoned discussion'. However, Rogers asked him to report to Canberra 'that we feel very strongly about this. Don't send back a report that we are taking this in our stride because we are not'.[57] Plimsoll had conveyed to Rogers that Whitlam 'wished to have good and close relations with the US and that he saw Vietnam questions as the only substantive matter of difference'. The problem with that proposition was that, seen from Washington, Vietnam had long been a core part of bilateral cooperation. It was from this that Whitlam now was departing.

The Vietnam peace agreement came into effect on 27 January 1973. Canberra felt that the agreement opened the way for establishment of diplomatic relations with North Vietnam. Plimsoll reported 'dismay' in the State Department at the speed of Australia's proposed action in this direction, as well as a lack of prior discussion with the US, such as the Americans had had with Canada and Japan. The US had hoped that friendly countries would hold back on such a step 'to see whether North Vietnam was ready to give effect to the agreement'. Plimsoll warned that a move towards diplomatic relations 'would be bound to touch a raw nerve in the White House' and recommended moving slowly.[58] However, on 26 February, Whitlam announced that Canberra and Hanoi had decided to establish diplomatic relations.[59] Nixon retaliated. Australia was included in a list of countries to be treated in a discriminatory fashion. The Ambassador was not to be received by the administration

---

55 *Reminiscential Conversations*, vol. i, p. 454.
56 Washington to Canberra, 8 January 1973, cablegram no. I2602, series A7976/1, NAA, Canberra.
57 *Reminiscential Conversations*, pp. ii, 176.
58 Washington to Canberra, 2 February 1973, cablegram no. I.13166, series A1838/2, item 3020/10/3, part 1, NAA, Canberra; Washington to Canberra, 2 February 1973, cablegram no. I.13039, series A1838/2, item 3020/10/3, part 1, NAA, Canberra; Washington to Canberra, 6 February 1973, cablegram no. I.12399, series A1838/2, item 3020/10/3, part 1, NAA, Canberra.
59 Edwards, *Nation at War*, p. 326; Washington to Canberra, 31 January 1973, cablegram no. I.11925, series A7976/1, NAA, Canberra.

or by senior officials. Embassy officers were to be received at no higher than desk level in the State Department. Marshall Green protested, but there was much angst in the White House.[60]

Plimsoll later recalled that it was a 'difficult period'. It testified to the high regard in which he was held that his contacts continued 'as much as ever'. Rogers, who much later spoke to Plimsoll of this White House edict, said that he and Green were not going to stop talking to him. As they could not see him on the golf course, Plimsoll not being a golfer, they saw him at his residence.[61] Rogers 'had a very high regard for Plimsoll as perhaps the best informed diplomat in Washington on several key United Nations issues and strategy'.[62] Of other members of the Cabinet, Attorney-General Richardson 'went out of his way to be helpful and co-operative'. The Secretary for Health, Education and Welfare, Caspar Weinberger, with whom Plimsoll had become friendly, blatantly disregarded the directive.[63]

Plimsoll seemed despondent and unhappy at the direction of the Whitlam Government, and constantly having to defend its new policies to the administration.[64] He, nevertheless, continued to provide forthright advice to Canberra, warning about possible effects of the new government's moves on relations with the US. Whitlam was 'attached to the principle of universality in our diplomatic relations', especially with communist countries, to assist in achieving the more 'independent' foreign policy to which he aspired.[65] Following an approach from Cuba about establishing consular relations, Plimsoll noted that many Latin American countries still did not support Cuban membership of the UN. Nor was there any US movement, either from the President or Congress, towards rapprochement with Cuba. For Nixon, Cuba was still 'a very personal issue'; the 1962 missile crisis remained much on his mind, while Bebe Rebozo, a Cuban émigré, was one of his closest friends. The US would regard any Australian move towards Cuba as 'a deliberately anti-American act since there would be little or no resulting benefit to Australia'. Plimsoll 'urged caution' and patience. To hold off

60   Fernandez, personal communication, 19 March 1997.
61   *Reminiscential Conversations*, vol. i, pp. 455–6.
62   Marshall Green, personal communication, 13 April 1997.
63   *Reminiscential Conversations*, vol. i, pp. 455–6; Plimsoll's diary, 19 January 1973, Plimsoll Papers, MS8048/3, NLA, Canberra.
64   Fernandez, personal communication, 19–20 February 2001.
65   Whitlam, 'Statement by the Prime Minister', *Australian Foreign Affairs Record*, December 1972, p. 59.

was not a matter of 'following' the US. Rather, looking at it from an Organization of American States regional perspective, 'there should be no conflict with the idea of the independent foreign policy in waiting on the countries of Cuba's own region to develop a position'. Canberra accepted Plimsoll's comments as 'generally valid' and was persuaded not to respond to the Cuban approach.[66]

Whitlam wanted to move quickly towards recognising North Korea. Plimsoll had had years of involvement in policy towards Korea. The Foreign Minister of South Korea, who frequently consulted him when visiting Washington, was 'very hurt' that Australia, as an old friend and ally, 'had canvassed its new moves with a number of other countries before talking them out with Seoul'.[67] Green told Plimsoll that the US disagreed with Australia 'making any decision at this stage in favour of recognition or diplomatic relations with North Korea or even saying that it was an objective'.[68] Plimsoll advised Canberra to proceed cautiously: 'Let the contacts with the [DPRK] grow rather than be created overnight',[69] he wrote before Whitlam received the visiting South Korean Foreign Minister in Canberra. Plimsoll recalled that earlier Australian policy on Korea had been bipartisan, noting Evatt's support in 1950 of the Menzies Government's decision to commit Australian forces in the defence of the South. Australia was well respected in Seoul; that was 'not something that should be lightly cast aside'.[70]

Getting Whitlam to the White House

During the first six months of 1973, Plimsoll assisted no fewer than six Whitlam ministers visiting Washington. But Nixon had let it be known at the end of March that he was 'so displeased' that he would not receive Whitlam himself. Whitlam professed surprise. He had thought that for him to visit the President should be 'as natural and relatively informal as his visit to a British Prime Minister'.[71] Getting Nixon to reverse his decision presented a major challenge. Whitlam's first idea was that, on

---

66   Washington to Canberra, 20 April 1973, cablegram no. 2124, Plimsoll Papers, DFAT; Canberra to Washington, 27 April 1973, cablegram no. 1933, Plimsoll Papers, DFAT.
67   Washington to Canberra, 24 February 1973, cablegram no. O.1775, Plimsoll Papers, DFAT.
68   Washington to Canberra, 3 March 1973, cablegram no. O.2045, Plimsoll Papers, DFAT.
69   Washington to Canberra, 29 January 1973, cablegram no. O.883, Plimsoll Papers, DFAT.
70   Washington to Canberra, 9 May 1973, cablegram no. O.4147, Plimsoll Papers, DFAT.
71   Whitlam, *Whitlam Government*, p. 46. Whitlam wrote that this message came via a 'planted story' in the *Washington Post*.

his way to the Commonwealth Prime Ministers' meeting in Ottawa, he could pass through the US. Chances of seeing the President would be improved if an ANZUS Council meeting could be held in Washington.[72] When Plimsoll raised with Rogers the possibility of Whitlam coming to Washington for an ANZUS meeting, the latter instantly reacted that this would include Whitlam meeting the President. 'Now was not the time to raise that' with Nixon, who was 'still smarting'.

Plimsoll reported that he 'spoke frankly to Rogers about forces at work inside the political parties in Australia and the resulting pressures and also limitations on freedom of action'. He pressed the desirability of the two leaders having 'a frank personal talk' soon.[73] Whitlam did not appear overly concerned, yet he did not want to be thought an unreliable ally or not a friend of the US.[74] The prospect of being unwelcome at the White House in his first year in office would not have appealed either.[75] Whitlam next tried sending Peter Wilenski, his principal private secretary, to Washington to talk to Kissinger. This cut across the normal role of the ambassador. Whitlam, although he respected Plimsoll, felt that it would be more appropriate to get a message of reassurance through to Nixon about the nature of the new Australian Government through Wilenski, who would be more familiar with the new ministers, not least the three 'mavericks'. Whitlam noted also, given his fascination with European history, that Kissinger and Wilenski each had been born only a few hundred kilometres apart.[76]

Wilenski's mission was most secret. Not even Plimsoll was informed. Whitlam had been afraid that a request to see Kissinger through the normal diplomatic channels, if refused, would leak to the press and make his government seem 'isolated from America' or even 'anti-American'. Whitlam personally telephoned Professor Ross Terrill at Harvard to ask him to arrange a meeting. Terrill, who knew Kissinger, was an Australian

---

72   GN Bilney to Secretary of Department, 28 February 1973, letter, series A138/369, item 686/2/1/5, part 1, NAA, Canberra. Bilney was in Whitlam's office, seconded from Foreign Affairs.
73   Washington to Canberra, 16 March 1973, cablegram no. I.30601, series A1838/369, item 686/2/15, part 1, NAA, Canberra.
74   Bilney, personal communication, 3 March 2008.
75   Whitlam, *Whitlam Government*, p. 46.
76   Whitlam, personal communication, 27 March 2008. See also Gough Whitlam, *Abiding Interests*, University of Queensland Press, Brisbane, 1997, p. 286.

Sinologist. It was only an hour before the meeting with Kissinger on 2 May that Plimsoll, who happened to be in the embassy, was informed of Wilenski's arrival, and that Wilenski had asked to see him.[77]

It was not an easy meeting. Wilenski sought Plimsoll's help in preparing to talk to Kissinger. Plimsoll was unhappy with being kept out of the picture, at Whitlam not asking him to talk to Kissinger, at the short notice of Wilenski's arrival, and at this last-minute request for advice before such an important meeting. He hardly knew Wilenski, and would have wondered what Wilenski could hope to achieve with Kissinger, one of the most powerful people in Washington. Not surprisingly, Plimsoll, according to Wilenski, was 'not at all helpful'.[78] Searching quickly for something to say, he annoyed Wilenski, of Polish background, with a suggestion that he refer to the common English-speaking background of both countries. Later in the evening Wilenski called on Plimsoll at the Residence to give him some account of his meeting,[79] Wilenski later told Terrill that with Kissinger there had been a 'reasonably conciliatory tone' and 'talk of wiping the slate if not clean, partly clean, reopening direct line of communication between the prime minister and the president'. On matters that they disagreed on, Kissinger 'adopted a lecturing tone', and kept reminding him 'of the responsibilities of a great power'. There were, nevertheless, hopeful signs that a Whitlam visit would take place.[80] At least one embassy officer considered Whitlam's initiative as 'an appalling, insensitive, stupid thing to do to Plimsoll', risking undercutting his standing with the Americans.[81] Plimsoll kept his counsel. It was a new way for Australian diplomacy even if it had several precedents in the international diplomacy of special envoys earlier in the century.[82]

In the next month, June, Andrew Peacock, a minister in the previous government, visited Washington on a US Leadership Grant. Plimsoll talked to him about the problems confronting a prime ministerial visit. He had a dinner for Peacock at which Republican Senator Charles

77   Ross Terrill, *The Australians: In Search of an Identity*, Simon and Schuster, London, 1987, p. 89; Terrill, personal communication, 16 July 2008.
78   Terrill, personal communication, 10 July 2008.
79   Plimsoll's diary, 2 May 1973, Plimsoll Papers, MS8048/3, NLA, Canberra; Terrill, personal communication 10 July 2008.
80   Terrill, personal communication, 10 July 2008.
81   Hughes, personal communication, 2000.
82   Waller, *Diplomatic Life*, p. 50. Later that year in China, Waller found it 'a bit gratuitous' that, given the limit on numbers present, Whitlam preferred to take Wilenski in to see Chairman Mao in preference to the Secretary of his department.

Percy was a guest. Percy later helped Peacock to meet other prominent Republicans, among them George HW Bush, then National Chair of the Republican Party.[83] Bush took Peacock to meet the Vice President, Spiro Agnew. In an 'ugly fifteen minutes', Agnew said the US was sick of being criticised by banana republics, and then having people (like Peacock) creep in to back down. Peacock replied that this was not the point. A refusal to receive Whitlam would boost his standing in Australia and, in the longer term, would have a bad impact bilaterally. Agnew would not budge, but Bush was impressed, and arranged for Peacock to see Nixon, who listened and said he would think about it. Next day, Bush, after accompanying Nixon on a plane flight, phoned Peacock to say that Nixon had taken the point: he did not want Whitlam to get a boost in the Australian electorate as a result of no invitation. Peacock told Plimsoll this before leaving the US on 15 June.[84] The next morning Plimsoll was telephoned by Lieutenant General Brent Scowcroft, Kissinger's deputy.[85] He extended 'an invitation on behalf of the president for Mr Whitlam to see him on 30 July'. Plimsoll immediately informed Canberra.[86] Scowcroft recalled that Nixon had been persuaded that refusing to receive Whitlam 'would be an affront', and regardless of what he and his ministers had said, 'would not be the right thing'.[87] Although the invitation came soon after the Peacock visit, Nixon's reversal was probably the cumulative effect of a number of such demarches and conversations, in Canberra as well as in Washington.[88] Plimsoll certainly pushed hard on this. Scowcroft recalled Plimsoll as a 'very skilful advocate at a very difficult time, trying to explain very different attitudes and policies'.[89]

When Whitlam came to Washington, he had some 40 minutes with Nixon during which he tried to establish 'some rapport and mutual confidence'. He felt this 'crucial test' came off very well. He was accompanied only by Plimsoll, whom he told not to give an account of the talk to anyone, 'and

83   Later President of the United States, 1989–93.
84   Peacock, personal communication, November 1996. Plimsoll saw Peacock several times at dinners between 1–15 June 1973; Plimsoll's diary, Plimsoll Papers, MS8048/3, NLA, Canberra.
85   Bob Woodward and Carl Bernstein, *The Final Days*, Simon and Schuster, New York, 1976, p. 196. Scowcroft was later National Security Advisor to President Ford (1974–76) and to President GHW Bush (1989–93).
86   Plimsoll's diary, 16 June 1973, Plimsoll Papers, MS8048/3, NLA, Canberra.
87   Brent Scowcroft, personal communication, 4 April 2008.
88   Fernandez, personal communication, 20 February 2001.
89   Scowcroft, personal communication, 4 April 2008. Also Roy Macartney, *Age*, reported from Washington that 'the Australian Ambassador's enhanced standing at the White House had helped prepared the way'. Quoted by Cameron in *Reminiscential Conversations*, vol. ii, p. 333.

that includes Wilenski'.[90] Along with others, Plimsoll also accompanied Whitlam on calls on Agnew, Rogers, Kissinger, and Congressional leaders.[91] The program for the visit was a shadow of the normal one for an Australian prime minister. There was no joint press conference and no lunch or dinner at the White House. Rogers and his wife, who had the Whitlams and Plimsoll to a late afternoon drink at their home on a Sunday afternoon, tendered the sole US hospitality. By contrast, some weeks later, Nixon hosted a dinner in honour of the Prime Minister of New Zealand, Norman Kirk.[92]

Plimsoll filled the gap in local hospitality by hosting three dinners and a working lunch at the Residence. His personal standing was such that, despite the coolness from the White House, he was able to attract many significant Americans to meet and talk with over meals, opportunities that Whitlam 'fully used'.[93] These included five Cabinet members: Rogers, Elliot Richardson, Weinberger, Earl Butz (Agriculture), and Claude Breniger (Transportation). Others had been prominent in previous Democratic administrations: Robert S McNamara, President of the World Bank and former Secretary of Defense; and Arthur Goldberg, former Labor Secretary, Justice of the Supreme Court and US Permanent Representative at the UN. Other guests included Senate Democratic Leader Mike Mansfield, and leading Congressional figures, the Administrator of NASA, and Leonard Woodcock, president of the United Automobile Workers.[94] At the Residence, Graham Freudenberg, Whitlam's speechwriter, had a sometimes spirited discussion with Plimsoll about the speech that Plimsoll had drafted Whitlam at the National Press Club in Washington. One issue was the US F-111 aircraft for the Royal Australian Air Force, costs of which had escalated in the 10 years since the original agreement. Freudenberg wanted Whitlam to attack the F-111 project. Plimsoll disagreed: regardless of the rights or wrongs of the original decision, Australia had the aircraft and 'ought to make the most of it. It's an asset, don't throw it away'. Whitlam said nothing, but later privately told Plimsoll that he would not mention the F-111 in the speech. 'In fact I'm glad we have got it, because I think it

---

90   *Reminiscential Conversations*, vol. ii, p. 332; Washington to Canberra, 1 August 1973, cablegram no. O.7136, Plimsoll Papers, DFAT, Canberra.

91   Plimsoll's diary, 30–31 July 1973, Plimsoll Papers, MS8048/3, NLA, Canberra.

92   Plimsoll's diary, 27 September 1973, Plimsoll Papers, MS8048/3, NLA, Canberra. Plimsoll attended this dinner.

93   Washington to Canberra, 1 August 1973, cablegram no. O.7136, Plimsoll Papers, DFAT, Canberra.

94   Plimsoll's diary, 28–31 July 1973, Plimsoll Papers, MS8048/3, NLA, Canberra.

is a good thing for the populous countries to the north of us to know that we've got a weapon like that. And I'm not going to do anything to disparage it.'[95]

The important thing about the visit was that it took place at all. Whitlam, moreover, felt that it had 'gone very well', and 'had more than achieved the purposes we had in mind'.[96] Few knew that Plimsoll's presence during the visit had been by no means assured. His health was 'beginning to play up a bit'.[97] At 5 am on 19 July, nine days before the visit, Plimsoll had 'fainted in his bathroom and fallen unconscious to the floor'. During the next few days he had visited two specialists, including a neurologist, and had undergone various tests. On 21 July, during a weekend, he was confined to bed with a cold and a temperature of 101°F (38°C). Plimsoll had accompanied Whitlam on his subsequent visit to New York and, on return to Washington, he had a further examination. Ultimately, he was assured that he was in good health but should reduce his weight.[98] Here was a case of an ambassador maintaining the high levels of energy and astute interpersonal management needed in Washington, at the expense of his health.

Eviction from Washington

Plimsoll had come to relish his role as ambassador, including 'the intellectual challenge presenting Australia's case at the highest level'. The richness of US political life 'was a source of endless fascination for him'.[99] He was well settled in Australia's most important post, from where he could exercise some moderating influence on the emerging foreign policy of the new government, given his attachment to providing frank and fearless advice, and his relationship with Whitlam. But others had different ideas. During Whitlam's visit, Plimsoll received a personal letter from Whitlam notifying him of the end of his posting in Washington and of his transfer to Moscow.

---

95 *Reminiscential Conversations*, vol. i, p. 392.
96 Washington to Canberra, 1 August 1973, cablegram no. I.7136, Plimsoll Papers, DFAT, Canberra.
97 Fernandez, personal communication, 19 March 1997. Fernandez thought Plimsoll had collapsed on two occasions in the Residence. Plimsoll had reminded Fernandez of standing instructions for the No. 2 to inform Canberra when the Head of Mission was ill – at the same time he did not want Fernandez acting 'precipitately' on this.
98 Plimsoll's diary, 19–23 July, 2 August 1973, Plimsoll Papers, MS8048/3, NLA, Canberra.
99 Lipski, personal communication, 28 August 1997.

The news would not have been a complete surprise. Some weeks earlier, Whitlam had told him that he was thinking of replacing him: where would he want to go? Plimsoll had asked for Moscow, Port Moresby, or the OECD in Paris. Whitlam said it would probably be Moscow, and then afterwards another big post such as London. Plimsoll said he would fit in wherever he was wanted.

Whitlam later told Richard Woolcott that he had been enormously impressed with Plimsoll's 'dedication and decency', in that few of Plimsoll's stature would be prepared to go from Washington to Port Moresby.[100] At the same time Plimsoll, for all he had said about being willing to fit in with changes, would have preferred to stay longer in Washington. And he found the rationale for his move unconvincing and upsetting. Unknown to him, a manoeuvre, involving movement of others as well, had been underway for some time. Whitlam had wanted to find a post for Bruce Grant, a leading journalist, one who had given him public support before the election.[101] Whitlam suggested Washington; Grant was hesitant. Then it was suggested that Grant become permanent representative at the UN in New York: Waller argued successfully that McIntyre should be allowed to remain because Australia had been elected to the UN Security Council. Wilenski suggested either Tokyo or Delhi. Grant was interested in Delhi, which he had discussed in the past with Plimsoll.[102] Sir Patrick Shaw, who had been in Delhi for more than three years, and wanted to end his career there, was informed that Grant would take his place. He was then offered either Tokyo or Washington. He preferred Tokyo, his wife preferred Washington: they chose Washington.[103] The Shaws were good friends of Plimsoll, who was surprised to be replaced, not by a political appointment, but another career officer, one whom he thought was 'less in sympathy with the Whitlam Government than I was'.[104] Plimsoll was upset that the first

100   *Reminiscential Conversations*, vol. ii, p. 324; Woolcott, personal communication, 12 December 1997.

101   In late 1972 Grant, along with others including Kenneth Baillieu Myer and Walter Crocker, had written a letter to the editors of leading Australian newspapers advocating a change of government.

102   Bruce Grant, personal communication, 1997; Waller, *Diplomatic Life*, pp. 48–9. Waller emphasised to Whitlam the 'highly professional position' of the PR at the UN.

103   Karina Campbell, personal communication, 19 February 2004. See also Roy Macartney, 'Musical Chairs in an Embassy', *Age*, 5 February 1974.

104   *Reminiscential Conversations*, vol. ii, p. 324.

he heard of his move was as a fait accompli, and that no one in the department, especially not Waller, had seen fit to tell him what was afoot.[105]

Plimsoll found an opportunity to discuss the matter privately with Whitlam while he was in Washington. Recapitulating their talk in a later letter, Plimsoll said he knew some 'might consider that I was unduly pro-American' but Whitlam had reassured him that he was 'not dissatisfied' with his performance. Nor was Whitlam 'doubtful of [his] loyalty as Ambassador to your Government'. Plimsoll undertook to go to Moscow if things had gone too far for the decision to be reversed. Whitlam told him he had been advised that Plimsoll's term had expired. Plimsoll contested this: since 1946 all his predecessors had served six years or more. Whitlam had said he would look into that. Some weeks later, in the absence of anything further from Whitlam, Plimsoll wrote to him, more in sorrow than anger. He had already been instructed to seek *agrément* for Shaw, while *agrément* had been sought for him in Moscow. Having rehearsed the points they had already discussed, he took issue again with the department's assertion that his term had expired. He repeated his view about the need for a five-year posting, given the time it took to get to know the US. He noted that nearly 40 foreign ambassadors currently in Washington had been there longer than he had.[106] Whitlam replied three weeks later. Whitlam 'did not take issue' with what Plimsoll had told him about the Washington posting, but this was now 'water under the bridge'. As to the failure to convey to him the view that his time had expired, Whitlam expressed 'regret that events took this course'.[107]

Waller had not been in good health after his time in Washington; this had been widely known. Plimsoll had later learned that Waller felt strongly that three years as Ambassador in Washington was 'as long as flesh and blood could stand'.[108] This was perhaps a view that few were aware of, and which he evidently had not shared with Plimsoll; not in three separate private talks that Plimsoll had had with Waller during his consultations in August 1972, nor during the four talks during

105 Waller, *Diplomatic Life*, p. 42.
106 Plimsoll to Whitlam, 3 September 1973, letter, Plimsoll Papers, item 8048/16/3, NLA, Canberra.
107 Whitlam to Plimsoll, September 1973, letter, Plimsoll Papers, item 8048/16/3, NLA, Canberra.
108 *Reminiscential Conversations*, vol. ii, p. 324.

Plimsoll's short visit at the end of that year.[109] Plimsoll considered that capacity to stand the strain of Washington depended on the individual. For his part, he 'certainly wasn't worn out',[110] an assertion that is at least open to question in view of his collapse before the Prime Minister's visit. Whitlam expressed understanding that 'your letter to me can have been no easier to write than has been this reply'. He assured Plimsoll of his confidence in him, and of his interest in Plimsoll's forthcoming posting to Moscow.[111] On 26 September, Whitlam announced Grant's appointment to New Delhi, Plimsoll's to Moscow, Shaw's to Washington, and Shann's to Tokyo.[112]

Final weeks

The year 1973 drew to a close. In January 1974, in Plimsoll's final weeks in Washington, the question of relations with North Korea rose again. It had been understood that Canberra would not move on this until March, which would have been after Plimsoll left. But it was decided that the issue should be 'out of the way' before the ANZUS Council meeting in February, but more especially by the beginning of February, before the resumption of parliament. Whitlam and Don Willesee (now Foreign Minister) feared that otherwise the Labor caucus might 'seize the initiative' and press for relations quickly, which would suggest 'Caucus is running foreign policy rather than the Government itself'. Willesee also directed that relations should be established 'even if the price for this would be to open an office with a Chargé in Pyongyang', although Alan Renouf, the new Secretary, had pointed out that the department thought this would be undesirable.[113]

Plimsoll, disappointed, said he had hoped that Australia would have delayed establishing relations in order to try further to get Pyongyang's agreement to the admission to the UN of both Koreas 'in accordance with the principle of universality', and because this would give an additional degree of recognition to the international status and de facto

---

109 Plimsoll's diary references to Waller, 15, 18, 25 August 1972; 22, 28, 29 December 1972 and 4 January 1973, Plimsoll Papers, MS8048/3, NLA, Canberra.
110 *Reminiscential Conversations*, vol. ii, p. 324.
111 Whitlam to Plimsoll, September 1973, letter, Plimsoll Papers, item 8048/16/3, NLA, Canberra.
112 Ministerial Press Release, *Australian Foreign Affairs Record*, vol. 44, no. 9, 1973, p. 622.
113 Renouf and Senator Willesee, 12 January 1974, note, series A1838/2, item 3125/10/1/3, part 2, NAA, Canberra.

boundaries of the two governments 'and would make it clear that an attack of one on the other would be an act of aggression'.[114] He gave up on getting approval to visit Seoul on his way to Moscow to discuss the development of relations between Seoul and Moscow. This had been at the invitation of Kim Dong-Jo, his former Republic of Korea colleague in Washington, now Foreign Minister of Korea.[115]

In a farewell call, Kissinger told him that basically bilateral relations were good. 'We had so many interests in common that it took a great deal of ingenuity on both sides to create trouble between us.' Although the US was 'unhappy' about the Australian approach to North Korea, it was not something that would affect the relationship.[116] Plimsoll later recalled Kissinger as 'an able man with a nimble mind, a profound thinker. But quite ruthless and completely cynical'.[117]

The US was becoming increasingly divided over Watergate. Plimsoll was guest of honour at a dinner in Spokane, Washington. Following the usual toast to the Queen, he responded with a toast to the President of the US. More than half those present refused to drink to the second toast, even though it was to the office, not the incumbent.[118]

It was ironic for Plimsoll to be moved not only when he was at his peak in Washington but after the considerable help he had rendered the Prime Minister in his role over the meeting with Nixon. Not long before his departure, Plimsoll accompanied the visiting Lance Barnard, Deputy Prime Minister and Minister of Defence, when the latter called on Kissinger. Kissinger told Barnard: 'You're mad to move Plimsoll. He's got contacts here and great influence, and you're mad to move him.'[119] Yet he was moved, as part of 'musical chairs' to facilitate a political appointment elsewhere. Since Plimsoll's time in Washington, most incumbents have served for around three years.

---

114 Washington to Canberra, 17 January 1974, cablegram no. I.8128, series A1828/2, item 3125/10/1/3, part 2, NAA, Canberra. In fact, things moved slowly. The Australian Chargé did not arrive in Pyongyang until 30 April 1975, more than a year later.
115 Washington to Canberra, 11 December 1973, cablegram no. I.144009, series A1838/2, item 3127/10/1, part 13, NAA, Canberra; Washington to Canberra, 21 December 1973, cablegram no. I.149483, series A1838/2, item 3127/10/1, part 13, NAA, Canberra.
116 Washington to Canberra, cablegram no. I.14594, series A1838/2, item 3125/10/1/3, part 2, NAA, Canberra.
117 *Reminiscential Conversations*, vol. ii, p. 170.
118 Ibid., vol. ii, p. 168.
119 Ibid., vol. ii, p. 325.

At the core of the Australia–US relationship, in Plimsoll's reckoning, was the ANZUS Treaty, by then more than 20 years old. There were times when Plimsoll felt that through ill-considered actions, its future was uncertain. On return home, in a speech early in 1974 in Melbourne, he said that Australia must 'hang on' to the ANZUS Treaty:

> Under it the President is able to act to help us without first consulting Congress. That was achieved in a climate that might be impossible to rediscover. ANZUS is like a precious vase, it could be broken into pieces, and it is irreplaceable.[120]

Plimsoll had, through his judicious counsel, unflagging and well-targeted advocacy in Washington, and adroit mediation between American and Australian prima donna leaders, protected the valuables in the relationship during an unprecedented period of turbulence.

---

120 Plimsoll, speech to AIIA, Melbourne, 25 February 1974. Recorded in diary of Alfred Stirling, 25 February 1974, DFAT, Canberra.

9

The career diplomats: Sir Patrick Shaw, Alan Renouf and Sir Nicholas Parkinson, 1974–82

David Lee

In the years from 1974 to 1982, the Whitlam and Fraser governments followed the precedent established with the earlier appointments of Sir Keith Waller and Sir James Plimsoll of sending career diplomats to Washington. In contrast with the position from 1940 to 1964, when non-career diplomats had been appointed, Sir Patrick Shaw, Alan Renouf and Sir Nicholas Parkinson were all senior Foreign Affairs officers with extensive diplomatic experience. Shaw was a Deputy Secretary of the Department of Foreign Affairs, Renouf was Permanent Secretary of the department before being appointed to Washington, and Parkinson was appointed head of the department between his two terms as Ambassador to the United States. The three ambassadors, Shaw, Renouf and Parkinson, helped repair the Australia–US relationship after the period of significant tension, particularly in 1972 and 1973 when the Whitlam Labor Government was consistently at loggerheads with the Nixon Administration. Shaw's term straddled Labor and Coalition governments, while Parkinson and Renouf served a Coalition Government.

During the time after the US had ended its military commitment in Southeast Asia, the Fraser Government worried that Jimmy Carter's administration was not paying sufficient attention to the Asia-Pacific region and that the Australia, New Zealand, United States Security Treaty (ANZUS) was consequently decreasing in importance. The Fraser Government was also apprehensive that a possible US–Soviet disarmament agreement in the Indian Ocean might be to the detriment of the alliance.

Renouf and Parkinson, as heads of mission in Washington from 1976 to 1982, maintained the strong tradition of previous ambassadors in Washington. They entreated the US to consult Australia and consistently emphasised the continuing importance of the ANZUS alliance and the significance of Australia as a partner in the Asia-Pacific region. The intensification of the Cold War in the late 1970s helped the envoys to achieve their objective. By the last year of the Carter Administration in 1980, the Soviet invasion of Afghanistan and developments in the Southeast Asian region had created a new geopolitical environment in which the ambassadors were able to help bring about intensified strategic cooperation between Australia and the US under ANZUS. Notwithstanding the revival of military cooperation under ANZUS, however, a wider problem loomed for Australian envoys in Washington of having to demonstrate Australia's importance to the American public as well as to the Executive and the Congress. Parkinson presciently identified a problem in 1982 that would be taken up by all his successors as head of mission in Washington.

Sir Patrick Shaw

Patrick Shaw was born on 18 September 1913 at Kew, Melbourne, the son of an Australian-born physician. He was educated at Ballarat and Scotch College and then the University of Melbourne.[1] After joining the Commonwealth Public Service in 1936, he transferred in 1939 to the Department of External Affairs, Australia's fledgling foreign office. In 1940, Shaw was posted as Third Secretary to the Australian legation in Tokyo and, after the outbreak of the Pacific War, was interned along with other legation staff until exchanged for Japanese diplomats in August 1942. Shaw subsequently served at the Australian High Commission in New Zealand from 1943 to 1945, and again in Tokyo in the late 1940s. From 1956 to 1959 he was Australia's Ambassador to

---

1   David Lee, 'Shaw, Sir Patrick (1913–1975)', *Australian Dictionary of Biography*, vol. 16, 1940–1980, Melbourne University Press, Carlton, 2002, pp. 220–21.

the Federal Republic of Germany and then Ambassador to Indonesia from 1960 to 1962. As Australian envoy in Jakarta he supported a policy, unpopular with the Menzies Government at the time, of acceding to Indonesia's wish to incorporate West New Guinea (Irian Jaya).[2] Shaw was Deputy Secretary to Sir Arthur Tange from 1964 to 1965 at the time when Australia began its military involvement with the US in South Vietnam. From 1965 to 1970 he was Australia's Permanent Representative to the United Nations, New York, and then High Commissioner in New Delhi from 17 April 1970. Shaw's apparent intention was to retire from the public service at the end of his diplomatic service in India.

His plans were altered by decisions of the Whitlam Labor Government. Sir James Plimsoll had commenced his appointment in Washington in 1970 at the same time as Shaw began his posting in New Delhi. Plimsoll had hopes of serving in Washington for as long a time as Keith Waller and Howard Beale before him. But, as Jeremy Hearder notes in the previous chapter, during Gough Whitlam's visit to Washington in 1973, Plimsoll received a personal letter from the Prime Minister advising him that, after three years in Washington, he would be transferred to Moscow.

As noted, Plimsoll's transfer to Moscow at Whitlam's behest was part of a series of appointments to key diplomatic posts. Sir Keith Waller, now the Permanent Secretary of the Department of Foreign Affairs, had been doing all he could to make Washington available for Shaw. Waller had attended the same school and university as Shaw and had formed a high regard for him. Indeed, Waller may have felt some sensitivity that he had risen to head the Department of Foreign Affairs while the exceptionally able Shaw had not managed to do so.[3] On 26 September 1973, Whitlam announced the appointment of Shaw to Washington, Plimsoll to Moscow, Grant to New Delhi and another senior Department of Foreign Affairs official, Keith Shann, to Tokyo.[4]

Shaw presented his letters of credence to President Richard Nixon on 13 March 1974. In doing so, Shaw remarked:

2   Ibid.
3   Jeremy Hearder, *Jim Plim: Ambassador Extraordinary: A Biography for Sir James Plimsoll*, Connor Court, Ballarat, 2015, p. 250.
4   Edward Gough Whitlam, 'Senior Diplomatic Appointments', *Current Notes*, vol. 44, September 1973, pp. 622–4.

> There is a fundamental continuity in Australian policies which is symbolised by ANZUS which remains Australia's most important and enduring treaty because it embodies permanent and natural elements in the relations between our countries.[5]

Shaw's term in Washington would be even shorter than Plimsoll's – from March 1974 until his untimely death in December 1975. In that period, however, he helped the Whitlam Government smooth the difficulties in the relationship that had surfaced in 1972 and 1973 when it had clashed repeatedly with the Nixon Administration.[6] The first year of Shaw's posting, 1974, was also consumed by the Watergate crisis that ultimately led to Nixon's resignation and his replacement by Gerald R Ford, who succeeded to the presidency on 9 August 1974. Shaw was increasingly called upon not only to explain Australian policy and attitudes to the US Government and public but to help explain changes in the US to the Australian public. Shaw was no less active than Plimsoll in making speeches and giving addresses across the US. The US reaction to the Watergate crisis, and an 'imperial presidency' that had developed since World War II, affected the Australia–US relationship by making US foreign policy initiatives more difficult and US commitments more fragile, particularly in the Asian region. After Watergate, presidential power was circumscribed and Congressional scrutiny of administration programs increased.[7]

By February 1975, Shaw was able to report to the Minister for Foreign Affairs, Senator Don Willesee, that the Whitlam Government 'could properly claim to have successfully brought a new understanding into Australia's relationship with the United States of America'.[8] Shaw remarked that the difficulties in the Australia–US relationship during 1973 were largely concerned with the divisive factor of the Vietnam War. But in Shaw's assessment, it was understandable that there would be differences of views between an Australian Labor Government in Canberra and a Republican Administration in Washington. He explained:

---

5   'Australian Ambassador to US Presents Letters of Credence', *Australian Foreign Affairs Record*, vol. 45, March 1974, p. 183.

6   See generally James Curran, *Unholy Fury: Whitlam and Nixon at War*, Melbourne University Press, Carlton, 2015.

7   'Call on His Excellency the Governor-General by Mr N.F. Parkinson, Australian Ambassador-designate to the United States', 8 October 1979, series A1838, item 1500/2/27/12 part 1, National Archives of Australia (NAA), Canberra.

8   Shaw to Willesee, 14 February 1975, letter, series A1838, item 250/9/924 part 1, NAA, Canberra.

One does not expect the views of the Australian Labor Government to coincide with those of the United States Republican Administration any more than one expects the views of the American Democrats in Congress to coincide with those of the [Republican] American Executive.[9]

Shaw noted to Renouf, the Secretary in Canberra, that the US State Department had prohibited any comment whatsoever on the Australian Labor Party Conference in Terrigal, New South Wales, in February 1975. At this meeting, the Australian Labor Party had passed a resolution calling for an Australian diplomatic relationship with the South Vietnamese Provisional Revolutionary Government (PRG). Shaw warned that Ford's administration would be concerned about the possible repercussions of Australia establishing relations with the PRG and recommended that the government weigh the future of Australia's relationship with the PRG against the damage to Australia's relations with the US. Shaw added:

> The achievement of the last year was noteworthy in that two Governments of two different political complexions saw beyond differences which were less important and probably temporary. If we can possibly avoid it, we do not want these less important differences to become part of the internal political debate in either country to the detriment of our overall relationship.[10]

Despite Shaw's admonitions, the Whitlam Government recognised the PRG in South Vietnam on 6 May 1975.[11] The Ford Administration, however, took the decision in its stride. Philip C Habib, a US Assistant Secretary of State visiting Australia at the end of May, noted that 'we seemed to have passed through the rough patches in bilateral relations' and that Whitlam's recent visit had been 'first class'.[12]

The visit to which Habib referred was Whitlam's third to the US; it took place in May 1975. During this visit, Whitlam had discussions with Vice President Nelson Rockefeller, Secretary of State Henry Kissinger and President Ford.[13] In a major address to the National Press

---

9   Ibid.
10   Ibid.
11   'South Viet-Nam: Australian recognition', *Australian Foreign Affairs Record*, vol. 46, May 1975, p. 296.
12   Discussions in Canberra between Australian officials and Philip C Habib, 23 May 1975, series A1838, item 250/9/1 part 23, NAA, Canberra.
13   'Visit of Mr Whitlam to the United States', *Australian Foreign Affairs Record*, vol. 46, May 1975, p. 264.

Club in Washington on 8 May 1975, Whitlam characterised the allied intervention in Indochina in the 1960s and 1970s as a tragic mistake foredoomed to failure, applauded the thrust of US policy in aiming for détente with the Soviet Union and announced that Australia 'had lent her voice to the maintenance of a zone of peace in the Indian Ocean'.[14] Throughout 1975, Shaw and the embassy staff in Washington were busy facilitating not only Whitlam's but also other ministerial visits. In 1975 Willesee visited the US twice – for a meeting of the ANZUS Council in Washington in April and then to attend the UN General Assembly in New York in September. Shaw joined Willesee in a small Australian delegation to the ANZUS Council meeting. Whitlam's Minister for Defence, Bill Morrison, also had discussions with the US Secretary of Defense James R Schlesinger in August.

In his role as Ambassador to the US, Shaw not only explained Australia to the US but he also helped the Australian public to understand its Pacific neighbour. For example, on a visit to Australia in September 1975, Shaw spoke on ABC radio about developments in the Australia–US relationship during his time in Washington. He noted that the change of government in Australia in 1972 had produced occasional harsh words, but that 'these have been put into perspective by the American leadership and both sides know they neither take one nor other for granted, but both accept the importance of the one to the other'.[15] Shaw concluded his address with the words:

> So if I have a message for you tonight, it is this, that Australia has a new sort of relationship with the United States, it's an independent one, it's one of mutual understanding and respect, but in ways which few of us have taken aboard, there is a new game being played in world diplomacy and in this Australia has a part to play, it's partly an independent line and also partly in co-operation with our main ally and friend, the United States of America.[16]

The convulsive political crisis of Watergate in the US in 1974 was paralleled by a constitutional crisis in Australia. On 11 November 1975 the Governor-General, Sir John Kerr, dismissed the Whitlam Government and installed the Leader of the Opposition, Malcom

---

14   Edward Gough Whitlam, 'Partnership in Peace', address to the National Press Club in Washington, DC, 8 May 1975, *Australian Foreign Affairs Record*, vol. 46, May 1975, p. 268.
15   Patrick Shaw, Radio Special Projects, 28 September 1975, series A1838, item 250/9/1 part 23, NAA, Canberra.
16   Ibid.

Fraser, at the head of a caretaker government pending a double dissolution election in December 1975. During this caretaker period, Shaw warned that the Ford Administration 'will be hyper-sensitive about commenting on anything which might be interpreted as interfering in the domestic process in Australia'.[17] He added that '[i]t will be a delicate and difficult time which I hope we can get through without damage to the Australian–American relationship'.[18] The caretaker period ended without damage to Australian–American relations, although there was periodic media questioning of whether the US Central Intelligence Agency might have had a role in the premature end of the Whitlam Government.[19] A coalition of the Liberal and National Country parties was elected in a landslide in the general election on 13 December 1975.

Fraser's electoral victory was met with relief in the US. Ford hailed the victory, conveying to Fraser his congratulations. Not long after the election, Shaw announced to a luncheon in New York on 17 December 1975:

> Now we turn back more to our old friends amongst those old friends the most important is the United States of America. We have never been non-aligned because we have the Australian–United States–New Zealand alliance, which is our prime security pact, and we have always kept that in the foremost parts of our minds and will continue to do so.[20]

Shaw prepared himself for a busy time after the election in introducing the newly formed Fraser Government to the Ford Administration. But in tragic fulfilment of Keith Waller's premonition that three years in Washington was 'as long as flesh and blood could stand',[21] Shaw suffered a heart attack. He died in Georgetown University Hospital on 27 December 1975. The strain of his two years in Washington had been exacerbated by an earlier assault on his wife outside the Residence.

---

17   Shaw to Andrew Peacock, Minister for Foreign Affairs, 12 November 1975, letter, series A1838, item 250/9/1 part 23, NAA, Canberra.
18   Ibid.
19   See Brian Toohey and William Pinwill, *Oyster: The Story of the Australian Secret Intelligence Service*, Heinemann, Port Melbourne, 1989.
20   Remarks by Sir Patrick Shaw to Australian Association Lunch, New York, 11 December1975, series A1838, item 250/9/1 part 23, NAA, Canberra.
21   *Reminisciental Conversations between Hon. Clyde Cameron and Sit James Plimsoll*, 1984, TRC 1967, vol. 11, p. 324, National Library of Australia (NLA), Canberra.

Shaw's death was followed by messages of condolence from leading members of the administration. The Secretary of State, Henry Kissinger, for example, cabled the Australian Government: 'We are shocked and saddened at the untimely death in Washington this evening of Sir Patrick Shaw. He has been an outstanding Ambassador, as well as friend and confidante to us all.'[22] Although Shaw's own political opinions were more in sympathy with the Coalition than with Labor, he was a loyal emissary of the Whitlam Government, accurately reporting from Washington and skilfully advocating government policy. The tributes that he earned on his death were testimony to the esteem in which he was held by members of the US Government and of Congress.

Nicholas Parkinson (first term)

The Fraser Government chose another seasoned diplomat, Nicholas Parkinson, to succeed Shaw as Ambassador to the US. Andrew Peacock, Fraser's Minister for Foreign Affairs, announced Parkinson's appointment on 1 February 1976.[23] Nicholas Parkinson was born in Horsham, England, on 5 December 1925, the son of the English-born Reverend Charles Tasman Parkinson, who migrated to Australia to become principal of King's School Parramatta, bringing his son Nicholas with him. Nicholas was educated at King's School Parramatta and then at the University of Sydney, from which he graduated with a Bachelor of Arts degree. After serving in the Royal Australian Air Force between 1943 and 1946, he joined the Department of External Affairs as a cadet and then studied in the School of African and Oriental Studies at the University of London in 1952 and 1953. He was a junior diplomat in Cairo from 1953 to 1956, then a Second Secretary in Hong Kong from 1958 to 1961. Postings followed in Wellington from 1963 to 1965 and Kuala Lumpur from 1965 to 1967. Between 1967 and 1970 he served as the assistant secretary responsible for the Joint Intelligence Committee before serving as High Commissioner to Singapore from 1970 to 1974. Parkinson was one of two deputy secretaries in the Department of Foreign Affairs from 1974 to 1976.

---

22   Embassy in Washington to Department of Foreign Affairs, 29 December 1975, cablegram no. 30242, series A1838, item 250/9/1 part 23, NAA, Canberra.
23   'Appointment of Ambassador to the United States', *Australian Foreign Affairs Record*, vol. 47, 1976, pp. 95–6.

Parkinson commenced his appointment in Washington on 6 March 1976 but spent less time in Washington than even Shaw, serving less than a year before returning to Canberra in order to succeed Alan Renouf as Permanent Secretary of the Department of Foreign Affairs. Parkinson presented his credentials to Ford on 16 March 1976. He commented to Canberra that the promptness of his presentation of credentials was an indication of the favour that the Fraser Government had found with the Ford Administration. He informed Canberra that the early presentation of credentials was 'intended as a deliberate gesture of friendship' and that 'the ceremony was specially arranged without other ambassadors in the queue'.[24] When Parkinson began his term in Washington, Sir John Kerr's dismissal of the Whitlam Government had exacerbated anti-American feeling that originated in a campaign against the allied war in Vietnam but later included opposition to uranium mining and to the possibility that the ANZUS alliance and the joint defence facilities might lead to the nuclear targeting of Australian cities. This growth of anti-American sentiment was highlighted in September 1976 when the president of the Australian Council of Trade Unions and future Labor Prime Minister, Bob Hawke, signed an advertisement pledging opposition to military alliances, foreign military bases and military interventions.[25] Hawke's signature was ironic in view of his subsequent strong support for the ANZUS alliance as Australian Prime Minister in the 1980s.

Notwithstanding the change from Whitlam to Fraser, some observers of the Australia–US relationship detected a longer-term change in Australia's attitude to the relationship in the 1970s that was independent of political allegiance. Writing in the *New York Times* on 21 December 1975, Australian journalist Harry Gordon wrote:

> Australia's recent attitude towards the United States has veered from the sycophantic to the abusive. This ambivalence is not just a consequence of varying periods of power by two opposing political parties in Australia. It reflects a love-hate condition that diplomats and historians down the years have chosen to call a 'special relationship'.[26]

The new Prime Minister, Malcolm Fraser, highlighted the change in the nature of the Australia–US relationship in the 1970s as compared with the relationship in the 1950s and 1960s when he told the House of

24   Parkinson to Department of Foreign Affairs, 16 March 1976, cablegram no. WH29577, series A1838, item 1500/2/27/10 part 1, NAA, Canberra.
25   'Hawke Calls for an End to ANZUS', *Sun News Pictorial*, 18 September 1976.
26   Harry Gordon, 'Australia's Foreign Policy Readjustments', *New York Times*, 21 December 1975.

Representatives that 'the interests of the United States and the interests of Australia are not necessarily identical. In our relations with the United States, as in our relations with other great powers, our first responsibility is independently to assess our interests'.[27] He continued:

> Of all the great powers with active interests and capabilities in the areas of critical concern to Australia, the United States is the power with which we have closest links … As long as Australia values freedom and respect for the individual, the United States is the power with which we can realistically establish close and warm friendship and with which we can most closely work to advance world peace and the humane values we share.[28]

Parkinson and the embassy in Washington facilitated a visit by Fraser to Washington in June 1976 after earlier trips he had made to Japan and China. The Ambassador was active in shaping the agenda of the discussions between Fraser and Ford, particularly on how the two leaders saw the Australia–US relationship being developed and what strategic insights Fraser had learned from his visit to China and Japan.[29] During his visit to Washington, Fraser evoked not the 'All the Way with LBJ' rhetoric of Coalition predecessors like Harold Holt, but rather a mood of 'calculated and pragmatic national self-interest'.[30] Fraser repeated what he had earlier told parliament in Canberra: that the interests of the US and the interests of Australia were not necessarily identical.[31]

One of Parkinson's great skills was in organising all aspects of Fraser's first visit as prime minister to the US. So successful was the embassy's management of the visit that Parkinson later sent the embassy's notes to the Department of the Prime Minister and Cabinet to be used as a template for future prime ministerial visits abroad.[32] Fraser was personally impressed by Parkinson's handling of the visit, a factor that

---

27 Quoted in Glen Barclay, 'Australia and North America' in Peter John Boyce and Jim R Angel (eds), *Independence and Alliance: Australia in World Affairs 1976–80*, George Allen & Unwin, North Sydney, 1983, pp. 146–7.

28 Ibid., p. 147.

29 Embassy in Washington to Department of Foreign Affairs, 9 July 1976, cablegram no. WH34793 series A1209, item 1976/1422 part 2, NAA, Canberra.

30 Barclay, 'Australia and North America', p. 146.

31 Ibid.

32 Parkinson to James Scholtens, Director, Office of Government, Ceremonial and Hospitality, Department of the Prime Minister and Cabinet, 10 August 1976, letter, series A1209, item 1976/1422 part 2, NAA, Canberra.

would lead to Fraser appointing him as Secretary of the Department of Foreign Affairs in the following year and sending the incumbent, Alan Renouf, to head the embassy in Washington.[33]

The appointment of Alan Renouf

Alan Renouf, like Sir James Plimsoll, was appointed as Australia's Ambassador to the US after heading the Department of Foreign Affairs. Renouf's appointment in Washington began on 1 February 1977 and finished towards the end of 1979. Born in Sydney on 21 March 1919, Renouf was educated at Sydney High School and then the University of Sydney. After service in the Australian Imperial Force from 1939 to 1943, he joined the Department of External Affairs. His career included several postings in the US. He was Counsellor in the Australian Permanent Mission to the UN, New York, from 1946 to 1949; First Secretary in Washington from 1954 to 1956; and Minister, deputy head of mission, in the embassy in Washington from 1963 to 1965. Prior to his appointment as Ambassador to the US, he had been head of mission in Nigeria from 1961 to 1963 and in Paris from 1969 to 1973. After Waller stepped down as Secretary of the Department of Foreign Affairs in 1974, Whitlam appointed him as his replacement, a position he held until 1977.

Renouf's appointment to Washington came about through a falling out with Fraser that began in 1975 when Fraser was Leader of the Opposition and Renouf was still the Permanent Secretary of the Department of Foreign Affairs. As Renouf recalled it, he had been invited to speak to an audience of more than 600 people at a Legacy Luncheon in the Great Hall in Newcastle in the second half of 1975. Renouf's Newcastle speech angered Fraser when the latter received reports that Renouf had been excessively vigorous in defending the Labor Government's foreign policy against Opposition criticism. Fraser rang Renouf to allege that 'I hear from the press that you made a speech in Newcastle at mid-day today which was very much in favour of the government and you spoke very much like a Labor Party minister'.[34]

---

33   Fraser to Parkinson, n.d. (August 1976?), letter, series A1209, item 1976/1422, part 2, NAA, Canberra.
34   Alan Renouf, interview, 23 November 1993, transcript, NLA, 138.

To Renouf's defence that he was only reciting government policy, Fraser retorted: 'Oh, you went much further than a public servant should go, according to what I hear.'[35]

After Fraser became Prime Minister in 1975, Renouf remained as head of the Department of Foreign Affairs, but the problems between the two men resurfaced when Fraser made a visit to the People's Republic of China in 1976 before making his first visit to the US. During this trip to China, Fraser floated the idea of a four-power military grouping between the US, Australia, the People's Republic of China and Japan. The Fraser Government was greatly embarrassed when a junior official in Australia's embassy in Beijing leaked copies of the top secret record of the meeting. Fraser placed the blame for the leak squarely on Renouf as Secretary of the Department of Foreign Affairs and, not long afterwards, he informed Renouf that he was removing him as Permanent Secretary. In an appointment with Fraser, Renouf remonstrated that 'as a permanent head I'm entitled to a position at the same level, and unless you offer me a position at the same level, which I'm prepared to accept, you can't get rid of me'.[36] Fraser then asked Renouf where he wanted to go to which Renouf replied that 'I'll only go to one place. I'll go to Washington'.[37]

Fraser agreed to Renouf's request and asked the Minister for Foreign Affairs, Andrew Peacock, to arrange it. As a consequence, the incumbent Ambassador to the US, Nicholas Parkinson, was brought back to Canberra and appointed Permanent Secretary of the Department of Foreign Affairs, while Renouf succeeded Parkinson in Washington. So incensed was Renouf about the manner of his removal as secretary that he declined the offer of a knighthood and also returned his Order of the British Empire. Renouf arrived in Washington in February 1977 and presented his credentials as Ambassador on 17 February. His connections in the US and understanding of the workings of the American political system gave him a strong advantage as immediately noted by Cyrus Vance, the US Secretary of State, who was able to comment that 'Australia had a great Ambassador here in Washington who had quickly established excellent contacts'.[38] Although Renouf had

---

35   Ibid.
36   Ibid., 148.
37   Ibid., 149.
38   Record of the Minister's Conversation with Secretary of State, Cyrus Vance, 25 March 1977, series A1838, item 250/9/10/2 part 6, NAA, Canberra.

a poor relationship with Fraser, his experience and contacts in the US made him an effective Ambassador in Washington during a time when Australia–US relations were not particularly close.

The ambassadors and the Carter Administration

By the time that Renouf commenced his appointment in Washington, the Democrat Jimmy Carter had commenced his single term as President from 1977 to 1981 and Renouf was immediately involved in facilitating visits to Washington by Fraser and Peacock and in seeking to ensure that the new administration took account of Australian views in making its foreign policy. Carter was a Southerner from Atlanta, Georgia. When Renouf saw his Secretary of State, Cyrus Vance, on 9 February 1977, he entreated the Carter Administration to consult with Australia, as an 'old and trusted ally'.[39] Renouf noted that the degree of such consultation in the past had not been 'satisfactory to the Australian Government which was one of those which had suffered from Kissinger's secrecy in years gone by (e.g. during the Vietnam peace negotiations)'.[40]

Renouf's concerns about lack of US consultation with Australia were quickly validated. Carter caused disquiet in Canberra when only two months into his administration he revealed that he had proposed to the Soviet Union that the Indian Ocean be completely demilitarised. The announcement came as a complete surprise to the Australian Government and Peacock remonstrated to Vance that the lack of prior consultation had 'hurt the Government of Australia'.[41] Carter also worried the Australian Government by promoting 'trilateralism', a term referring to a preference for concerting agreement between North America, Japan and Western Europe. The Fraser Government worried that such an emphasis would marginalise Australia and the ANZUS alliance.

---

39   Renouf to Department of Foreign Affairs, 9 February 1977, cablegram no. WH43999 series A1838, item 250/9/10/2 part 4, NAA, Canberra.
40   Ibid.
41   Record of the Minister's Conversation with Secretary of State, Cyrus Vance, 25 March 1977, series A1838, item 250/9/10/2 part 6, NAA, Canberra.

Renouf and the embassy arranged a visit by Peacock to the US in the latter part of March 1977. They organised meetings with Vice President Walter Mondale, with Secretary of State Vance and senior officials of his department, with Zbigniew Brzezinski, Carter's adviser on National Security Affairs, and with Paul Warnke, Director of the Arms Control and Disarmament Agency. Peacock reported that in these first extensive talks at the ministerial level with the Carter Administration, he had secured a positive response from Vance.[42] The Secretary of State indicated to Peacock that while the Carter Administration viewed Australia primarily in terms of its important responsibilities in the South West Pacific Area, it would be seeking Australian advice 'across the board' on Southeast Asia and the Pacific.[43] Peacock also took the advice of Renouf and his staff in Washington that there were limits to the degree to which the US would consult Australia. Peacock noted in a submission to Cabinet on 13 May 1977 the 'asymmetric' nature of the relationship, the fragmented nature of the policymaking process in the US, and Carter's penchant for 'thinking out loud' as reflected by his comments on demilitarisation of the Indian Ocean.[44]

Renouf then arranged a visit for Fraser with Carter in June 1977. This proved a more difficult task. In February, Renouf reported from Washington that considerable difficulties were being encountered in making firm arrangements for high-level visits to Washington to meet Carter.[45] Renouf had to deploy all his skills to persuade the State Department to press Carter to agree to an official visit by Fraser.[46] Finally, on 11 March 1977, Renouf went to Vance, telling him that Fraser led a Coalition Government that had 'constantly stuck with the United States through thick and thin' and that, on coming to power, his government had 'immediately set out to repair and repaired the damage done to that relationship by the previous Labor Government'.[47] Vance's response was 'terse' and Renouf sensed that the 'Americans are becoming a little resentful of the pressure being applied on them'.[48]

42   Peacock to Cabinet, 13 May 1977, submission, series A1209, item 1244, NAA, Canberra.
43   Note of Minister's visit to the United States, c. March 1977, series A1838, item 250/9/10/2 part 5, NAA, Canberra.
44   Peacock to Cabinet, 13 May 1977, submission, series A1209, item 1244, NAA, Canberra.
45   Henderson to Peacock, 9 February 1977, cablegram no. CH471698, series A1209, NAA, Canberra.
46   Renouf to the Department of Foreign Affairs, 9 March 1977, cablegram no. WH45450, series A1209, NAA, Canberra.
47   Ibid.; Renouf to the Department of Foreign Affairs, 11 March 1977, cablegram no. WH25632, series A1209, item 1977/33 part 1, NAA, Canberra.
48   Ibid.

Eventually, however, Renouf's diplomacy paid off when the White House agreed to an official visit by Fraser. An exasperated Renouf remarked that the episode brought out vividly that the:

> long-standing tendency in Washington to take Australia for granted persists and perhaps has even become stronger now that Atlanta has 'occupied' Washington, with the partial eclipse of the W.A.S.P. and Yankee establishment and with the prevailing input from what is left of the establishment being 'trilateral'.[49]

Renouf drew the lesson: '[i]t is only from being tough, when necessary, and even nasty, when necessary, can we hope to have proper influence in Washington'.[50]

Despite the difficulties in organising it, the prime ministerial visit was a success. Carter welcomed Fraser in an elaborate ceremony on the South Lawn of the White House. He spoke warmly of the many values shared with Australia and Fraser reciprocated the common concern of the two countries over the 'inability of many countries to escape from poverty, growing concern over the availability of energy resources, and the denial of fundamental freedoms to many people in many countries'.[51] Carter added that Australia was 'setting an example for us and other nations to emulate. And our nation's commitments to non-proliferation will certainly be strengthened and enhanced by the fine example that has been set by Prime Minister Fraser and his own government in Australia'.[52]

Carter was referring with approval to the decision of the Fraser Government to export Australian supplies of uranium to other countries subject to safeguards. The US applauded this decision because Carter's nonproliferation policy was aimed at preventing a plutonium-based energy economy and discouraging fast-breeder nuclear reactors, the likeliest source of weapons-grade fissile material.[53] Avoiding such a plutonium-based energy economy meant supplying enough uranium to countries to avoid their having to reprocess the mineral and thus produce a much more dangerous form of plutonium that might produce

---

49   Renouf to Parkinson, 21 March 1977, cablegram no. WH46070, series A1209, item 1977/33 part 1, NAA, Canberra.
50   Ibid.
51   Barclay, 'Australia and North America', p. 148.
52   Ibid.
53   Coral Bell, *Dependent Ally: A Study in Australian Foreign Policy*, Oxford University Press, Melbourne, 1988, p. 152.

sufficient fissionable material for a military device.[54] Australia was important here because of its world-class deposits of uranium, many of which had been discovered in the late 1960s and early 1970s.[55] Fraser thanked Renouf for organising the visit but reserved his most effusive gratitude for Denis Argall, counsellor in the embassy, whom he asked to pass on to colleagues in the embassy the gratitude of all the delegation that visited the US.[56]

While Australia's decision to export uranium was a positive for the Australia–US relationship, in important respects Australia–US relations drifted during Renouf's term as head of mission in Washington from 1977 to 1979. Indeed, the Fraser Government became concerned that the security relationship between Australia and the US was 'withering on the vine' as it became apparent that the US was winding down its military commitments in the Pacific and Indian Oceans.[57] The academic FA Mediansky had highlighted this drift in May 1976 when he commented:

> The diminishing role of the ANZUS alliance in United States eyes is related to America's reduced military power and interests in South East Asia. The defence relationship was more important in the 1960s when the United States was the most powerful military nation in South East Asia. By contrast the last four years have seen the run-down of its military capability in Indo-China and Thailand with possible reductions in the Philippines to follow. The awesome encirclement of China is now a thing of the past.[58]

The US had withdrawn its forces from Thailand and Taiwan and was planning to leave the Korean Peninsula by 1984. What made these developments of greater concern to Australia was that the Soviet Union at the same time had deployed twice the naval tonnages and five times the number of aircraft in the region. A July 1977 brief from the Australian Department of Foreign Affairs made the observation that the 'confidence of Australia's regional associates in continued US

---

54 'Mondale likely to discuss nuclear treaty', *Sydney Morning Herald*, 21 February 1978.
55 Carter to Fraser, 29 June 1977, letter, series A1209, item 1977/33 part 1, NAA, Canberra.
56 Fraser to Argall, 11 July 1977, letter, series A1209, item 1977/33 part 1 NAA, Canberra.
57 Barclay, 'Australia and North America', p. 149.
58 Fedor Alexander Mediansky, 'The diminishing role of ANZUS', *Sydney Morning Herald*, 4 May 1976.

support was thoroughly shaken by Vietnam and has not yet been fully recovered'.[59] Carter's 1977 announcement of plans to demilitarise the Indian Ocean only exacerbated Australian anxieties.

Consequently, the Fraser Government waged a political campaign that lasted more than a year after Carter's Indian Ocean announcement to secure a tacit or de facto interpretation of the ANZUS Treaty to make it clear to other parties that the pact concerned the Indian Ocean as well as the Pacific Ocean. The text of the ANZUS Treaty referred specifically to Pacific territories, but it also spoke of the 'metropolitan territory of the powers' that in Australia's case included the section of its coastline that faced the Indian Ocean.[60] During the last year of the Ford Administration, Fraser had succeeded in having the ANZUS Council give its 'informal approval' to Australia and the US developing defence cooperation in the Indian Ocean.[61] The communiqué after the 1977 ANZUS Council specified that any arms limitation agreement in the Indian Ocean must be 'consistent with the security interests of the ANZUS parties'.[62]

Renouf worked hard to achieve the Australian Government's objective. He helped persuade Vance to provide a letter assuring the ANZUS partners that if the US secured an agreement on the Indian Ocean with the Soviet Union, it would not 'in any way qualify or derogate from the US commitment to Australia or limit [US] freedom to act in implementing our commitment under the ANZUS Treaty'.[63] Then, during the meeting of the ANZUS Council in Washington in June 1978, Renouf had the wording of the communiqué amended to read that any agreement between the US and the Soviet Union on the Indian Ocean 'must' not – rather than 'would' not – detract from the ANZUS alliance.[64]

Renouf ended his term as Ambassador to the US in July 1979. Some years after his retirement from the public service he made one more intervention relating to his time in Washington. This was to remedy

---

59 Strategic and International Policy Division, Department of Foreign Affairs, 'United States: Strategic Policies and Perceptions', series A1838, item 686/2/19 part 1, NAA, Canberra.
60 Bell, *Dependent Ally*, p. 149.
61 Frank Cranston, 'ANZUS Role Approved', *Canberra Times*, 8 August 1976.
62 Bell, *Dependent Ally*, p. 150.
63 *Sydney Morning Herald*, 10 June 1978; brief for Visit of Vice President Mondale 10–11 April 1978, series A1838, item 250/9/30 part 1, NAA, Canberra.
64 Renouf to the Department of Foreign Affairs, 6 June 1978, cablegram no. WH67624, series A1838, item 250/11/18 part 2, NAA, Canberra.

177

the situation that prevailed when he was Ambassador and when the Australian Government was regarded as such a bad payer of hotel bills in the US that hotels across the country had refused credit to Australian representatives travelling on official business. Renouf told an Australian parliamentary inquiry in June 1982 that, during his term as Australian Ambassador to the US, he was distressed by delays in the payment of bills.[65] He pleaded:

> I really believe the Australian Department of Finance should be told in Canberra to stop trying to save money by not paying bills on time ... We achieved the reputation in the United States that we were a bad credit risk.[66]

Nicholas Parkinson (second term)

Renouf returned from Washington in July 1979 and retired from the public service in August of that year. By that time Parkinson had been suffering from an affliction in his eyesight that made it hard for him to continue his duties as Secretary of the Department of Foreign Affairs. Consequently, Peter Henderson, a Deputy Secretary in the Department of Foreign Affairs, was appointed to succeed Parkinson as Secretary, while Parkinson presented his credentials as Ambassador to the US for the second time on 28 November 1979. In his welcoming remarks, Carter noted that 'an old friend has returned to us after a brief absence, and we are pleased to see that friend again'.[67]

Vietnam's invasion of Kampuchea in 1978 and China's subsequent incursion into Vietnam helped to revive US interest in Southeast Asia. This focus was extended to Southwest Asia and the Indian Ocean on 12 December 1979, a month after Parkinson arrived in Washington, when a Russian regiment seized the airport near Kabul, beginning 10 years of Soviet military intervention in Afghanistan. The Americans feared that extension of this intervention from Afghanistan to neighbouring Pakistan would bring the Russians to the shores of the Arabian Sea and in a position to threaten oil routes from the Middle East to the West. In support of the US efforts to restrain Soviet Union

---

65 'Australia—the bad payer', *Sydney Morning Herald*, 3 June 1982.
66 Ibid.
67 Embassy in Washington to Department of Foreign Affairs, 28 November 1979, cablegram no. WH84240, series A1838, item 1500/2/27/12 part 1, NAA, Canberra.

expansion, the Fraser Government attempted to persuade members of the Australian team to boycott the Olympic Games in Moscow. In addition, Fraser announced that he had '[i]mmediately made an offer to the United States to consult with them concerning greater Australian involvement in patrolling and surveillance of the Indian Ocean'.[68]

In the aftermath of the Soviet intervention in Afghanistan, Australia's stocks with the Carter Administration rose high. Parkinson organised another prime ministerial visit to Washington from 30 January to 1 February 1980 at which Fraser and Carter discussed the situation in Afghanistan and the revolutionary situation in Iran where officers of the US embassy in Tehran had been taken hostage. During that visit, Fraser declared that the Russian invasion of Afghanistan had established a 'more dangerous situation than that which prevailed in Berlin, or Cuba, or Korea in earlier times'.[69] Carter shared this assessment. In his State of the Union Address on 23 January 1980, the President declared that an attempt to gain control of the Persian Gulf region would be repelled by all necessary means 'including military force'.[70] The ANZUS Council meeting in Washington on 26 and 27 February 1980 noted that Australia would deploy a carrier taskforce in the Indian Ocean and that consultations at operational and policy levels 'take on a new urgency in the uncertain strategic prospects resulting from the present South-West Asia crisis, that operational planning in response to the crisis is well under way, and that additional measures are being explored'.[71] For historian Glen Barclay, '[b]arely a year after reaching its nadir of irrelevancy, ANZUS was at last looking and sounding like a vehicle for genuine military cooperation that Australia had always wanted it to be'.[72] In the beginning of the 1980s the Fraser Government further strengthened military cooperation by permitting US aircraft based at Guam to conduct training flights over Northern Queensland and to stage through Darwin on training and surveillance flights into the Indian Ocean.

---

68   Barclay, 'Australia and North America', p. 153.
69   Embassy in Washington to Department of Foreign Affairs, 31 January 1980, transcript of the Prime Minister's Press Conference, cablegram no. WH86510, series A1209, item 1980/64 part 1, NAA, Canberra.
70   Barclay, 'Australia and North America', p. 153.
71   Ibid., pp. 154–5.
72   Ibid., p. 155.

Parkinson ended his second term as Ambassador to the US prematurely at the end of 1981 because of the persistence of the problem with his eyesight.[73] On his return to Canberra, in an informal briefing to a subcommittee of the Joint Committee of Foreign Affairs and Defence on 25 February 1982, Parkinson emphasised that Australia in 1982 was regarded more seriously than ever before by what he called the US 'establishment' (that is, by the US Administration and Congress). He argued that the 'establishment' in the US had become 'more conscious of the strategic importance of Australia in a changing world situation and of the potential of Australia's resources'.[74] On the other hand, Parkinson referred to the problem of what he labelled Australia's 'vanishing constituency' in the US. By this he meant the gradual disappearance from public life of the wartime generation that had forged that ANZUS alliance – including the likes of Eisenhower, John F Kennedy, John Foster Dulles, Dean Acheson and Dean Rusk. For this reason Parkinson thought that there was more reason for Australian diplomats to try to reach the 'voter' level, the ordinary public, more effectively. Far more than the letter of the ANZUS Treaty for Parkinson was that the American public should be aware of Australia. In the 1980s the challenge of extending Australian influence to Congress and the broader American public would become an increasing focus of the ambassador and the embassy in Washington.

Conclusion

The time 1972 and 1973 was a period of great instability in the Australia–US relationship and a major challenge for Sir James Plimsoll. Succeeding Plimsoll after 1973 were three career diplomats who worked hard to repair Australia–US relations. By the beginning of 1975, Sir Patrick Shaw had helped the Whitlam Government achieve what he described as a more independent relationship between Australia and the US. Shaw also navigated a period of political instability in two countries – the Watergate Crisis in Washington in 1974 and the dismissal of the Whitlam Government in 1975.

---

73   Parkinson to Henderson, 1 September 1981, letter, series A10476, TC-NFP part 2, NAA, Canberra.
74   Sir Nicholas Parkinson, former Australian Ambassador in Washington, to Joint Committee on Foreign Affairs and Defence, 28 February 1982, informal briefing, series A1838, item 250/9/1/7 part 1, NAA, Canberra.

Shaw died in December 1975 before introducing a new Australian Coalition Government to Washington. This task fell to another experienced diplomat, Sir Nicholas Parkinson, who organised a successful visit by Fraser to Washington in 1976 before returning to Canberra to take up the position of Permanent Secretary of the Department of Foreign Affairs. Parkinson's successor, Alan Renouf, had perhaps the best preparation of any head of mission in Washington to that time, having served in the embassy twice before, once as deputy head of mission. He arrived in Washington in 1977, embittered by his removal as Secretary of the Department of Foreign Affairs. Nonetheless, he worked effectively to influence the Carter Administration and to combat what one interpreter described as the 'withering on the vine' of the security relationship. Renouf helped the Fraser Government achieve the tacit interpretation of the ANZUS Treaty to cover the Indian as well as the Pacific Ocean. He was succeeded at the end of 1979 by Parkinson again. In his second term, Parkinson presided over a security relationship that was much closer than the relationship of the mid-1970s because of developments in Southeast Asia and Southwest Asia. For Parkinson, however, one of the major challenges ahead in the 1980s was for the embassy in Washington to extend its influence in the US beyond the executive government.

The three ambassadors confronted different problems. Shaw had to deal with a relationship that had been fractured by ideologically opposed governments in the early 1970s. Hampered by a prime minister who distrusted him because of his supposed political affiliations, Renouf had to work especially hard to register Australian interests with the Carter Administration, which seemed to have downgraded Australia's political and strategic importance. Parkinson, struggling with the physical disability of his failing eyesight, identified Australia's 'vanishing constituency' in the US as a longer-term problem for all Australian governments. All three envoys were effective in different ways. Parkinson was an exemplary organiser, Renouf an assiduous networker and Shaw the persuasive advocate of a reforming government.

10

Australia's ambassadors in Washington, 1982–89

David Lee

This chapter examines Australia's ambassadors in Washington during the period from 1982 to 1989 with a focus on two major episodes: the Australia, New Zealand, United States Security Treaty (ANZUS) and Missile-eXperimental (MX) missile crises of 1984 to 1986; and the issue of agricultural protectionism in the second half of the 1980s.[1] The election in 1972 of the first federal Labor Government in Australia since 1949 had seen Australia–US relations reach their nadir, as the Nixon Administration reacted adversely to criticisms of US policy in Vietnam by Prime Minister Gough Whitlam and his ministers, and as the Whitlam Government renegotiated arrangements over the joint facilities. The return to power of a Liberal–National Country party coalition led by Malcolm Fraser in 1975 saw the embassy in Washington assist the Fraser Government to seek closer defence ties with the US extending into the Indian Ocean. Liberal Party Senator Sir Robert Cotton, who was appointed Australian Ambassador to the United States in 1982, headed the embassy when Bob Hawke came to power in 1983.

---

1   See Henry S Albinski, *Australian External Policy Under Labor: Content, Process and the National Debate*, University of Queensland Press, St Lucia, 1977; Coral Bell, *Dependent Ally: A Study in Australian Foreign Policy*, Oxford University Press, Melbourne, 1988; Glen St John Barclay, *Friends in High Places: Australian–American Diplomatic Relations since 1945*, Oxford University Press, Melbourne, 1985; and James Curran, *Unholy Fury: Whitlam and Nixon at War*, Melbourne University Press, Carlton, 2015.

Hawke was the head of an Australian Labor Party calling for strong action to counter nuclear proliferation and some of whose members were advocating an end to the ANZUS alliance. Cotton was succeeded in 1985 by seasoned career diplomat Rawdon Dalrymple.

The 1984 election of a Labour Government in New Zealand opposed to visits by nuclear warships to its ports precipitated a crisis in the tripartite ANZUS alliance and threatened to unravel the *modus vivendi* achieved in the Australian Labor Party (ALP) on Australia–US relations during 1983. Adding to the political difficulties in the relationship was the resentment among Australian farmers in 1985 about subsidies to US agriculture that threatened unsubsidised Australian exports. The chapter shows how the embassy in Washington, under Ambassadors Sir Robert Cotton and Rawdon Dalrymple, assisted the Australian Government to navigate the ANZUS crisis of 1984 to 1986 and the economic crisis precipitated by the 1985 US Farm Bill in a way that left the Australia–US relationship much stronger by the end of the 1980s than it was at the end of the 1970s.

Cotton, the Hawke Government and ANZUS, 1983–84

Throughout 1983 and 1984 the Hawke Government pursued its first-term foreign policy on two different strands. One was Hawke's support for the US alliance and his personal rapport with President Ronald Reagan and Secretary of State George Shultz, both of whom he talked to on his first visit to Washington as Prime Minister in June 1983. On that first visit, Hawke took care to emphasise that Australian foreign policy had taken on a bipartisan character in the 1980s, that the ANZUS Treaty yielded mutual and reciprocal benefits, and that the provisions of the treaty did not 'derogate from Australia's right of national decision-making in foreign and defence policy'.[2] The other strand of Australian foreign policy after 1983 was the advocacy by Minister for Foreign Affairs Bill Hayden of a comprehensive nuclear test ban treaty, a South Pacific Nuclear Free Zone (SPNFZ) and disarmament negotiations

---

2   Bob Hawke, speech, Washington Press Club, 15 June 1983, *Australian Foreign Affairs Record*, vol. 54, 1983, p. 269.

between the superpowers in multilateral forums.[3] On 22 November 1983, Cabinet agreed on a package of disarmament measures, including measures to halt and reverse the nuclear arms race; to uphold the nuclear non-proliferation treaty; to promote a comprehensive and verifiable ban on nuclear testing; to develop the concept of a nuclear-free zone in the South Pacific; to support the achievement of a ban on chemical weapons; to support the process of negotiation and the achievement of balanced and verifiable arms control agreements; and to take an active role in pursuing arms control and disarmament. Hayden, who had been a senior minister in the Whitlam Government, took a much more critical position than Hawke towards the US.[4]

The Ambassador to the US from the time of his appointment by Fraser in 1982 to 1985 was Sir Robert Cotton. Cotton had been a Liberal senator for New South Wales from 1965 to 1978, Minister for Civil Aviation from 1969 to 1972, Minister for Industry and Commerce from 1975 to 1977 and Consul-General in New York from 1978 to 1982 before being appointed to Washington. Cotton remained as the Australian envoy to Washington after the election of the Hawke Labor Government. 'I didn't leave and they didn't ask me to – and they still pay me', he joked to an American audience in 1984.[5] It helped Hawke's aim of demonstrating the bipartisan character of Australian foreign policy to retain a Liberal of Cotton's standing as Ambassador to the US. Relaxed and jovial, Cotton, like Hawke, was popular in America. Not a diplomat by profession, he irreverently said of his job: 'I'm the chief import for politics here.'[6] Cotton performed the vital role of helping to introduce a new Australian Government to the Reagan Administration and of assuring the administration that the election of a Labor Government in 1983 would not affect the Australia–US relationship as the election of the Whitlam Government had done in 1972. The fact that Cotton was a Liberal appointed by the Fraser Government assisted in making

3   On the Hawke Government's foreign policy see Alan Burnett, *The A-NZ-US Triangle*, Strategic and Defence Studies Centre, The Australian National University, 1988; Andrew F Cooper, Richard A Higgott and Kim Richard Nossal, *Relocating Middle Powers: Australia and Canada in a Changing World Order*, Melbourne University Press, Carlton South, 1993; Bob Hawke, *The Hawke Memoirs*, William Heinemann Australia, Port Melbourne, 1994; Paul Kelly, *The Hawke Ascendancy*, Angus & Robertson, North Ryde, 1984.
4   Bell, *Dependent Ally*, pp. 227–9.
5   Barbara Gamarekian, 'Beyond Billabongs and Koala Bears', *New York Times*, 28 August 1984.
6   Ibid.

Hawke's case for the continuity of the Australia–US alliance. Cotton, like Beale, was a good networker in Washington and, like Plimsoll before him, made an effort to travel widely throughout the US.

Notwithstanding the calibre of Australia's ambassadors to the US, that Australia did not always rate highly in the global scale of US concerns had been graphically illustrated in 1983. In a reshuffle of responsibilities in the US State Department in that year it was decided that Australia, New Zealand and the Pacific Island countries no longer needed their own Deputy Assistant Secretary of State and were instead handed to one whose major responsibility was China. Cotton's successor, Rawdon Dalrymple, formed the impression in 1985 that there were few ambassadors, perhaps only five or six, who had relatively easy access to the Secretary of State and another half dozen or so who could get to see him if they pressed hard enough. The rest of other countries, and that category included Australia, could only get in to see him if they were accompanying a head of government or senior minister from their own country.[7] This state of affairs was in marked contrast to the 1950s and 1960s when Australian Ambassadors Percy Spender and Howard Beale had much easier access to senior administration officials and to the President himself. The Washington of the 1950s and 1960s was a much smaller place than the American capital in the 1980s.

During his ambassadorship, Cotton called on Shultz five times, always in the company of visiting Australian ministers: with Minister for Foreign Affairs Tony Street in 1982 and 1983, with Hawke in 1983 and 1985 and with Hayden in 1983. He made three other requests for appointments that were declined: the first, a courtesy call, the second before a meeting of the 1984 Association of South East Asian Nations' Foreign Ministers and the ANZUS Council meeting, and the third a farewell call.[8] It was, however, the case that the New Zealand ships and MX crises – which reached their denouements in 1985 and which will be analysed below – heightened the importance of Australian envoys in Washington and brought Australia to the attention of the President and senior administration figures much more often than had been the case in the late 1970s.

---

7   Rawdon Dalrymple to GC Allen, Chief of Protocol, Department of Foreign Affairs, 9 September 1985, letter, series A1838, item 250/9/4/5 part 9, National Archives of Australia (NAA), Canberra.

8   Paper, Department of Foreign Affairs, 'Calls on Mr Shultz by Sir Robert Cotton', series A1838, item 250/9/4 part 10, NAA, Canberra.

In 1985 the embassy was staffed by 34 Australia-based officers from the departments of Foreign Affairs, Trade, Primary Industry, Treasury, Finance, Immigration and Ethnic Affairs, as well as the Attorney-General's Department and the Department of Defence, and supported by 176 locally engaged staff.[9] Its chancery at 1601 Massachusetts Avenue was a modern building comprising seven storeys above a ground floor and two basements and a head of mission residence, which was described in 1985 as a building 'in a state of advanced general deterioration' that had 'not been renovated since the early 30s'.[10]

While the relationship of Cotton and the embassy with Hayden was sometimes strained, that with Hawke and the Department of the Prime Minister and Cabinet was much more cordial. Cotton accompanied Hawke during his first official visit to Washington in 1983 and had further discussions with him at Kirribilli House in January 1984 about the state of Australia–US relations and Cotton's plan to expand the embassy's 'constituency' in the US.[11] What Cotton meant by this was the problem, as he saw it, that Australia, unlike in many other countries, had no ethnic political base in the US and faced the problem of a 'vanishing constituency'.[12] He noted, however, that Australia's victory in the 1983 America's Cup, the success of Australian films, and the contribution of sporting persons and music groups had led to a remarkable rise in American interest in Australia. In these circumstances Cotton considered that:

> We now have an unprecedented opportunity to build on a new respect for Australia's achievements, to demonstrate that we are a country with a future, a considerable economic potential, a contribution to make, and one to be taken seriously not only as an ally but as a focus on a broad range of American interests in our highly populated and fast growing region.[13]

Cotton sought to enlist Hawke's support in building on this new American interest in Australia by securing an adequately funded and coordinated program of information, cultural and promotional activities in the US, citing as an example support for the Australian–American

---

9   Paper, 'Washington', Department of Foreign Affairs, n.d., 1985, series A1838, item 250/9/4/5 part 9, NAA, Canberra.
10   Ibid.
11   Cotton to Hawke, 9 May 1984, series A1209 1985/1053 part 5 and series A1838 250/9/4/5 part 8.
12   Ibid.
13   Ibid.

Bicentennial Foundation's ambition to promote Australian studies in America. Cotton was successful in engaging the interests of a group of Americans headed by Charles W Parry, chairman and chief executive officer of Alcoa, to work with the Australian Government on planning for the Bicentenary.[14]

Cotton led the embassy during a period when it assisted the government in the review of ANZUS that Hawke had promised during the election campaign. The review concluded that the ultimate value of ANZUS lay in the assurance it provided against the subjugation of Australia by major military force and the overall deterrent value of having a relationship with a country having large military resources and global reach. At a more immediate and practical level, the review found that there was substantial and irreplaceable value in the many-sided cooperation with the US in such matters as consultation with the Americans on strategic matters; being treated as a favoured customer in defence purchasing; gaining access to US defence scientific and technological information; and receiving a large volume and wide range of intelligence reporting. While such benefits were normally presented as flowing from the tripartite ANZUS Treaty, in reality they stemmed from Australia's association with the US.

The review noted that the joint facilities were not a necessary consequence of the ANZUS Treaty and did not derive from any particular ANZUS arrangement, but that the agreements that established them referred to the treaty. It found the risks that the facilities posed of making Australia a nuclear target were justified by the contribution they made to the deterrence of nuclear war and that they involved no derogation from Australia's sovereignty and independence.[15] But whereas earlier Coalition governments had sought what Coral Bell has described as 'maximalist' interpretations of the ANZUS Treaty, Hayden was content for ANZUS to be defined as a 'regional' treaty.[16] By the end of 1983, Hawke and Hayden, assisted by the embassy in Washington, had secured a *modus vivendi* in the Labor Party based on support for the ANZUS alliance combined with an active foreign policy aimed at mitigating the nuclear arms race through support for such measures as a Comprehensive Test Ban Treaty and the SPNFZ.

---

14 Ibid.
15 Department of Foreign Affairs to Hayden, 12 March 1985, cablegram no. CH267301, series A1838, item 686/1 part 42, NAA, Canberra.
16 Bell, *Dependent Ally*, pp. 232–3.

The aftermath of the 1984 New Zealand election

The election of a New Zealand Labour Government in July 1984 greatly complicated the foreign policy of the Hawke Government. The embassy in Washington and the ambassadors were called on thereafter to help the government salvage a fracturing ANZUS alliance and prevent through diplomacy infighting over ANZUS in the governing ALP. In 1984 the New Zealand Labour Party ran on a platform of banning from New Zealand ports all visits from nuclear-armed and nuclear-propelled ships; denuclearising the ANZUS alliance through renegotiation of the ANZUS Treaty; refocusing it on ensuring the economic, social and political stability of the South East Asian and South Pacific regions; and promoting the SPNFZ. Although the governing New Zealand National Government did not make foreign policy and protecting ANZUS a major line of its attack on its Labour opponents, the US embassy in Wellington took the extraordinary step of intervening during the New Zealand election campaign.

US Ambassador to New Zealand Monroe Browne distributed a statement about the ANZUS alliance and sought to refute Lange's suggestions that an earlier New Zealand Labour Government had prohibited nuclear ships visits between 1972 and 1975. In fact, a New Zealand National Party Government had suspended visits of nuclear-powered vessels in 1964 because of the absence of clear processes of indemnification in the event of a nuclear accident involving such vessels.[17] They had not resumed visits to New Zealand until 1976 after US indemnification legislation had been passed, although 22 visits by nuclear-capable ships had taken place between 1972 and 1975.[18]

---

17   Paper, Department of Foreign Affairs, 'US views on ANZUS and port access', n.d., series A1838, item 686/1 part 30, NAA, Canberra.
18   High Commission in Wellington to Department of Foreign Affairs, cablegram no. WL20102, 11 July 1984, series A1838, item 919/18/1 part 4, NAA, Canberra; AD Campbell to Hayden, 19 October 1984, submission, series A1838, item 686/1 part 30, NAA, Canberra.

When Labour's David Lange won the election resoundingly on 14 July 1984, many senior figures in the Hawke Government were relieved that the ALP Conference had taken place before the New Zealand election and not after it because of the boost that Lange's election would have given those in the ALP who wanted to replicate the platform of the New Zealand Party. Lange would later tell Hayden that he had received hundreds of letters from Australians seeking to use events in New Zealand as leverage in internal battles in the ALP.[19] As it was, the centre and right of the ALP were able to defeat proposals from the Socialist Left faction that would have required Australia to withdraw from the ANZUS alliance and close down the joint facilities in Australia. The conference permitted visits of US ships to Australian ports although limiting the pattern and frequency of US naval visits so that they did not amount to 'home porting'.[20]

In the immediate aftermath of the New Zealand election, an ANZUS Council meeting – in fact, the last ever tripartite ANZUS Council meeting – took place in Wellington on 16 and 17 July 1984, with ministers from the caretaker New Zealand National Party Government representing New Zealand, as Lange's ministers had not yet been sworn in. Ominously, in a press conference after the meeting, Shultz confirmed that it was essential for any alliance that the military forces of members had to be able to have contact with each other.[21]

In responding to the New Zealand election and its consequences for ANZUS, Hawke and Hayden had differing approaches. Hawke did not want the US to make a deal that accorded exceptional treatment to ship visits to New Zealand for fear that members of his own party would press for Australia to be given the same treatment and potentially to reopen the whole debate over ANZUS that appeared to have been settled in Australia in 1983. Conversely, he worried that if New Zealand were able to implement the ship ban without US reprisals, the chances of being able to keep the existing Australia–US relationship intact would be slim.[22] That was why Shultz had been so uncompromising at

---

19   Hayden and Lange, New York, 26 September 1984, record of conversation, series A1209 1985/1053 part 5, NAA, Canberra.

20   Deborah Snow, 'Nuclear Ships to Again Ruffle ANZUS', *Australian Financial Review*, 16 July 1984.

21   Department of Foreign Affairs to High Commission in Wellington and embassy in Washington, 15 July 1984, cablegram no. CH209514, series A1838, item 919/18/1 part 4, NAA, Canberra.

22   'Lange's Threat to ANZUS', *Sydney Morning Herald*, 9 August 1984.

the Wellington ANZUS Council meeting about US ship visits – he was less worried about New Zealand ports than he was about the possible reaction of the ALP.[23]

Hayden, on the other hand, instinctively wanted to pursue an even-handed policy to the US and New Zealand. In frank discussions after the Wellington ANZUS Council meeting, Lange bluntly told Hayden that US vessels were not needed in New Zealand and had no bearing on New Zealand's defence strategy.[24] Hayden countered with an explanation of Australia's accommodation with the US on the US joint facilities, B-52 flights over Australia, and US ship visits. Of his own experience, he recalled: 'We went down that lane in 1982. There is blood on my feet still.'[25] Hayden was referring to the embarrassment he had felt in 1982 when Prime Minister Malcolm Fraser had exploited ambiguity and uncertainty in ALP policy over US ship visits. This incident had contributed to Hayden's replacement by Hawke as leader of the ALP in the following year. Hayden then elaborated his thinking about the benefits that ANZUS gave to Australia – in sharing of intelligence, managing the relationship with Indonesia, and accessing US defence equipment and valuable defence and scientific information.[26]

Hayden came to a perceptive early assessment that Lange would be unable to resist the overwhelming sentiment in the New Zealand Labour Party on ship visits.[27] In these circumstances, he thought that expelling New Zealand from ANZUS because of its new policy – which was not an explicit obligation under the treaty – would cause a 'nasty' reaction in both New Zealand and Australia, as would a scenario where both Australia and the US withdrew from the tripartite treaty. As did embassy officials in Washington, Hayden warned Shultz and the State Department against bullying New Zealand or taking economic action against it. He predicted to Hawke that New Zealand actions would make the next ALP Conference in Australia difficult, but he was confident of winning if arguments were made in a reasonable way or in a way that could be characterised as not blindly following the US:

23   Ibid.
24   High Commission in Wellington to Department of Foreign Affairs, 18 July 1984, cablegram no. WL20205, series A1838, item 686/1 part 26, NAA, Canberra.
25   Ibid.
26   Ibid.
27   Hayden to Hawke, 20 August 1984, cablegram no. MC12525, series A1838, item 686/1 part 26, NAA, Canberra.

In saying this I am not proposing criticism for the sake of being fashionable. On the contrary, I am proposing that we express our concerns, and where necessary in good common sense, our criticisms, only on a limited number of occasions when it may be required to protect our national interests. A middle power like Australia cannot be on exactly the same course as a superpower like the U.S. no matter how close our formal alliance and our friendship, on all matters.[28]

Hayden advised Hawke that the Australian Government should not overreact: Australia had its own policy on ship visits and should leave New Zealand to work out its policy with the US. Above all, Hayden considered that Australia had to pursue its specific interest of preserving an appropriately structured defence partnership with the US, entailing a willingness to support an American strategic presence in the region as part of a system of reciprocal obligations and benefits.[29]

In the second half of 1984, the Australian Ambassador in Washington and his staff fulfilled one of the most vital functions of Australia's overseas diplomats in their close reporting of the thinking of the Reagan Administration on the New Zealand crisis. This reporting helped the Australian Government to maintain a nuanced and even-handed approach to the political rupture between two of Australia's closest allies. On 20 September 1984, for example, Cotton and his deputy head of mission, Tim MacDonald, met with Paul Wolfowitz, Assistant Secretary of State, Bureau of East Asian and Pacific Affairs, in the company of Peter Henderson, Secretary of the Department of Foreign Affairs. Wolfowitz indicated that the US would try to work out a compromise with New Zealand, but that the State Department was nervous about making concessions to New Zealand because of the major political and strategic problems that this would create for more important relationships, particularly Japan and Australia. Military thinking in the US, moreover, was that ANZUS as a tripartite arrangement was less important to the US than the relationship with Australia.

The State Department kept the embassy abreast of US–New Zealand negotiations. Wolfowitz, for example, relayed to the Australians the substance of a discussion between Shultz and Lange in which the American had proposed the compromise based on an agreement reached with Norway – that is, a prohibition of the stationing of nuclear weapons

---

28   Ibid.
29   Ibid.

in New Zealand coupled with an acceptance of ships visits without any questioning of their nuclear status. Lange countered with a different kind of compromise – a policy of not stationing nuclear weapons on New Zealand soil in conjunction with a formula that acknowledged no need for the US to deploy nuclear weapons in defence of New Zealand.[30]

Towards the end of 1984, the State Department informed embassy officials that it could not afford to extend unilaterally the post–New Zealand election moratorium on ship visits because that would be giving a signal to other allies that, in response to political difficulties, the US was prepared to adopt a self-denying ordinance. There was some sympathy on the part of the Americans for giving the New Zealand Government a 'fig leaf' to cover a back down, but Shultz was becoming increasingly irritated with Lange's inability to resolve the situation to the satisfaction of the US. During these and other discussions, Australian diplomats in Washington under Cotton's guidance adopted the approach of counselling the administration to maintain a patient attitude to New Zealand since the way that the issue was handled would have important implications for the Pacific, for Australia's traditional ties with New Zealand and for Southeast Asia due to the effects on the attitudes of Singapore and Malaysia towards the Five Power Defence Arrangements (the series of agreements signed in 1971 between Australia, New Zealand, the United Kingdom, Singapore and Malaysia providing for immediate consultation on possible actions in the event or threat or an armed attack on Malaysia or Singapore).[31] In this respect, Cotton and his staff proved adept in advocating the policies of the Hawke Government.

Not long before his own second visit to Washington, at the beginning of 1985, Hawke sent Lange a letter of advice as the New Zealand Government considered the prospects of a US ship visit. He warned Lange that New Zealand policy was imposing a grave risk to two of Australia's most important bilateral relationships – those with New Zealand and the US. He advised Lange: 'We could not accept as a permanent arrangement that the ANZUS alliance has a different meaning, and entail different obligations, for different members.'[32] Hawke's admonitions were unavailing. Not long after sending the letter,

---

30   Embassy in Washington to Department of Foreign Affairs, 25 September 1984, cablegram no. WH53706, series A1209 1985/1053 part 5, NAA, Canberra.
31   Embassy in Washington to Department of Foreign Affairs, 1 September 1984, cablegram no. WH52686, series A1838, item 686/1 part 26, NAA, Canberra.
32   Hawke to Lange, 10 January 1985, letter, quoted in Gerald Hensley, *Friendly Fire: Nuclear Politics & the Collapse of ANZUS, 1984–1987*, Auckland University Press, Auckland, 2013, p. 95.

on 17 January 1985, the US embassy in Wellington requested a visit to New Zealand by the destroyer *Buchanan* on 17 January 1985 while Lange was holidaying in Tokelau. Although the ship's obsolescent status meant that it was unlikely to be carrying nuclear weapons, its armaments included the ASROC anti-submarine missile (of 20,000 such weapons produced, 850 had nuclear capabilities). Since acting New Zealand Prime Minister Geoffrey Palmer could have no categorical assurance that the ship did not carry nuclear weapons, he declined the US request for the *Buchanan*.[33]

The MX and New Zealand ship visits crises

Before the New Zealand decision, on 25 January 1985, Cotton sent an analysis to the Department of Foreign Affairs in Canberra, giving his advice on a forthcoming visit to the US that Hawke was about to make.[34] One of the most important roles of the Ambassador in Washington was to advise on, and help prepare for, prime ministerial discussions with the President and his Cabinet. Cotton performed this role with great care and diligence. While noting that the overall Australia–US relationship was harmonious, Cotton pointed to irritants such as over Australia's lobbying for a Comprehensive Test Ban Treaty and some criticisms of US policy in Central America. He also noted a feeling in some parts of the Reagan Administration that events in Australia's region were moving contrary to US interests – on ships visits, growing pressures from disarmament movements, the SPNFZ and Soviet pressures in Pacific Island countries. Cotton recommended disaggregating the issues and explaining the Australian Government's position on each. He did not, however, mention in his cable an issue that would cause a storm during Hawke's visit.[35]

Before Hawke arrived in Washington, a political crisis had developed in Australia and in the ALP caucus over testing of MX missiles. Its origins went back to 1979 when a tri-service US defence committee began a study aimed at finding new international sites for the testing of US intercontinental ballistic missiles. The committee completed its

---

33   Gareth Evans, Minister for Minerals and Energy to Hayden and Beazley, 16 March 1985, memorandum, series A1838, item 370/1/20 part 33, NAA, Canberra.
34   Cotton to Department of Foreign Affairs, 25 January 1985, cablegram no. WH59133, series A1209 1984/1287 part 1, NAA, Canberra.
35   Ibid.

report in September 1981, recommending Sydney as a base for the staging and refuelling of US aircraft in their monitoring of missile tests. After taking office in 1981, the Reagan Administration unveiled a plan to add thousands of additional warheads to the US arsenal including a new land-based strategic missile (the MX). Since the MX was more precise and powerful than other missiles, many considered it to be a destabilising first-strike weapon. Adding to the controversial nature of the MX missile was the Strategic Defense Initiative, which Reagan had unveiled on 23 March 1983. With arms negotiations deadlocked, Reagan announced plans to develop a space-based antiballistic missile system that would render nuclear weapons obsolete. Reagan's launching of a massive build-up of nuclear arms and an expensive effort to build a defence against strategic missiles exacerbated tensions with the Soviet Union and catalysed anti-nuclear activism in the US and around the world.[36]

In 1982, the Reagan Administration obtained the agreement of the Fraser Government to provide logistic support for monitoring of long-range missile tests with the splashdown point near Australia. After Fraser's defeat at the polls, the administration tested whether Hawke's sympathies towards the US matched those of its predecessor by pressing him to confirm Fraser's decision. Hawke agreed and later, on 16 November 1983, Hawke, Hayden and the Minister for Defence, Gordon Scholes, formally agreed to the request with certain modifications. But they asked the US to remove the impact zone of the missiles outside Australia's exclusive economic zone and give an assurance that the flight path would essentially be limited to international waters. Cabinet ratification of the decision of the three ministers came only on 29 January 1985 at the first meeting since the re-election of the Hawke Government in 1984.

As Hawke left for Washington in 1985, shockwaves reverberated throughout the ALP over the publication of the decision in the Australian media. Left faction Labor MP Gerry Hand described the decision as 'the best-kept secret since the Government has been in office' and warned that there was a 'very real question of survival' for the Labor Party if Hawke continued with his policy.[37] Concern over the policy was not restricted to the Left as members of both the Centre-Left and Right factions criticised the decision, and federal member for Capricornia

---

36   See generally Ronald E Powaski, *Return to Armageddon: the United States and the Nuclear Arms Race 1981–1999*, Oxford University Press, New York, 2000.
37   David O'Reilly, 'Left Seeks Centre's Support over MX', *Australian*, 4 February 1985.

and Hawke supporter Keith Wright urged that Australia should become the 'Switzerland of the South Pacific'.[38] Hawke's difficulty in sticking to his decision on the MX missile was exacerbated by the perception of many Australians that the Reagan Administration had overreacted to the New Zealand Government's policy on visits by nuclear-armed warships in the previous year. For the Australian Government to agree to the US request, at the same time as some were criticising it for siding with the US against New Zealand, would have been a provocative and risky step to take.[39] It did not help that Hawke's letter to Lange about his stance on nuclear ships had been leaked to the *National Times* newspaper and had provoked a strong backlash in sections of the ALP.

Both Hawke and Hayden could argue that their policies on ANZUS and nuclear ship visits were consistent with party policy, since the 1984 ALP Conference had specifically endorsed the US alliance, the continuation of the ANZUS Treaty and the use of Australian ports by US nuclear-armed ships. However, the proposal that Australia assist in the monitoring of MX missile testing appeared at odds with ALP policies on nuclear testing and nuclear non-proliferation. It would be difficult for the Hawke Government to defend MX missile testing on the same basis as it defended the joint facilities – that the facilities contributed to nuclear deterrence. This was because the MX program involved the threat of escalation of the arms race. Moreover, the Hawke Government's proposed SPNFZ treaty was already being criticised for the fact that it would still allow the passage of nuclear-powered and nuclear-armed warships. Helping an ally in test-firing missiles that were designed to carry nuclear warheads into the Pacific was much harder to defend as consistent with the proposed treaty.

As Hawke embarked for Washington, many senior figures in the Australian Government hoped that the US would quietly drop their request for Australian support for monitoring the MX missiles; otherwise the Hawke Government may be forced to decline it. In a press conference in Brussels before heading to Washington, Hawke intimated the possibility of a change in policy on the MX missiles by stating that

---

38   Ibid.
39   Geoff Kitney, 'Why Bob Hawke will have to say no', *National Times*, 1 February 1985.

'I'll be making it very clear to the United States' Administration that the Australian Government is not giving support to the strategic defence initiative'. [40]

Cotton and the embassy helped resolve a major potential problem by convincing the Reagan Administration that Hawke had moved ahead of the opinion of his caucus on the MX missile issue and that the administration would need to rescue him from a difficult domestic position. Shultz, who was a personal friend of Hawke, took an indulgent and helpful attitude. Hawke had a conversation with Shultz and Caspar Weinberger facilitated at an embassy dinner. Following the meeting, the two US Cabinet members instructed their departments to solve Australia's MX problem. It was a measure of Hawke's stature in the US and the Australian embassy's deft handling of the issue that Hawke and Shultz issued a joint statement to the effect that Hawke had raised the community concern in Australia on the testing of the MX missile and that the US had taken the decision to conduct the MX tests without the use of Australian support arrangements.[41]

In his first press conference after returning to Australia, Hawke explained that a decision to provide support facilities for MX missile tests would have placed the alliance with the US and the joint facilities in jeopardy and would have impaired the capacity of Australia to carry out its disarmament policies.[42] Hawke feared such a rebellion in his caucus as would have led to a re-examination of the whole US alliance. Adding to Shultz's assistance of Australia on the MX issue, the Assistant Secretary for Asia and the Far East, Wolfowitz, later gave the broadest and most unequivocal assurances yet about the US commitment under ANZUS at a conference at Pennsylvania State University in March. Ironically, in view of the fact that Hayden had sought to lower expectations about the treaty's meaning, Wolfowitz remarked: 'In the case of an attack on Australia, for example, our commitment remains firm whether

---

40   Transcript, Prime Minister's Press Conference at Brussels Hilton, 4 February 1985; Brussels to Department of Foreign Affairs, 5 February 1985, cablegram no. CH257659, both series A1209 1984/1287 part 1, NAA, Canberra.
41   Hawke and Shultz, Washington, 6 February 1985, joint statement; Embassy in Washington to Department of Foreign Affairs, 6 February 1985, cablegram no. WH59609, both series A1209 1984/1287 part 1, NAA, Canberra; see also United States, *Department of State Bulletin*, vol. 85, no. 2097, April 1985, pp. 60–1.
42   Paul Malone, 'Alliance in jeopardy: PM gives his reasons for MX Decision', *Canberra Times*, 20 February 1985.

the attack should come from the Pacific or Indian Ocean approaches. Our commitment to the defence of allies is not limited to any particular threat; it applies to any particular aggressor.'[43]

In supporting the MX missile tests, Hawke had been trying to demonstrate that he was as pro-ANZUS as the Liberal–National Party Opposition, which his party had defeated at the polls for a second time on 1 December 1984. The problem with this strategy, as the MX crisis revealed, was that it seemed to have aligned Labor too closely with the view that the integrity of the alliance demanded Australia's and New Zealand's absolute compliance with US wishes. While the Opposition was exhorting Hawke to crush New Zealand, Hayden and Scholes's successor as Defence Minister, Kim Beazley, urged that such an approach to New Zealand was not in Australia's interests.[44] Thus, when the Reagan Administration urged the Australian Government to issue a joint statement cancelling the 1985 ANZUS Council meeting, Hayden and Beazley convinced Hawke to decline the overture. As Hayden noted on 2 March 1985, he did not want Australia to be seen as dropping New Zealand or pushing them into a 'laager mentality'.[45] So Australia issued a statement by itself on the cancellation, lest it appear to be siding with the US against New Zealand, while also agreeing to go ahead with bilateral consultations with the US.[46]

On 24 June 1985, Rawdon Dalrymple replaced Cotton as Australia's Ambassador to the US. Dalrymple was a highly regarded professional diplomat. Born in Sydney in 1930, he was educated at Sydney Church of England Grammar School and then took a Bachelor of Arts degree at the University of Sydney before winning the New South Wales Rhodes Scholarship in 1952. He took first-class honours in Philosophy, Politics and Economics at Oxford University and returned to Australia to lecture in philosophy at Sydney University in 1955 and 1956. In 1957 he joined the Department of External Affairs and, after postings in Bonn, London, Manila and Jakarta, was appointed Ambassador to Israel from 1972 to 1975 and then Ambassador to Indonesia from 1981 to 1985.

---

43   Peter Cole-Adams, 'The Untidy History of 34 Years of ANZUS', *Age*, 23 March 1985.
44   Geoff Kitney, 'Ministerial Moves to Cool the ANZUS Debate', *National Times*, 8–14 March 1985.
45   Hayden, 2 March 1985, note, series A1838, item 686/1 part 40, NAA, Canberra.
46   Australian Government media statement, 4 March 1985, series A1838, item 686/1 part 40, NAA, Canberra.

While Dalrymple had been appointed a Deputy Secretary in the Department of Foreign Affairs on 21 March 1985, other aspirants to the post in Washington included the Secretary of the Department of Foreign Affairs from 1981 to 1984, Peter Henderson, and Bill Morrison, a former Minister for Defence in the Whitlam Government. Moreover, Hayden and Hawke each had their own preferences for the post among other senior Foreign Affairs officials. Against Henderson was that Hayden felt him too close to the previous government. Just before Henderson resigned as Secretary of the Department of Foreign Affairs, Hawke had indicated that he intended to make a political appointment in Washington. This did not happen. Hayden and Hawke could not agree on their own candidates; Morrison was sent to replace Dalrymple in Jakarta and Dalrymple was appointed as envoy to the US. The factor that likely proved advantageous to Dalrymple was the respect of Hawke, who had been Western Australia's Rhodes Scholar in 1952, and knew him from their years together at Oxford University. This highly skilled and experienced diplomat inherited from Cotton the task of helping the Hawke Government through the New Zealand ANZUS crisis and dealing with another major problem in the relationship, the US decision to subsidise American agricultural exports.

Noting Cotton's difficulty in securing audiences with Shultz by himself, Dalrymple early in his term urged that more messages to the US Government be passed through him as a way of helping him to see and influence Shultz and other senior administration officials more often on political matters. In November 1985, he reported that he could not recall instructions from Canberra that would have given him access to Shultz or his deputies, although he often received ones that took him to comparable figures in the administration on matters such as trade and Australia's forthcoming bicentennial celebrations in 1988.[47] Dalrymple's remarks also highlighted that the Australian Government had the option of using diplomatic channels other than the embassy in Washington. For example, more often than not Hawke would, either personally or through his own office, or on the telephone, pass on his views directly to Reagan and Shultz.

---

47 Garry Woodard, Acting Deputy Secretary A, to Miller, 11 November 1985, minute, series A1838 250/9/4/5 part 9, NAA, Canberra.

Dalrymple took charge of the embassy at a critical time in the ANZUS crisis. As some members of the administration and Congress contemplated ending the ANZUS arrangement altogether, the Hawke Government faced the unpalatable possibility of having to negotiate a new bilateral agreement with the US including possible pressure to codify key clauses of arrangements including on the joint facilities, Pine Gap, North West Cape and Nurrungar. This issue had the potential to erupt in the ALP caucus. Another problem was that Australia was unlikely in the mid-1980s to get anything like the commitment it had obtained from the US under the ANZUS Treaty 1951.

Talks that Hayden held in October 1985 with Shultz, Weinberger, the Secretary of Defense, and Robert MacFarlane, the National Security Adviser, thus shaped up as what one commentator described as the most critical meeting held between Australia and the US since World War II.[48] At its conclusion, Hayden reported that he had agreed with Shultz that direct bilateral arrangements under the ANZUS Treaty would be maintained and that the Hawke Government intended to maintain support for activities under the ANZUS Treaty, including access to Australian ports by US naval vessels. In the meantime, Hayden asked the embassy in Washington to advise how the US Government was likely to react to legislation that the Lange Government had foreshadowed on nuclear ships visits.[49]

The departments of Hayden and Beazley canvassed exhaustively which options were best for Australia. They agreed that termination, withdrawal by one or more parties from it or denunciation would destroy the treaty and that any effort to secure a replacement bilateral security treaties would 'create enormously difficult problems for Australia'. On the other hand, suspension of US obligations to New Zealand under the treaty would trigger no formal legal consequences and support the Hawke Government's policy objectives of maintaining the ANZUS Treaty and allowing Australia to maintain its close bilateral relations with both Australia and New Zealand.[50] Hayden agreed and instructed the embassy to support a measured response to New Zealand through informal suspension that, 'while constituting an unambiguous signal to

---

48 Andrew Clark, 'ANZUS Breakdown has become a Messy Divorce', *Bulletin*, 9 October 1985.
49 Department of Foreign Affairs to Embassy in Washington, 7 November 1985, cablegram no. CH323649, series A1838, item 250/11/18 part 27, NAA, Canberra.
50 Beazley to Hayden with attachments, 16 October 1985, letter, series A1838, item 250/11/18 part 26, NAA, Canberra.

New Zealand (and to her western allies) that it was not "getting away" with its port access policy, would not cause serious problems for the maintenance of the ANZUS treaty'.[51]

Michael Costello, Hayden's private secretary, reinforced the point by arguing that, if New Zealand–US military cooperation were suspended, the Australian Government should publicise the fact that its own military relationships with both the US and New Zealand remained intact: 'In this scenario we would have two sets of bilateral relationships governed by the full effect of the ANZUS Treaty. Australia would be the pivot of the western association of nations in this part of the world.'[52] The efforts of Hawke's ministers acting in part through Dalrymple and his staff to persuade the US Administration of the desirability of the suspension option were successful. In August 1986 Shultz sent a letter advising that the US was:

> [s]uspending its security obligations to New Zealand under the ANZUS Treaty due to the continuing failure of that country to restore normal access to allied ships and aircraft. I wish to reaffirm the view of the United States that the commitments between the United States and Australia remain unaltered in any way.[53]

Export enhancement and the economic relationship

When Hayden confirmed to Shultz in 1986 that the Australia–US leg of the ANZUS arrangements would continue unimpaired despite the New Zealand–US leg having been suspended, his message contained a sting in its tail. As captured in a departmental briefing paper, Hayden asked:

> What exactly is the value of the alliance to both its partners?

> Where manageability of the alliance is threatened is when one partner takes action which damages the fundamental interests of its alliance colleagues …

---

51 Hayden to Hawke, 27 November 1985, letter, series A1838, item 686/1 part 59, NAA, Canberra.
52 Costello to Hayden, 25 October 1985, note, series A1838, item 686/1 part 58, NAA, Canberra.
53 Text of letter from George Shultz to Bill Hayden, 11 August 1986, *Australian Foreign Affairs Record*, vol. 57, 1986, pp. 739–40.

... A few weeks ago, Secretary of State George Shultz told Prime Minister Lange that New Zealand would remain a friend but not an ally. Now the Congress is telling Australia that it is an ally but not a friend.[54]

The object of Hayden's barb was the US Export Enhancement Program (EEP), a US initiative that was causing consternation among Australian farmers. On 15 May 1985 the US Secretary of Agriculture, John Block, had announced a US$2 billion plan to provide subsidies in cash or kind to US farm exporters to ship to designated markets, enabling them to sell at subsidised prices in those markets. The intent of the EEP and the 1985 Farm Bill that followed was to apply pressure to the rest of the world by directly subsidising American agricultural exports. The US had decided to use targeted agricultural subsidies in order to compete with subsidies provided to its farmers by the European Economic Community (EEC), as a way of pressing the EEC to lower or dismantle its agricultural protection.

In supporting the EEP, the Reagan Administration was reacting against a fall in the value of US farm exports by 13 per cent between 1981 and 1984 from US$44 billion to US$38 billion. The effect of the Farm Bill on Australian farmers, who received no export subsidies from government, was dramatic. For example, Australia's share of the wheat and flour market declined from nearly 20 per cent in 1985–86 to about 11 per cent in 1988–89, while the US share of the market soared from 28.7 per cent to about 43 per cent.[55] At the same time the EEC, against which the EEP was targeted, increased its share from about 17.4 per cent to very nearly 20 per cent over the same period.[56] From 1985 to 1988 the bilateral relationship between Australia and the US was particularly affected by the impact of US governmental action on Australia's farm sector, especially for wheat, cotton and rice. As one Australian-based US official commented:

54   Department of Foreign Affairs Backgrounder, 13 August 1986, quoted in Burnett, *The A-NZ-US Triangle*, p. 179.
55   Don Kenyon and David Lee, *The Struggle for Trade Liberalisation in Agriculture: Australia and the Cairns Group in the Uruguay Round*, Department of Foreign Affairs, Canberra, 2006, p. 136.
56   Ibid.

At its peak, between 1985–88, the EEP issue generated levels of Australian official and public outage directed against the US unequalled since the Vietnam War. A fundamental difference between the two issues is that Australians, like Americans, were divided on Vietnam – but are unified on the EEP issue.[57]

US economic measures aimed at the EEC were not the only ones to cause problems for Australia. In 1983 the Reagan Administration had also pressed the Japanese Government led by Nakasone Yasuhiro to redress the economic imbalance in the Japanese–US economic relationship through such measures as taking more imports of coal and beef from the US. As with measures aimed at the EEC, those aimed at Japan had consequences for Australia. Despite US coal being unable to compete in price or quality with Australian coal, Australian coal exporters found themselves squeezed by increased Japanese purchases from America. Similarly, in 1985 a rise in the quota of US beef consumed in Japan entailed a lesser quantity of Australian beef being sold on the Japanese market. By the beginning of 1985 the Australian Government found itself in the position of fighting a rear-guard action to preserve its market share across a range of commodities.[58]

The problems in the ANZUS relationship were largely resolved, at least as far as Australia was concerned, by 1986. In the second half of the 1980s, a major focus of the Australian Government and the embassy in Washington was on economic and trade issues. In the embassy, Australian actions on the trade front were led by an experienced Department of Trade official, the Minister (Commercial) Greg Wood, much of whose work was targeted at Congress. A Department of Foreign Affairs briefing paper in 1986 noted that power in the US was shared between the administration and the Congress and that when the American leadership faced domestic imperatives it would put aside principles and friends. Noting that Dalrymple had proved adept in lobbying and reporting, the Department of Foreign Affairs still felt that he needed extra support with work on Capitol Hill.[59] Part of the

---

57   Quoted in Pemberton, 'Australia and the United States' in Peter John Boyce and Jim R Angel (eds), *Diplomacy in the Marketplace: Australia in World Affairs, vol. 7, 1981–90*, Longman Cheshire, Melbourne, 1992, p. 130.

58   See John Welfield, 'Australia's Relations with Japan and the Korean Peninsula', in Peter John Boyce and Jim R Angel, *Diplomacy in the Marketplace, vol. 7, 1981–90*, Longman Cheshire, Melbourne, 1992, pp. 253–68.

59   DFA paper, 'Australia and the U.S.A.' n.d., 1986, series A1838, item 250/9/4 part 11, NAA, Canberra.

solution to the problem came in 1987 when the Hawke Government created a new position in the embassy, that of Minister (Congressional and Public Affairs), a position filled until 1989 by a future Australian Ambassador to the US, John McCarthy.

Indicative of the degree of importance that trade and economic issues were assuming from the mid-1980s on was Hawke's visit to Washington in April 1986. It was the first prime ministerial visit to the US in which trade and economic issues were the sole reason for the visit. The principal purpose was to convey the Australian Government's concern at the highest level towards the impact of the US Farm Act on the export of Australian farm products.[60] In Washington Dalrymple and his staff facilitated and managed the series of meetings Hawke had with senior members of the Reagan Administration – discussion and lunch with Reagan, extensive discussions with Shultz, a morning one-on-one golf game followed by a lunch hosted by Shultz and a dinner hosted by Hawke. Hawke also saw the Secretary of Agriculture, Richard Lyng, and the Chairman of the Federal Reserve, Paul Volcker. A difference between the 1986 visit and previous prime ministerial ones was the number of meetings arranged between Hawke and Congressmen, a program that also reflected the increasing energy that embassy officials were directing towards Congressional liaison. Hawke called on Senator Bob Dole, the Senate Majority leader; Senator Robert Byrd, the Senate Minority leader; as well as the House Majority leadership Chairman, Tip O'Neill, Jim Wright and Tom Foley. These meetings, along with conversations with the Congressmen who attended Shultz's dinner for Hawke, enabled him to communicate the consequences of the Farm Act to a country that the US regarded as a friend and expected to continue to be a close ally.[61] The administration was engaged to soften the effects of Congressional legislation and to support trade negotiations in multilateral forums. Hawke conveyed to Reagan the severe hardship that Australian farmers were facing, sought to have the administration's reassurance that the EEP would continue on a targeted basis essentially at markets of subsiding exporters and secured US agreement to have agriculture accepted as a key issue for a new round of multilateral trade negotiations in Geneva.[62] In his remarks on the visit on 17 April 1986,

---

60   David Reese, Counsellor, Embassy in Washington, to Colin MacDonald, 28 April 1986, letter, series A1838, item 250/9/4 part 10, NAA, Canberra.

61   Ibid.

62   Prime Minister's Departure Statement from the White House, April 1986, series A1838, item 250/9/4 part 10, NAA, Canberra.

Reagan indicated that the US would 'be responsive to the extent we can to Australian interests'. Reagan explained that the US aimed at a truly free international agricultural market but that in the interim measures were necessary to counter unfair subsidisation.[63]

In trilateral meetings of the ANZUS Council before 1985 economic issues had been kept out. However, in the Australia–US ministerial talks held in San Francisco on 10 and 11 August 1986, economic issues had assumed such a dimension the US was persuaded that they must be made a major item at the talks and were a significant part of the communiqué.[64] During 1986 there had been a range of ministerial delegations to the US, not only the prime ministerial visit, but ultimately an all-party parliamentary delegation to lobby against the EEP and the 1985 Farm Bill. There were also innumerable industry delegations to Washington in the period from 1986 to 1990.

As well as lobbying the administration and Congress, the Australian Government pursued an energetic campaign to include agriculture in negotiations in the General Agreement on Tariffs and Trade (GATT) in Geneva from 1985 and reinforced this campaign by forming and leading a coalition of agricultural free traders known as the Cairns Group. Australia and the Cairns Group found common cause with the US delegation in Geneva, which articulated an international strategy of working towards the elimination of protection for agriculture while maintaining the right to keep its protectionist defences as long as other countries subsidised agriculture. In Geneva, Australia and the US worked closely together with the common objective of achieving real agriculture policy reform in the period from 1985 to 1990. Bilaterally, however, both sides were at loggerheads over US policies on agricultural protection and export subsidies that were prejudicial to Australia's interests.[65] In these circumstances, the embassy in Washington had to work hard to reduce mutual mistrust as Australian ministers and officials came to question whether the US was genuine in its strong support for agricultural reform in Geneva, or whether the Geneva stance of US officials was simply a diversionary ploy.

---

63   Remarks by Reagan and Hawke, 17 April 1986, series A1838, item 250/9/4 part 10, NAA, Canberra.
64   David Reese to Australian Consuls-General in the US, 20 August 1986, letter, series A1838, item 250/9/4 part 11, NAA, Canberra.
65   Kenyon and Lee, *The Struggle for Trade Liberalisation in Agriculture*, p. 134.

US Government spending on farm support declined from a peak of US$25.8 billion in 1986 to more 'normal' levels of US$10.89 billion in 1989. In the lead-up to the framing of the 1990 US Farm Bill, the Australian Government kept up the pressure on US agriculture policy by lodging a complaint against the US sugar program in the GATT in 1989. The government and the embassy in Washington also sought to soften the protectionist aspects of the 1990 Farm Bill by pressing for it to be broadly consistent with US negotiating proposals in Geneva that were aimed at reducing market-distorting subsidies and trade barriers. Although multilateral negotiations in Geneva would continue for several more years beyond 1990, the end of the Uruguay Round in 1993 saw substantial liberalisation of trade in agriculture and a significant reduction of export subsidies. The gradual movement of the US downward from the peak of its farm support in the mid-1980s laid the basis for a more harmonious Australia–US relationship by the end of the 1980s than that which prevailed in 1985–86.

Conclusion

The period from 1972 to 1975 had been one of considerable strain in Australia–US relations, and Australia's embassy in Washington had had to work hard to improve the relationship in subsequent years. When the Hawke Government took office in 1983, the new Labor Government sought to achieve a consensus in the ALP based on strong support for the Australia–US alliance, combined with regional and multilateral efforts to mitigate nuclear proliferation. This consensus threatened to unravel after 1984 with the MX missile affair and the election of a New Zealand Labour Government, one of the policies of which was to prohibit the entry of nuclear-armed or nuclear-propelled ships into New Zealand ports.

Strong pressure was exerted on Hawke to follow New Zealand's lead and many feared that the consequence of the crisis would be that the ANZUS alliance would be terminated without any adequate replacement. Under Cotton and Dalrymple, the Australian embassy in Washington played an important part in steering the Reagan Administration away from punitive sanctions against New Zealand and in favour of remodelling ANZUS into a bilateral alliance in the form of Australia-US Ministerial Consultations (AusMin) that continued nonetheless to be based on the tripartite ANZUS Treaty of 1951. By 1986, the embassy and the government had been successful in solving the ANZUS problem to Australia's satisfaction, and had also helped to avert potential trouble for Hawke over his MX missiles policy.

By that time, however, economic and trade problems centred on US subsidisation of agriculture were causing as significant a strain in Australia–US relations as the ANZUS crisis had. Now focusing its efforts on economic issues and targeting Congress as well as the administration, Dalrymple and his staff worked relentlessly to persuade the administration and Congress of the harmful effects of agricultural protectionism on innocent victims like Australia in the American–European trade war. By the end of the 1980s and beginning of the 1990s, the embassy's diplomatic efforts as well as Australian efforts in multilateral trade negotiations had helped bring about an international solution to the problems of international trade in agriculture. Cotton and Dalrymple had played an important part in this process, but their efforts were nonetheless supplemented by other channels of communication between Australia and the US, for example direct communication between heads of government and communication between the US embassy in Canberra and the Australian Government.

11

Diplomacy in the 1990s: Issues for the Washington embassy

James Cotton

The 1990s was a period in Australian foreign relations and diplomacy book-ended by two major geopolitical events: at the beginning, the destruction of the Berlin Wall and the collapse of socialism in Eastern Europe (though at the same time its resurgence in China), and at the end, the terrorist attacks of September 11. The former led to what appeared to comprise an entirely new international environment, opening the way for many diplomatic and regional initiatives; the latter, according to Richard Clarke's memoir, was hardly anticipated even at the highest levels in Washington,[1] and thus raised problems for a future time, and especially for Prime Minister John Howard who was physically present.

This chapter reviews the policy responses of successive Australian Governments to these major changes in the environment, paying particular attention to their consequences for relations with the United States. These policies need to be outlined at the outset since, with the ease of communications and the frequent practice of visiting personal diplomacy by members of government, the activities of ambassadors were highly constrained by the priorities of Canberra. The chapter

---

1   Richard Clarke, *Against All Enemies: Inside America's War on Terror*, Free Press, New York, 2004. On Australia and the end of the Cold War era, see Coral Bell (ed.), *Agenda for the Nineties: Australian Choices in Foreign and Defence Policy*, Longman Cheshire, Melbourne, 1991; Stuart Harris and James Cotton (eds), *The End of the Cold War in Northeast Asia*, Lynne Rienner, Boulder, 1991.

subsequently considers the personnel and work of the Australian embassy in Washington, drawing upon such materials as are available on the public record.

The 1990s transition in Australian diplomacy: The Hawke and Keating governments

While any starting point can be seen as arbitrary, and one defined by date is almost bound to be so, it will be argued here that the 1990s in Australian foreign policy began in the final two months of 1989 with the appearance of two landmark texts, both of which sought to redefine Australia's approach to Asia. Both carried major implications for the future place of the US and for the alliance in Australian diplomatic calculations. To some extent they may be seen as bids for policy space, given that in the bilateral relationship with the US, defence and Defence ministers had become principal focus and actors respectively.

The Garnaut Report – Professor Ross Garnaut had been Hawke's principal economic adviser and then Ambassador to China – was prepared on prime ministerial direction to outline national policies appropriate for the rise of Asia. It described an era in which the further development of the Northeast Asia economies would draw Australia into their trading and investment orbits, provided that sufficient domestic reforms were enacted to maximise the opportunities presented.[2] The notion that at some future time Australia might be required to 'choose' between the US and China was hardly to be anticipated, and in general Garnaut assumed that these economies would prosper to the extent that they liberalised, and economic liberalisation would bring social and ultimately political freedoms in its train. Garnaut thus anticipated, in light of the transformation of the Soviet bloc, that Marxist authoritarianism in China would fade and, accordingly, that North Korea would either reform or experience isolation and irrelevance.

A month after the Garnaut Report, Foreign Minister Gareth Evans delivered a ministerial statement on Australia's regional security. Its focus was principally upon Southeast Asia, where Evans declared

---

2   Ross Garnaut, *Australia and the Northeast Asian Ascendancy: Report to the Prime Minister and the Minister for Foreign Affairs and Trade,* Australian Government Publishing Service, Canberra, 1989.

Australia was moving beyond the conventional security preoccupations and anxieties of former times to a more confident era of 'comprehensive engagement'. While the text did address powers and regions beyond the immediate Australian environment, its message was that though the US remained 'the strongest player', Washington's focus was bound to shift from geopolitical to economic concerns. Moreover, in the longer term, the US would also find itself in a world in which in relative terms other powers, notably the European Union and Japan, would play a more prominent role.[3]

Taken together, these texts delivered mixed messages.[4] Both agreed that, in the calculations of states, geopolitical considerations were giving way to economic concerns and to a great extent security was taking on a multidimensional aspect to include economic and social means as well as ends. However, if Garnaut was right that Australia's main game was in Northeast Asia, then Evans' evident preoccupation with Southeast Asia was misplaced and perhaps even somewhat old-fashioned, especially given that his statement made no secret not only of Australia's economic standing but also its technological edge in conventional force capabilities. To be strictly accurate, of course, Garnaut's text was not a direct statement of policy, though Prime Minister Bob Hawke's remarks on its launch suggested many of its recommendations would be followed, and indeed on that occasion he announced initiatives that directly implemented some of them.[5] More were soon to follow.

Nevertheless, the implications for Australia's relations with the US were clear from both documents. If economics trumped security, and if Australia's economic future lay in Northeast Asia, then the US would matter less in two respects. Important aspects of the security alliance would be outmoded, and over time whatever the volume of Australia's trade and investment links with the US they would grow less important. Commentators at the time recognised the former: according to the remarks of Russell Trood at a 1996 workshop, 'Australia's security dependence on Washington has declined appreciably over the last

---

3   Gareth Evans, 'Australia's Regional Security', Ministerial Statement, Department of Foreign Affairs and Trade, Canberra, 1989.
4   Nancy Viviani, 'Of Voices, Visions and Texts', in Greg Fry (ed.), *Australia's Regional Security*, Allen & Unwin, Sydney, 1991, pp. 22–31.
5   Australian Government Department of the Prime Minister and Cabinet, *Speech by the Prime Minister: Launch of the Garnaut Report 'Australia and the Northeast Ascendancy' Sydney*, (Robert Hawke), 22 November 1989, pmtranscripts.pmc.gov.au/release/transcript-7826.

twenty years'.[6] It should be recalled that the security context for this observation was the East Asia Strategy Initiative, which led to an appreciable downsizing of US military deployments in Asia. The launch of Asia-Pacific Economic Cooperation (APEC) in 1989 may be seen, in part, as preparation for the eventuality of a diminishing US economic impact on Australia. APEC was designed to facilitate the economic complementarity and potential of the Western Pacific rim that was Garnaut's focus, while providing an alternative trade vehicle if the Canada–US Free Trade Agreement (FTA – negotiated in 1987) provided a successful foundation for a North American Free Trade Agreement (NAFTA) (subsequently agreed in 1993) or an FTA embracing all of the Americas, turning the US away from the region. At the time the inward-looking nature of the European Union was taken as a given.

Under Paul Keating, APEC became the centrepiece of the government's pursuit of regional enmeshment. And from the first he strenuously sought to involve the US. It should be recalled that in its original conception, the proposed membership of APEC excluded the US, although then Secretary of State James Baker persuaded Prime Minister Hawke to extend an invitation to Washington for the inaugural meeting in Canberra.[7] Even with the emergence of APEC as a major architectural advance in the region, the 1990s remained, beyond the conclusion of the Uruguay Round of the General Agreement on Tariffs and Trade (GATT), a decade of trade tensions.

President George HW Bush visited Australia in 1991. Expecting nothing more taxing than golf with Bob Hawke, he found himself instead in an intense and somewhat one-sided briefing on the issue of regional architecture with the new prime minister. According to Paul Kelly's account, after Keating had expounded to the President his vision for the US to shift its emphasis from the Atlantic to leadership in the Pacific, Bush's National Security Adviser Brent Scowcroft remarked that this was an idea that the US was yet to formulate even for itself.[8] Nevertheless, the ideas floated at their meeting led to the establishment of the Australian American Leadership Dialogue.

---

6   Russell Trood, 'The Australian–American Alliance: Beyond Demystification', in William Tow, Russell Trood, Toshiya Hoshino (eds), *Bilateralism in a Multilateral Era*, Japan Institute of International Affairs & Centre for the Study of Australia–Asia Relations, Tokyo, 1997, p. 135.
7   James A Baker III, *The Politics of Diplomacy: Revolution, War and Peace, 1989–1992*, Putnam's Sons, New York, 1995, pp. 609–13.
8   Paul Kelly, *The March of the Patriots: The Struggle for Modern Australia*, Melbourne University Press, Melbourne, 2009, p. 161.

One of the innovations Keating proposed was a regional heads of government conclave.[9] This idea, which Keating pressed on both Bush and Bill Clinton, transformed APEC from a second-tier and somewhat experimental forum to a major focus for regional diplomacy. Keating was fulsome and no doubt accurate in his claims for being the originator of this innovation – on his account, Bush remained unconvinced, but Clinton grasped the opportunities presented – however, Clinton's memoirs, in which Keating is not mentioned, assert it was his own idea.[10]

Consistent with his December 1989 Security Statement and with the government's emphasis upon building regional structures, Gareth Evans pursued the idea of an Asia-Pacific-wide security dialogue on the lines of the Commission on Security and Cooperation in Europe. He aired this proposal at an Association of Southeast Asian Nations (ASEAN) post-ministerial in Jakarta in 1990, and in a subsequent opinion piece.[11] The initial American reception was hostile. While by this time there was acceptance of regionalism as a benign economic mechanism, security initiatives of this kind were seen as simply serving the Soviet objective of constraining US power, and Secretary of State James Baker told Evans so.[12] However, with the collapse of the Soviet Union, Baker came around to the idea by 1992.[13]

Evans went so far as to formulate – with a little help from his department and academic advisers – a new approach to security, 'co-operative security', which seemed to portend an era where a change in state norms of behaviour, new collective regimes, and a strengthened UN system would be able to head off or remediate most forms of conflict. Evans' book had little to say on exactly what role the US might play in this new world arrangement beyond noting that the management of the world's multiform security challenges was beyond even America's resources as the sole superpower.[14] The overview of Australia's foreign policy he had published (with Bruce Grant) in 1991 was a little more forthcoming,

9   Paul Keating, *Engagement: Australia Faces the Asia-Pacific*, Pan Macmillan, Sydney, 2000, p. 195.
10   Keating, *Engagement*, pp. 29–30, 82, 86–93; Bill Clinton, *My Life*, Knopf, New York, 2004, pp. 560–1, 930.
11   Gareth Evans, 'What Asia Needs is a Europe-Style CSCA', *International Herald Tribune*, 27 July 1990.
12   James A Baker to Australian Foreign Minister, Senator Gareth Evans, 19 November 1990, published in 'Security, in letter and spirit', *The Australian Financial Review*, 2 May 1991, p. 24.
13   James A Baker, 'America in Asia: Emerging Architecture for a Pacific Community', *Foreign Affairs*, vol. 70, no. 5, 1991/92, pp. 1–18.
14   Gareth Evans, *Cooperating for Peace: The Global Agenda for the 1990s and Beyond*, Allen & Unwin, Sydney, 1993, p. 5.

though it devoted twice as much space to Southeast Asia alone. This text cautioned against regarding the US as in any way exceptional: 'Impressive though its achievements and authority are, the United States is not so much an all-powerful force as a nation like any other, with interests like any other, and domestic pressures upon it to act ... like any other.'[15] Perhaps indicative of a cooling in relations, the 1993 Australia–US Ministerial Consultations (AusMin) due to be hosted by Australia was delayed until March 1994. In a diplomatic forum that began with security and foreign policy in mind, the communiqués of which were otherwise predictable platitudes regarding closeness of world views and values, from 1990 successive American delegations had been required also to defend their use of subsidies for primary produce exports and to acknowledge – if tacitly – the potential damage posed by this practice to Australian exports of like commodities.[16]

In the immediate neighbourhood, the Agreement on Maintaining Security with Indonesia, negotiated in great secrecy, was signed in December 1995. By this time a number of commentators were of the view that the distance between Australia and the US was growing, and correspondingly that the alliance was diminishing in importance as the web of regional security linkages grew more complex.[17] However, a note of caution is in order in summarising the trends under the Hawke and Keating governments. The various strategic overviews proceeding from the defence establishment, as might be expected, alerted policymakers to the risks and dangers in the new environment while still stressing the many advantages to Australia of the Australia, New Zealand, United States Security Treaty (ANZUS) and its associated arrangements.

The Howard Government

Although foreign policy was not a significant factor in the change of government in 1996, the Coalition made clear during the election campaign of that year that they would bring a different style to

15   Gareth Evans and Bruce Grant, *Australia's Foreign Relations in the World of the 1990s*, Melbourne University Press, Melbourne, 1991, pp. 302–3.
16   For AusMin documents see dfat.gov.au/geo/united-states-of-america/ausmin/pages/ausmin-australia-united-states-ministerial-consultations.aspx.
17   Roger Bell, 'Reassessed: Australia's Relationship with the United States', in James Cotton and John Ravenhill (eds), *Seeking Asian Engagement: Australia in World Affairs 1991–95*, Oxford University Press and AIAA, Melbourne, 1997, pp. 207–29.

its management. The touchstone for policy would be its service of 'the national interest', which was understood to mean Australia's physical security and prosperity, and the safety of its citizens. In addition, the Coalition proposed a 'reinvigoration' of the US alliance, claiming that 'Asia' had supplanted the American alliance in the management and prioritising of foreign policy.[18] In its first month in office, the Coalition's commitment to the alliance was manifest in the supportive remarks made regarding the US decision to deploy major naval units as a response to Chinese missile tests in the waters off Taiwan – this tactic was evidently designed to pressure the Taiwanese who were conducting elections for the presidency. Beijing responded with a virtual freeze on relations that lasted into 1997.

The new government took advantage of the fact that they were the hosts of AusMin in July 1996 to place their stamp on the relationship. In a joint declaration, which was given the grandiloquent title, 'the Sydney Statement', they rehearsed what they regarded as the overwhelming value of the alliance:

> Australia and the United States place enduring value on the alliance because of its significance in maintaining and consolidating Australia's capability for self-reliant defence, and because it constitutes a crucial element in the United States' permanent presence in the Asia Pacific region. Both governments reaffirm their commitment to that presence through forward-deployed US forces, access arrangements and exercises. We both attach importance to continuing Australian access to United States technology, close cooperation in intelligence matters, the assurance of resupply and logistics support in a crisis, and combined exercises and training to promote interoperability.[19]

The concrete outcomes of the AusMin meeting, however, were limited to the announcement of new joint training arrangements and the extension of the life of the joint intelligence facilities. Significantly, the 1996 communiqué included the observation that Australia 'welcomed'

---

18   James Cotton and John Ravenhill, 'Australia in World Affairs 1996–2000', in James Cotton and John Ravenhill (eds), *The National Interest in a Global Era: Australia in World Affairs 1996–2000*, Oxford University Press/AIIA, Melbourne, 2001, pp. 3–9.
19   AusMin, *Australia–United States Ministerial Consultations: 1996 Sydney Statement*, Department of Foreign Affairs and Trade, Canberra, 1996, dfat.gov.au/geo/united-states-of-america/ausmin/Pages/australia-united-states-ministerial-consultations-1996-sydney-statement.aspx.

the recent US–Japan agreement on alliance responsibilities;[20] it also contained some remarks on trade, distinctly muted by comparison to the earlier communiqués of the decade.

The wider context of these sentiments was an effort by the US to revivify its Asian alliances, endeavouring to persuade its partners to assume further responsibilities not only for their own defence but also in relation to regional US priorities. Japan had already agreed to relax restraints upon what was always a somewhat one-sided relationship, being the product of exceptional historical circumstances.[21] While the post-1990 draw-down of US forces in Asia was an encouragement to such a re-evaluation, both parties were mindful of the emergence of new China–Taiwan tensions and of the need to maintain vigilance given North Korea's admission of its pursuit of a nuclear program (the resulting crisis constrained – temporarily as it turned out – by the 1994 'Agreed Framework').

The new government then turned its attention to drafting a foreign policy White Paper that further signalled the essentials of its distinctive style: not only would national interest – conceived in somewhat constrained security and economic terms as well as with reference to certain 'values' – henceforth constitute the standard for national policy, but a priority would be placed on bilateral strategies. Bilateralism was described as 'the basic building block',[22] and it would take the place of the previous government's (allegedly excessive) enthusiasm for multilateralism. While the White Paper devoted a good deal of attention to Asia – some of its projections soon undermined by the regional financial crisis – the US was identified as a member of the nation's most important partnerships and one the government was determined to broaden and strengthen, including in relation to joint participation in Asian regional institutions. The White Paper conceded that while the US was 'a key economic partner', nevertheless there remained the likelihood of differences continuing to appear in trade and trading strategies. Significantly, the document envisaged the emergence of Japan as 'a more important defence partner' in the context of the US alliance.

---

20   Tomohiko Satake, 'The origin of trilateralism? The US–Japan–Australia Security Relations in the 1990s', *International Relations of the Asia–Pacific*, vol. 11, no. 1, 2011, pp. 87–114.
21   Ministry of Foreign Affairs of Japan, *The Japan–US Joint Declaration on Security, Alliance for the 21ˢᵗ Century*, 17 April 1996, www.mofa.go.jp/region/n-america/us/security/security.html.
22   Department of Foreign Affairs and Trade, White Paper, *In the National Interest: Australia's Foreign and Trade Policy*, Department of Foreign Affairs and Trade, Canberra, 1997, p. 53.

A reinvigorated alliance required more, however, than words. As Defense Secretary William Cohen noted at AusMin in 1998, Australia was the first power to volunteer forces to deal with the contingency generated by Saddam Hussein's threat to expel weapons inspectors.[23] Yet at the same time Cohen was telling his Australian colleagues, if journalists' reports are accurate, that Australia was not spending sufficient funds on defence and there was only so much that the US could do for partners who did not equip themselves appropriately.[24] However, the Howard Government only later began a significant and continuing augmentation of the defence budget as a response first to the East Timor commitment and then to the events of 2001.

Accordingly, US support for Australian intervention in the East Timor crisis of 1999 was crucial for the success of the International Force for East Timor (INTERFET). Yet in the days immediately following the independence ballot there were anxious moments in Canberra when the Clinton administration seemed reluctant to offer support for the intervention that was clearly needed in order to deal with the mayhem in the territory. The view was taken in the US that this crisis should receive an 'Asian' response, this position reflecting both the desire not to derail Indonesia's democratic transition and also the preoccupation with the Kosovo crisis. National Security Adviser Sandy Berger was reported as being opposed to any direct American role.[25] In the event, as it became clear that INTERFET would have to become largely an Australian operation, American support was promised. En route to the Auckland summit of APEC, Clinton made it plain that Indonesia would suffer potentially severe financial penalties if cooperation in the deployment of a multinational force was not forthcoming. Though US troops would not be deployed, logistic and intelligence assets were mobilised, and Washington earmarked mobile forces to be available as reserves if called upon. Yet the initial fear that the US would choose to ignore Australia's articulated security concerns in the interests of better relations with the

23   Joint Press Conference at the Conclusion of the AusMin Talks with Secretary of State Madeleine K Albright, Secretary of Defense William Cohen, Australian Minister for Foreign Affairs Alexander Downer, and Australian Minister for Defence Ian McLachlan, HMAS *Watson*, Sydney, 31 July 1998.
24   Greg Sheridan, 'US warns of defence risk', *Australian*, 31 July 1998.
25   Sandy Berger, National Security Advisor, and Gene Sperling, National Economic Advisor, press briefing, 8 September 1999. On the East Timor issue, see James Cotton, *East Timor, Australia and Regional Order: Intervention and its Aftermath in Southeast Asia*, Routledge, London, 2004.

major (and now democratising) Southeast Asian regional power recalled an earlier time when just this calculation was followed: the West New Guinea dispute of the early 1960s.[26]

From the American perspective, there was certainly the expectation that reciprocity could be expected from Australia in security crises. On a private visit to Australia in 1999, Richard Armitage – already a keen proponent of the project to remove Saddam Hussein, he would later progress as Deputy Secretary of State in the George W Bush Administration – asserted that if Australia did not participate with the US in a conflict over Taiwan, the alliance would be at an end.[27] While this was a personal opinion, the readiness with which Australia subsequently became engaged first in Afghanistan and then Iraq was remarkable. In retrospect it is clear that no proper assessment was made of the likely costs or consequences, which suggests that the American lead was the crucial factor in these decisions. Yet it is perhaps unsurprising that, witnessing September 11 from the vantage point of Washington, John Howard invoked the ANZUS Treaty. Whether Keating would have taken this step, while a hypothetical, might be doubted; Hawke is more likely to have done so.

The ambassadors: Michael Cook and Don Russell

Australian emissaries to Washington have generally been either senior diplomats or political figures with Cabinet experience. At the beginning of the 1990s, Michael Cook held the position. Though a Cambridge man with more than three decades of experience in the department, Cook had not held the usual brace of ambassadorships of his peers (apart, significantly, from a 10-month sojourn in Saigon). The historical context of his movement to the position is of considerable relevance. In February 1985 Hawke, after significant public pressure, had withdrawn from an undertaking to the US to facilitate the testing of

---

26 Stuart Doran, 'Toeing the Line: Australia's Abandonment of "Traditional" West New Guinea Policy', *Journal of Pacific History*, vol. 36, no. 1, 2001, pp. 5–18.
27 William T Tow and Leisa Hay, 'Australia, the United States and a "China Growing Strong" Managing Conflict Avoidance', *Australian Journal of International Affairs*, vol. 55, no. 1, 2001, pp. 37–54; Greg Sheridan, 'What if bluff and bluster turn to biff?', *Australian*, 10 March 2000.

nuclear-capable MX missiles in the Western Pacific.[28] While Secretary of State George Shultz diplomatically facilitated this change of course, he and his colleagues were suspicious of the trend in Australian policy, especially in relation to nuclear weapons. In the same year, the initiative to construct a South Pacific Nuclear Free Zone (SPNFZ) was realised in the Treaty of Rarotonga and Australia also continued to campaign for a Comprehensive Test Ban Treaty (a measure finally realised in 1996 but which Washington has yet to ratify; neither had the US signed on to SPNFZ).

Cook was the next Hawke Government appointee to the position of Ambassador (following Rawdon Dalrymple, 1985–89). Having served as an adviser to Malcolm Fraser, Cook was Fraser's appointee in 1981 to become Director-General of Office of National Assessments (ONA) and thus the nation's most senior intelligence figure, a position he held until 1989. He was also a person of strong conservative views (as is still apparent from his published writings)[29] who prided himself on his closeness to important figures in the US Republican Party. According to one account, Cook while at ONA had raised with Justice Robert Hope, then reviewing the Australian intelligence community, the suggestion that Foreign Minister Hayden's suspicion of the US had obstructed information cooperation with Washington.[30] As one journalist wrote at the time of his appointment, 'Some Foreign Affairs officials are concerned about what they describe as Mr Cook's conservative, pro-US views'.[31] It may be postulated that his appointment was intended to reassure Washington that Australia would not be taking the New Zealand route out of the alliance.

The appointment also indicated Hawke's close control of the relationship with the US; he was reported to have spent a good deal of time with Cook while he was at ONA. As Ambassador, Cook played a direct role in the events that led to the Australian commitment to the Gulf War. The key telephone call from Bush to Hawke on 10 August 1990 was made

---

28   Cabinet Minute, Security Committee, 29 January 1985, item A13979, series 4613/SEC, National Archives of Australia (NAA), Canberra.
29   Michael Cook, 'Why Australia Fights Other People's Wars', *Quadrant*, vol. 57, no. 9, 2013; also 'ANZUS and the Monroe Doctrine', *Quadrant*, vol. 57, no. 12, 2013; 'The American Alliance and the Shaping of the World', *Quadrant*, vol. 58, no. 4, 2014.
30   Brian Toohey and William Pinwill, *Oyster: The Story of the Australian Secret Intelligence Service*, Heinemann, Melbourne, 1989, p. 255.
31   Tom Burton and Helen O'Neil, 'It's musical chairs as diplomats are shuffled', *Sydney Morning Herald*, 25 November 1988, p. 7.

as a result of a request from the Ambassador as intermediary. Though Hawke stated that his decision to commit forces to the Gulf stemmed from that conversation, it transpired that the decision had actually been taken the previous day by a small group of ministers. Cook was a central figure in the process whereby this decision was made.[32]

Nevertheless, not all members of the Cabinet were so impressed with Cook's appointment. It was alleged by journalists that the relationship between Evans and Cook was poor, with the Foreign Minister admonishing his envoy for his failure to develop sufficiently close relations with both sides of US politics, thus prejudicing Australia's interests when Clinton defeated Bush in the 1992 elections. It was noteworthy that Cook had decided not to attend that year's convention of the Democratic Party, though he was present at the Republican Party's equivalent. Indeed, notoriously media averse – diplomacy was certainly a different art at that time – rather than submit to an interview himself, Cook had recommended to an Australian journalist writing his profile to consult leading Republican security figures Douglas Paal and Richard Armitage for assessments of his role. In any event, the journalist came to the conclusion that from the point of view of Keating's agenda, Cook was out of step with the current government's worldview:

> So for those in Canberra who are eager to see Australia stretching into new relationships in the region, in which the US is but one of many friends, rather than the special friend it's been, Cook is part of an old school that makes him the wrong man for the times.[33]

According to the *Washington Post* correspondent subsequently sent to Canberra, the Ambassador was known for offering 'not much availability' to the media.[34] Nevertheless, Cook was not oblivious to the shifting emphases of Canberra's strategy. One of his rare forays into the American press took the form of a spirited defence of the efficiencies of the Australian sugar industry, pointing out the inequity perpetrated

32   Alan Ramsey, 'President Bob rolls over for a tickle', *Sydney Morning Herald*, 11 August 1990, p. 25; Paul Grigson, 'How we begged to go to the Gulf', *Sydney Morning Herald*, 1 September 1990; Bob Hawke, *The Hawke Memoirs*, Heinemann, Port Melbourne, 1994, pp. 511–20. On the Gulf commitment see Murray Goot and Rodney Tiffen (eds), *Australia's Gulf War*, Melbourne University Press, Melbourne, 1992.

33   Pilita Clark, 'Ambassador on the Warpath', *Sydney Morning Herald*, 11 March 1993, p. 13.

34   Kathleen Burns, comments at 'Don Russell address at the National Press Club on 9 March 1994'. See also Kathleen Burns, 'A Stranger in Paradise? A Foreign Correspondent's View of the Parliamentary Press Gallery', Papers on Parliament, No. 23, Australian Parliament House, Canberra, 1994, www.aph.gov.au/binaries/senate/pubs/pops/pop23/c03.pdf.

by the GATT-inconsistent quotas placed in its way in the US market.[35] He also defended Australia's refusal to offer rights of settlement to boat people found not to be genuine refugees, a practice that he argued should be seen in the context of the generous national refugee quota.[36]

Following Cook, the Keating Government appointed Don Russell, an economist and (still youthful) former career official, though from Treasury and not from External/Foreign Affairs as his bureaucratic predecessors had been. This appointment can be seen to reflect those specific regional priorities that Keating had espoused. As has been shown, Keating was especially concerned to secure the enthusiastic participation of the US in the emerging economic regionalism of the Asia-Pacific.[37] It should be recalled that the trade priorities of the Clinton Administration at the outset were by no means clear, and in the circumstances, an envoy with a close knowledge of the relevant issues would be advantageous. In addition to his background, Russell had most recently worked very closely with Keating, becoming, in Neal Blewett's estimate, his 'most influential economic adviser'.[38] In his memoir, Keating records Russell's personal role in convincing the American administration that APEC should involve a leaders' meeting; he also states that in Jakarta, Clinton had remarked that 'he should get Don a desk and chair in the East Wing of the White House'.[39]

Where Cook remained a figure behind the scenes, Russell – in some respects in a tradition pioneered by Casey – took a good deal of trouble to address (if not always court) the many constituencies in the US. His principal focus was undoubtedly economic. As a contemporary commentator observed regarding his appointment, it 'clearly reflects [Keating's] conviction that Australia's relationship with the US has entered a crucial new phase in which trade and economic policy will play a role as important as strategic security was during the Cold War'.[40]

---

35 Michael Cook, Letter to the Editor, *New York Times*, 1 July 1989.
36 Michael Cook, 'Deadline for Boat People', *Washington Post*, 21 June 1990, p. A18.
37 Tony Wright, 'Keating Adviser to be US Envoy', *Sydney Morning Herald*, 12 June 1993, p. 1; Mike Seccombe and Tony Wright, 'The Don: Keating's Hard Man Goes to Washington', *Sydney Morning Herald*, 17 June 1993, p. 11.
38 Neal Blewett, *Cabinet Diary*, Wakefield Press, Kent Town, 1999, p. 45; John Edwards, *Keating: The Inside Story*, Penguin Books, Ringwood, 1996, pp. 287–90.
39 Keating, *Engagement*, pp. 92, 45.
40 Wright, 'Keating adviser to be US envoy', p. 1.

Eschewing some of the conventions of regular diplomacy, Russell was not afraid to volunteer frank remarks to American audiences on the difficult task of trade reform. Although the plan to form the NAFTA was originally seen in Canberra as a move towards exclusionary trading blocs, Russell soon saw that a failure on Clinton's part to win Congressional support for NAFTA would considerably weaken the President's standing just as he was due to host the first APEC leaders' meeting in Seattle, and voiced his fears.[41] Later in the year, Russell played a part in Cairns Group lobbying in Washington in an attempt to convince the US that agricultural subsidies were damaging the agricultural industries of the member countries.[42] Although (along with Trade Minister Peter Cook) he had managed to extract an undertaking from US Trade Representative Mickey Cantor to restrain the use of its Export Enhancement Program (EEP) that subsidised grain exports, the US had subsequently struck a deal with France, which allowed both parties to continue parallel practices.[43]

The Ambassador's focus on Asian trade issues was thoroughly on display in 1994. In that year, economic tensions between the US and Japan reached unprecedented heights. With the failure of the US–Japan Framework Talks conducted by Clinton and Prime Minister Hosokawa, Washington revived Super 301 (1974 Omnibus Trade Act) to mandate retaliatory trade actions and a trade war loomed. Don Russell was prominent in warning against the attendant risks, and even went as far as criticising the harshness of US tactics.[44] The US was also in dispute with China on human rights issues, with consideration being given to withdrawing China's Most Favoured Nation (MFN) status unless there were undertakings in Beijing to accept international standards. Russell was reported to have addressed a closed briefing for members of Congress on policy towards China, arguing the case for retention of MFN and suggesting that the Australian approach – then recently developed – of pursuing a parallel human rights dialogue with Beijing

---

41   Pilita Clark, 'Awkward in Aspen: Don the Diplomat', *Sydney Morning Herald*, 27 September 1993, pp. 1, 4; Pilita Clark, 'Jittery World at Free Trade, Protectionism Crossroads', *Sydney Morning Herald*, 16 November 1993, p. 11.
42   Pilita Clark, 'US Hints at Compromise on Subsidies', *Sydney Morning Herald*, 2 December 1993, p. 10.
43   Pilita Clark, 'Farm Compromise to Cost Australia Dearly', *Sydney Morning Herald*, 9 December 1993, p. 7.
44   Ben Hills, 'Japan Digs in for Trade War with US', *Sydney Morning Herald*, 17 February 1994, p. 1; Pilita Clark, 'Christopher Gives Pledge on Cheap US Wheat', *Sydney Morning Herald*, 4 March 1993, p. 1.

might improve relations while also assuaging domestic critics.[45] In the preparations for the APEC meeting that embraced the Bogor targets for regional trade liberalisation, Russell's embassy played an important role in the consultations between Clinton and Keating that ensured the US would take the lead, working hard to overcome some last minute wobbles on the 2010/2020 liberalisation targets (for industrialised and developing economies respectively).[46]

The year 1994 was also one in which the US considered legislation to institutionalise the outcomes of the Uruguay Round of the GATT. Australia's greatest concern was whether promised restraints on the use of the EEP, and also of its equivalent for dairy products, the Dairy Export Incentive Program (DEIP), would remain. Russell vigorously lobbied Cantor to stick to a verbal undertaking to this effect.[47] In the event, Congress allowed the EEP to continue, but under new restraints.

Returning to Canberra for the 1994 AusMin, Russell addressed the National Press Club, giving a positive and sometimes amusing overview of the Australia–US relationship. In response to a question suggesting otherwise he was quick to insist that Australia's 'new role in the region' was 'of great interest' to the US where policymakers, he claimed, respected Australian knowledge. While emphasising the seriousness of the tensions between Japan and the US on trade as well as accepting the American premise that many sectors of the Japanese market were effectively closed, Russell took the view that these differences would ultimately be resolved.[48]

Yet the trading rules established in 1994 produced less surety than the Australian Government and its ambassador had anticipated. In 1995 tensions rose over increased DEIP expenditures.[49] Then the EEP was employed to offer cheap wheat to China; just at the time there was a bilateral dispute between Washington and Beijing over issues including

45   Pilita Clark, 'Australia asks America to Renew China's Low-Tariff Trade Status', *Sydney Morning Herald*, 21 May 1994, p. 15.
46   David Lague and Pilita Clark, 'Keating, Clinton Put Trade Strategy in Place', *Sydney Morning Herald*, 2 September 1994, p. 2.
47   Pilita Clark, 'US Offers Sympathy but no Guarantees on Subsidies', *Sydney Morning Herald*, 28 September 1994, p. 6.
48   Don Russell, speech, National Press Club, Canberra, 9 March 1994, National Library of Australia (NLA), Canberra.
49   Pilita Clark, 'Dairy War Looms Over US Subsidies', *Sydney Morning Herald*, 1 January 1995, p. 1.

intellectual property.[50] An exasperated Russell went on the record to point out the inconsistency involved: 'It seems a bit strange if you are trying to be a bit stiff with the Chinese that you offer them cheaper-than-cheap wheat … It is a big gift to the recipient.'[51] He also found time to defend Australia's policy on East Timor and sought to explain Australia's opposition to French nuclear tests.[52] However, perhaps the limits of the relationship with Washington were best illustrated by the *Kanimbla* incident. Australia had sent a naval crew to pick up one of two former US Navy landing ships that had been purchased; the Pentagon supplied an admiral and Russell attended the handover ceremony that had been arranged. At the last moment, it was discovered that Congress had failed to sign off on the transfer, and was then headed for recess; no amount of pressure from the White House could overcome the delay. It took months to resolve the problem.[53]

Unlike his immediate peers, Russell found a later occasion to reflect at length on the nature of the Australia–US relationship, offering commentary in 2007 especially on differences regarding trade that were undoubtedly informed by his experiences in Washington. He characterised the pattern of trading linkages in the following terms:

> Australia's traditional export relationship is based on Australia's comparative advantage in the production of agricultural products and natural resources. On the face of it, this should provide Australian industry with attractive market opportunities. The [US] market is relatively open and attractive to low-cost producers. However, many key Australian exports are covered by quotas and other barriers to trade. Unfortunately, export industries such as wool, sugar, and dairy, where Australia is a highly efficient producer and where there is scope to expand production, are the very industries most heavily protected in the United States. This keeps Australia's trade negotiators active, but over the years such activity has not produced major gains for Australia. The result has been constant friction and irritation between the two countries.[54]

---

50   Pilita Clark, 'US Wheat Offer "Gift" for China', *Sydney Morning Herald*, 9 February 1995, p. 9.

51   Russell, quoted in David Sanger, 'US to Sell China More Wheat Despite Trade Rift', *New York Times*, 8 February 1995, pp. D1, D7.

52   Letters to the Editor, *New York Times*, 8 June 1994, p. A24, also 17 July 1995, p. A12.

53   Tony Wright, 'Bungle leaves Sailors Shipshape, Shipless', *Sydney Morning Herald*, 30 June 1994, p. 2.

54   Don Russell, 'Economic and Business Aspects: An Australian Perspective', in Jeffrey D. McCausland et al. (eds), *The Other Special Relationship: the United States and Australia at the Start of the 21st Century*, Army War College, Strategic Studies Institute, Carlisle, Pennsylvania, 2007, p. 217.

In a remark that may be taken as a personal reflection, Russell added: 'Australians often are shocked over the lack of consideration afforded Australia when it comes to market access for traditional Australian exports and the [US] willingness to protect its industries in such a blatant way.'[55]

On the decision to pursue an FTA with the US, though Russell noted the advantages that might be gained by the existence of close security relations, he was under no illusions that this connection would result in many material gains: 'U.S. negotiators have become expert at using the intransigence of the American Congress and the importance of the U.S. market to extract concessions from other countries while giving up little, if anything.' Nevertheless, there were positive lessons to be learned. For a figure associated with the favourable appraisal of Australia's traditional bureaucratic practices and the virtues of their need to remain insulated from excessive or partisan external pressures,[56] Russell's experience in trade negotiations evidently convinced him that the exigencies of working closely with the US demanded different strategies. He concluded that the approach and resources of the Department of Foreign Affairs and Trade were insufficient to the task of dealing with the US, finding in the preparedness of US trade negotiators to harness the resources and input of business and the private sector a strategy that Australia might advantageously emulate.[57]

The ambassadors: John McCarthy, Andrew Peacock, Michael Thawley

Russell was succeeded by John McCarthy, another polished product (Cambridge) who was returning to the city of his birth where he had also served twice previously. By the end of his diplomatic career, McCarthy's seniority and standing can be gauged by the fact that he had held all the ambassadorial posts that mattered. An early responsibility was to explain the rationale behind the Agreement on Maintaining Security (AMS) with Indonesia, despite having been given no prior notice of its impending announcement, a predicament he shared with his Indonesian

---

55   Ibid.
56   Parliament of Australia, Don Russell: 'The Role of Executive Government in Australia', Papers on Parliament, No. 41, December 2003, retrieved 1 December 2014, www.aph.gov.au/senate/~/~/link.aspx?_id=0C347E23897C4885BB8B5E5875D21141&_z=z.
57   Russell, 'Economic and Business Aspects', pp. 224, 226–7.

counterpart in Washington. Canberra subsequently sent a delegation led by Michael Thawley to explain the AMS to the State Department. Meeting with Winston Lord, Assistant Secretary of State for East Asian and Pacific Affairs, and Stanley Roth, Senior Director for Asian Affairs at the National Security Council, McCarthy was made aware of American displeasure of their complete lack of information regarding this development.[58] Coming into the position at the end of the Keating era, McCarthy's consummately professional approach undoubtedly facilitated Washington's understanding of the shift in the government's attitude towards the US relationship that was then the product of the domestic political cycle.

McCarthy remained in the post into the Howard Administration, his tenure including Howard's first prime ministerial visit to Washington. He then moved to Jakarta after the department's original choice for the post, Miles Kupa, was denied *agrément* as a result of an in-house assessment he had written that was critical of Suharto's New Order (which, in the event, was only to last until 1998). McCarthy was somewhat less visible than his predecessor, partly because of his status as a professional diplomat, but also as a product of the fact that – with the completion of the Uruguay Round and the creation of the World Trade Organization (WTO) – there was a strong expectation that clearer rules were beginning to emerge that would lead to more harmonious management of bilateral trade differences. Accordingly, McCarthy maintained the trade and Asia focus of his predecessor, the stress on the latter necessitated by Washington's preoccupations at the time with the Balkans. However, his speeches also contained more than a few references to lamb export quotas. His previous postings had provided the basis for a firm grasp of the importance of Congress where he engaged consistently to promote Australia's interests.

He worked to accommodate the new priorities that emerged in Canberra's approach to the alliance. As he later observed: 'There was ... a desire by the new Coalition Govt. to upgrade the security aspects of the relationship. Washington thought it was fine anyway, but agreed they would train a few more marines in Oz if we really wanted that.'[59]

---

58   John McCarthy, seminar, Alfred Deakin Research Institute, 2 October 2014.
59   John McCarthy, personal communication, 23 August 2014.

Such were the beginnings of the current US military presence in Darwin. McCarthy did not serve his full term, leaving in early 1997 to make way for his successor.[60]

In 1997, the precedent set by Richard Gardiner Casey, Percy Spender and Howard Beale was followed by the dispatch of Andrew Peacock (Ambassador 1997–99), former foreign minister and leader of the opposition.[61] Interestingly, McCarthy had served as his private secretary when he was foreign minister. With his long business and social connections with the US, Peacock was particularly skilful in maintaining a guest list of prominent figures in Washington, though there is no suggestion that his relationship with Shirley MacLaine was pursued for diplomatic and media advantage (though it seems to have had that effect). Without Peacock in Washington it is hard to imagine how Howard would have had the opportunity to sit next to the actress at a Foreign Policy Association dinner in New York in 1997.[62] Peacock also found time to pursue his passion for racing, owning a racehorse and regularly visiting the track.

In 1999 Peacock was required to appear before the US International Trade Commission to argue the case against the American industry's demand for restrictive quotas to be placed upon Australian and New Zealand lamb imports.[63] The Prime Minister was due to visit Washington in July, and with exquisite timing the Clinton Administration announced early that month that a new tariff rate would be imposed upon lamb imports, in addition to setting a quota on the basis of 1998 import levels.

When Howard arrived in Washington shortly afterwards, Peacock was able to organise a glittering array of talent at a barbecue at the embassy, the guest list including Secretary of State Madeleine Albright; US Federal Reserve chair, Alan Greenspan; the Mayor of Washington, Tony Williams; and the Secretary of the Interior, Bruce Babbitt. Among the distinguished Australian residents in the US was World Bank President James Wolfensohn. In his talks with the President, however, the Prime Minister could make no progress on mitigating the blow to the lamb

---

60   Peter Edwards to John McCarthy, interview, 25 June 2001, NLA, Canberra.
61   Jennifer Hewett, 'Mr Peacock Goes to Washington', *Sydney Morning Herald*, 28 September 1996; Jennifer Hewett, 'Punting with Peacock', *Sydney Morning Herald*, 21 June 1997, p. 5.
62   Jennifer Hewett, 'Shirley Catches Up on the Snooze', *Sydney Morning Herald*, 2 July 1997, p. 1.
63   Jennifer Hewett, 'Washington Bleats About Lamb Imports', *Sydney Morning Herald*, 27 February 1999, p. 25; John Howard in *Commonwealth Parliamentary Debates*, House of Representatives, 3 June 1999, p. 5990.

industry, despite his forceful presentation of the Australian case.[64] As a sign of the slow but steady evolution of the global trading order, the issue was eventually resolved not by bilateral diplomacy but through the dispute resolution procedures of the WTO.

In September 1999, shortly before he left his post, Peacock helped in Washington to focus American attention on the East Timor issue. According to Howard, he worked with Richard Holbrooke, US Ambassador to the UN, who advised him – with Holbrooke's Bosnian experience in mind – of the importance of a strong mandate for any international force that would enter the territory.[65] In the event, at the UN Australia insisted upon a 'Chapter VII' mandate for INTERFET – that is, the mandate conferred by the UN Charter, Chapter VII, providing for action with respect to threats to the peace, breaches of the peace, and acts of aggression.

Peacock's replacement was Michael Thawley, who though a career diplomat and bureaucrat had been very close to Howard as foreign policy adviser and was thus, to an extent, a conservative equivalent of Russell. When Howard made his visit to Washington in 2001, it was noticed that while the flamboyant *bon viveur* Peacock could only manage two members of Clinton's Cabinet at his barbecue for the Prime Minister, no fewer than six of Bush's Cabinet, along with Vice-President Dick Cheney, attended Thawley's equivalent gathering. While an early media profile described him as 'media shy', he impressed journalists as being extremely focused on marshalling the support of American players in order to maximise the prospects of an FTA:

> [H]e has relentlessly focused on securing a free-trade agreement with the US, helping build a coalition of 120 business groups supporting a deal and calling on members of Congress until they grew tired of him. If there was any criticism of Mr Thawley it was that he had been at times 'too energetic' in his advocacy, said one US official, who has heard as much about the glories of free trade with Australia as he can stand.[66]

---

64   Michelle Grattan, 'Barbeque, Then Lamb Beef with Clinton', *Sydney Morning Herald*, 12 July 1995, p. 5; Michelle Grattan, 'Washington Power Party Puts Andrew in the Pink', *Sydney Morning Herald*, 13 July 1999, p. 2; Jennifer Hewitt, 'Mr Peacock Rules Washington', *Sydney Morning Herald*, 17 July 1999, p. 37.
65   John Howard, *Lazarus Rising. A Personal and Political Autobiography*, HarperCollins, Sydney, 2010, p. 349.
66   Gay Alcorn, 'Free Trade Loser, Barbecue Winner', *Sydney Morning Herald*, 12 September 2001, p. 10.

With an FTA on the agenda (to be realised in 2004), a new era of mutual economic exchange beckoned, though in the interim Thawley found himself making the same arguments as his predecessors on such vexed issues as lamb exports. Giving evidence in 2000 to the US International Trade Commission, he was quoted as arguing forthrightly that '[t]he import restrictions invited questions from many Australians about the sincerity of the US position on international trade'. He posed the question: 'Is the United States in favour of free trade only for itself and not for others?'[67]

In the event, Thawley's evident affinity with Bush and his circle rendered him an ideal appointment for the transformation of the alliance that was to be the product of the September 11 terrorist attacks. Australia's direct invoking of ANZUS has been attributed to his advice. The destabilisation of the entire Middle East was the longer-term result of Bush's policies, as became manifest in events from 2014.

There are two further and final points to ponder regarding this brace of Australia's emissaries. Two – Cook and Thawley – are Geelong Grammar School 'old boys' and Peacock attended Scotch College. If this referent is a measure of membership of the old money elite, then they qualify. A consideration of their subsequent activities throws some additional light on their personal trajectories, and perhaps also on the perspectives they brought to bear on their diplomatic roles. After his retirement from the Department of Foreign Affairs and Trade, McCarthy remained directly active in the foreign policy community, serving as President of the Australian Institute of International Affairs from 2009 to 2015. Following a break during the Howard years, mostly in the financial world abroad, Russell returned to Canberra to serve as a departmental head. Cook retired to the UK, where he had once been Deputy High Commissioner; he has however, in recent years, published some personal commentary on the history of Australian foreign affairs. Having retired from Australian service, Peacock and Thawley took up residence in the US, respectively in Texas and in Washington, the former to attend to his many business interests, the latter to join a fund management entity. While Peacock subsequently had little to say on issues of current policy, Thawley has contributed to the Australian debate – delivering for example the 2005 Annual Menzies Lecture at Monash University –

---

67   Gay Alcorn, 'Hope of No More Clinton Rough Trade', *Sydney Morning Herald*, 15 December 2000, p. 11.

and has also funded an Australia–US research scholarship at the Lowy Institute. He returned to Canberra to head the Department of the Prime Minister and Cabinet in November 2014 in the final months of the Tony Abbott prime ministership.

Conclusions

The bookend years noted at the beginning suggest a significant transition in Australian foreign policy behaviour, namely, from a growing priority on regionalism with an economic focus to a return to the security embrace of the US alliance. From what is on the public record of the activities of Australia's diplomatic emissaries in this period, their roles conformed – in some cases proactively – to the requirements of this transition. Cook was familiar with the Republican 'hard men' at the time of Australia's participation in the first Gulf War, but this was deemed to be of growing irrelevance with the advent of the Clinton Administration and the rise of the regionalist agenda. Russell's close personal relationship with the Prime Minister, as much as his academic and policy backgrounds and activist style, made him a good advocate for Keating's economic objectives. McCarthy's charm and professionalism were indispensable in the transition phase when the Howard Administration was finding its feet in international affairs. Peacock's flamboyance and personal connections with the American business elite gave the embassy a prominence it would not otherwise have had. Thawley's Republican connections served him well especially with the turn to the preoccupation with terrorism.

Yet several cautions are in order for the effectiveness of representation in these years to be correctly judged. For all his cultivation of the media and the Washington policy community, Russell had to battle against the same commercial interests with which Cook had engaged. Despite his visibility, Peacock was still in the same position. With the invoking of ANZUS and the later negotiation of the Australia–US Free Trade Agreement, Thawley's difficulties were hardly apparent in the period under review. However, he was later to be embarrassed by his obligation to defend before a Congressional committee the conduct of the Australian Wheat Board (AWB), which, the Volcker Inquiry subsequently found, had paid – from July 1999 – an estimated AU$29 million to Saddam Hussein's regime in violation of UN sanctions in order to guarantee a continued market for Australian wheat.

If, finally, events in the years 1991 and 1998 are chosen as significant markers of the underlying trend, the narrative takes on quite a different aspect. As has been noted, in 1991 the Hawke Government committed forces to the First Gulf War; in 1998 the Howard Government sent an SAS military contingent to the same theatre in preparation for possible coalition action against the Saddam Hussein regime. Despite all the talk of seeking security in Asia and planning for defence self-reliance, the dispatch of expeditionary forces in support of great power projects remained the preferred response. To be sure, in both of these cases UN legitimation was a factor, yet when it was absent in 2003 it did not prevent resort to the same strategy. The 'Sydney Statement' of 1996 may have been presented as a breakthrough in alliance security cooperation, but it is worth recalling that the 'Agreement Between the Government of Australia and the Government of the United States of America Concerning Reciprocal Defense Procurement' was originally a proposal of Labor Defence Minister Robert Ray in 1995; though it was signed as a memorandum at the AusMin of that year it did not clear Congressional approval until after the start of the new millennium. And a further note of continuity can be detected in the outcome of the issue that appeared set to embarrass all those involved in the AWB scandal; despite harsh words while in opposition – including making the point that the issue was potentially damaging to relations with the US – the Rudd and Gillard administrations did not pursue the matter once they occupied the government benches.

12

Reflections: From 1940 to the post-9/11 world[1]

Kim Beazley
Australian Ambassador
to the United States, 2010–16

Every student of Australian foreign policy is aware of wartime Prime Minister John Curtin's 'turning to America' article in the *Herald* on 27 December 1941. It was dramatic, yet I don't think as dramatic as Curtin's short speech to the House of Representatives during the Battle of the Coral Sea in May 1942. That was more redolent of immediate danger delivered as it was at a non-conclusive point in the action:

> As I speak those who are participating in the action [Australian but overwhelmingly American sailors] are conforming to the sternest discipline and are subjecting themselves with all they have – it may be for many of them the 'last full measure of their devotion' – to accomplish the increased safety and security of this territory.[2]

This was reality, not projection, or analysis of future strategy. Here, six months after war on Japan had been declared, American ships were blocking a Japanese attack on Australia's bastion in Port Moresby.

---

1   This reflection was written in October 2014.
2   John Curtin in *Commonwealth Parliamentary Debates*, House of Representatives, 8 May 1942, retrieved via Hansard, 17 July 2015, parlinfo.aph.gov.au/parlInfo/genpdf/hansard80/hansardr80/1942-05-08/0121/hansard_frag.pdf;fileType=application%2Fpdf.

Those ships were fighting in what is now Australia's Exclusive Economic Zone. Bombers out of Queensland were joining in. One could not have had a more dramatic changing of the guard a few months after the ignominious collapse of Singapore.

Coral Sea is a misty part of the commemorative calendar in Australian official life. For ambassadors here in the US it resonates with clarity. Its commemoration here is in the hands of our Naval Attaché. It is recognised by a dinner or reception that attracts each year the most senior American naval representatives. Its 70th anniversary, which occurred soon after I arrived, also saw a major event at the US Naval Memorial. Americans take commemoration more seriously than we do. They avidly read the historical pamphlets the embassy produces for them and it sits in the minds of our American political and defence interlocutors. A commemorative coin helps, and skilfully distributed here it breaks through the cloud of a myriad of concerning global issues dominating American minds to help keep our agenda on the US table.

I think of Curtin a great deal while I am here. Reminders occur all the time. The Curtin–MacArthur relationship was a big feature of a conference in Milwaukee, Wisconsin, in 2014 commemorating the General's life. One of the 'big books' this year, the must reads for US political types, is British historian Nigel Hamilton's *The Mantle of Command*. Hamilton deals with Franklin Delano Roosevelt's strategic leadership in the first two years of the US' World War II. I suspect Hamilton's work reflects the first sign that we are distant enough from World War II to dispense with sentimentality in our historiography. Though he admires Winston Churchill, he roasts him. His analysis of the collapse of Britain's capacity to defend Australia is devastating. His detailing of the meticulous American focus on blocking a Japanese capacity to isolate Australia is thought-provoking.[3]

One million American service personnel passed through Australia in World War II. We were commanded by an American General, Douglas MacArthur, but until 1944, when the Philippines were recovered, we contributed the majority of his troops. Important though the US was for our equipment, a unique feature of Australia's war was that, unlike any other American ally, we supplied US fighting forces with the bulk

---

3   Nigel Hamilton, *The Mantle of Command, FDR at War, 1941–1942*, Houghton Mifflin Harcourt, Boston and New York, 2014.

of their logistics. Politically we were intensely focused on securing an American priority on our region both during and after the war and ensuring we had feet under the deliberative table.

Our early representatives to the US, Keith Officer, Richard Casey, Owen Dixon, Frederic Eggleston and, immediately postwar, Norman Makin, had to build an infrastructure of interconnections from scratch to make the shift to a massive web of infrastructure from nothing. It was a simpler time, with minds concentrated by war, but I don't know how they did it. They laboured under the political handicap that our American General was unpopular in Washington DC, and after the early emergency the US Navy that dominated the Pacific War wanted the fight back on a trajectory from the central Pacific, not the southwest. This might explain something of our unique role as an American supplier. Now we are intricately embedded in decision-making points in the US bureaucracy. Then, the US interlocutors were getting to grips with the fact that Australians were approaching them from somewhere other than the British embassy.

I rehearse this period because I argue that until this point we have never been as close to American priorities, or they more important to us, as was the case then. That has now changed. The first charge on our ambassador here is to completely understand their country's strategic situation and how it fits into American global priorities. The first surprise for me working back into the alliance brief was the realisation that the alliance was more important to us now than was the case in the Cold War. I was our last Cold War Defence Minister.

Then the joint facilities we hosted were critical to the US strategic deterrent and the US–Soviet discussion on controlling the arms race between them. On this basis we became a nuclear target and accepted this because the nuclear balance was critical to the avoidance of global nuclear devastation. The relationship produced benefits. We gained first-class intelligence on our region and more broadly. Likewise access to quality military equipment – the type that really worked – and training. We had the deterrent effect of a powerful ally. All of this was very useful. Our region, however, was not heavily challenging. Our gross domestic product (GDP) at the time that we wrote our 1987 Defence White Paper was greater than that of the Association of Southeast Asian Nations (ASEAN) combined and not far behind China (who hardly featured in the paper at all). In the area of military equipment, the US material was good. European equipment was, however, highly competitive: we preferred an Austrian individual weapon for the Army to an American one. On balance it could be said that, with nuclear factors considered, the US consumed our security – unusual for a Western ally. Committed as we were to the Western side in the frozen global architecture of the Cold War, the challenge for Australian statespersons was not how close we were to the US (we were close enough), but how we created space in our region and globally for Australian initiatives.

Things have changed dramatically. International structures and relationships (including alliances) are more fluid. Nuclear issues are not so prominent now. Crisis events that engage the US see it seeking much more complex foreign political arrangements. They seek partners beyond old allies. Keeping the attention of a much busier, more internally disputatious ally, is a difficult exercise. More important, the defence focus among our regional neighbours has changed markedly. No longer do they concentrate on internal security. Force projection interests them as they contemplate disputed borders. Something of an arms race in the region is underway. Improved economies drive this. Indonesia alone now of ASEAN partners is passing our GDP.

In the 20 years since the fall of the Berlin Wall there has been a military technological revolution. Just as maintaining a technological edge in our region has become difficult and critical, the capacities built into weapons platforms by the US has moved substantially ahead of its competitors. Nowhere can the consequences of this be more clearly seen than in the massive upgrade of our air defence. We are tracking for the best air defence we have had. Satellite surveillance, a product of the US intelligence partner, provides a strategic picture of the region. Our world-class over-the-horizon radar for strategic/tactical purposes was developed in the first instance with the US Airborne Early Warning aircraft, ASW/general surveillance aircraft, F-18 classic fighters, Super Hornet fighter bombers, Growlers, F-35s for strike – all of this massive capability is American. No more Mirages and Canberra bombers. Our strike and surveillance aircraft in the US order of battle are operated by the US Navy. As a result we are the US Navy's top foreign military sales partner.

The US security guarantee, whatever the argument about its applicability in various circumstances, immensely complicates the calculations of any potentially hostile nations in our region. The joint facilities are still important to our allies and ourselves. At least for the moment they are no longer nuclear targets. Whereas they constituted overwhelmingly

America's main interest in us, this is now balanced by the growing significance to the US of our zone. The US during the Cold War focused on Europe, North Asia and the Middle East. We inhabited a strategic backwater influenced further by discomfort suffered by the US in the Vietnam War. Now we are the southern tier of the new centre of American attention. Asia drives global prosperity and the US is responding. We are a more significant ally geographically than at any time since World War II. Just as the US is devising more complex ways of assessing the friendship of other powers, we have their heightened attention. It is argued that our proximity to the US burdens our relations with the region. As during the Cold War, our alliance is at least a private comfort to most in the region. Those locally who argue the opposite have a multiplicity of reasons for doing so. Among them none has the notion that by advocating more distance for Australia from its US ally they are improving Australian security.

Coming in as Ambassador, I have been challenged by the fact the US is more important to us, but at the same time there is more internal American argument about American priorities (including a serious isolationist stance among some powerful players). The US also confronts multiple crises in which it is expected to play a role. It looks for friends in all of them, and but can fit them into no ready paradigm as was the case during the Cold War. Alliance management for the US has become more difficult as it has become more important. What the US wants in a situation is harder to predict, changes more frequently, but requests of friends are nevertheless emphatic. Australian interests (beyond the general one of wishing the US success) are less easy to calculate. As the relationship has become more critical it has become more complex.

This is a picture the Ambassador to the US has at the back of their mind as they approach their representational task. One thing that is important to understand is that I do not represent the Australian people. The Australian Government represents the Australian people. The ambassador represents the government. The full title of an ambassador has not left its centuries-old nomenclature. Ambassadors once had the power to make wars and treaties. That is not so now. The ambassador is a cog in a giant wheel of policy advice and delivery. Through driving exercises in public diplomacy and in arguing the case privately, there is ample opportunity to present a unique perspective on the setting and history of the points at issue. The policy, however, comes from only one source: the government at home represented by its ministers. The most critical moments organisationally during the year revolve around prime ministerial and ministerial visits. Foreign ministers, trade ministers and defence ministers are most important but all ministers are significant. The visits by principals are helpful for many reasons not least because they force an ambassador to update their understanding of subtle policy changes or new policies.

When representation first began here, ministerial control and direction was distant and light. Arguably the most significant ambassador we have had here was in the 1950s, Sir Percy Spender. The then government allowed him a licence on all fronts (including treaty-making) that would have made him recognisable to a 19th-century plenipotentiary. My circumstances are very different.

The first humbling thing for an ex-minister to note is that your ministerial equivalents here barely want to talk to you (Hillary Clinton was a little different on this) but are very prepared to phone their counterparts in Australia. We have to work harder to get up a prime ministerial–presidential call, but when it comes, as with the ministerial calls, we are not on either end of the conversation. We are not always in the know when a conversation takes place. We receive summaries from both ends that are useful on detail but negligible in tone. Politicians and some public servants are active communicators with their American friends. Ministers not only reach their counterparts but delve into other areas of government, notably Congress and down the administration hierarchies. Particularly in the White House and the National Security Council (NSC), senior officials would rather talk to a senior adviser to the minister or Prime Minister than the Ambassador. Thankfully they still answer their emails (sooner or later).

In my time, the most extensive extra-ambassadorial communicator was former prime minister Kevin Rudd. He was nonstop at all levels and branches of government. So ubiquitous was he that, when he briefly returned to office, excited individuals at the White House said they were forming the Rudd Letter Committee. That was brought into existence, they assured me previously, because it was the only way to handle the regular written communication from the Prime Minister.

While this leadership communication creates information problems in the embassy, it is an unmitigated good thing. Our comfort matters little. Rapport between principals matters a great deal. Ministers, prime ministers, secretaries and presidents think outside their briefing notes.

They know the real decision-makers better than their public servants, probably before they get into office and certainly after six months in it. Second-track diplomacy bodies like the Australian American Leadership Dialogue have been invaluable in this regard. The job of the Ambassador is to work with it.

Australians and the Australian media are fascinated by the proximity of Australian leaders to their American colleagues. In my time in politics and since, the closest relationship was between John Howard and George W Bush. That relationship was forged during Howard's presence in the US during the 9/11 atrocity. It deepened with the war in Afghanistan and then the war in Iraq. Bush is a man who seeks deep friendships and appreciated them when politically embattled here.

The nearest equivalent was the relationship between Bob Hawke and George Shultz (Secretary of State, not President). That friendship was crucial when Hawke sought to extract Australia's support for a test of the then developmental MX missile. At the time the US was placing medium-range cruise missiles in Britain and foreshadowing the deployment of Pershing missiles in Europe. These posed political problems of enormous dimensions. A test seemed paltry alongside those commitments. Hawke persuaded Shultz that to persist would bring the joint facilities into more intense political debate in Australia. Shultz overrode the objections in his own department and the Pentagon. When the Reagan Administration departed, Schultz left. By then, Hawke had substantial international stature, which made him a strong partner for the new President, George HW Bush. This was intensified by support during the Kuwait War.

Paul Keating was a kindred spirit, in many ways, with another visceral politician in Bill Clinton. The three prime ministers I have served have all in their different ways enjoyed good relations with President Barack Obama. His associations are more cerebral. The current Prime Minister, Tony Abbott, though of a different political persuasion, has nevertheless managed a strong relationship. The search for MH370 has been a source of fascination here. The shooting down of MH17 and Prime Minister Abbott's response to it has evoked great sympathy in the administration. The developing picture in Iraq and Syria has started to assume some of the character of engagement in relationships manifest in the previous involvements in Iraq and Kuwait. Already there seems a more intense relationship developing between the President and those at the forefront of his coalition. It has certainly lifted the already high appreciation the President has of his relationship with Prime Minister Abbott. It seems mutual engagement in conflict is the catalyst for the type of interpersonal relationship the public expects. Foreign ministers' personal engagement is also important. All have been well-placed here. In recent times the current minister, Julie Bishop, has developed a particularly close relationship with Secretary Kerry. Possibly his deep engagement in the Middle East has helped. He needs good interlocutors in the Indo-Pacific region.

There is another reason the phenomenon of close prime ministerial and ministerial engagement in which the embassy may be out of the contact loop does not matter. We are essential to building structure beneath the policy formulations of ministers. This can only be done by an embassy. To sustain serious policy initiatives and functional connections requires deep, detailed work often across countries. Sustained activity in the embassy generates, or contributes to, well-constructed solutions. This is particularly so when engagement in military conflict is involved, or a major policy initiative has to have meat added to it to make it work, or when our ally's or our minds need to be changed. A continual drumbeat on this front has been provided by the conflict in Afghanistan. Likewise has been the development of the so-called 'pivot' in US policy to an Asia-Pacific priority. Currently underway is an intense campaign to secure an agreement for the Trans-Pacific Partnership and trade agreement and see it through Congress. These will be discussed with other matters below.

In pursuing our supportive diplomacy it is worth looking at our current assets. When I came here, the embassy was our second biggest (Indonesia was our largest). With the integration of AusAID into the Department of Foreign Affairs and Trade (DFAT), we have dropped to third (Papua New Guinea moved ahead). Our personnel by function break down this way: Defence has 104, DFAT has 107, Intelligence, Police and Customs have 15, Immigration has 19, Austrade have 12, Agricultural/Treasury/ The Australian National University (ANU)/Education/Industry has 12. A-based staff at Post number 93, locally engaged 176. Of the 93, 48 are Defence. Defence has 496 attached to the embassy out-posted and Customs and Attorney-General's 3.

Another asset is our property. We have good entertainment spaces. We are able to stage substantial cultural outreach in them and we are a popular location for social events. For officers, we are within walking distance of State, White House, Treasury and the Eisenhower

Building. The chancery is tired and its replacement has been announced. Increasingly, we have been using the Ambassador's Residence as a multifunctional representational asset. Until the middle of 2015 we have had in my time 600 events at the residence. It is a representational machine with a small staff. My wife has devoted herself to improving its grounds and entertainment spaces. Most of these events are the types of functions one would expect at a residence – receptions, formal meals, garden parties. Increasingly, however, we are using the residence for conferences. Particularly noteworthy, as the US honed the direction of its diplomacy in Southeast Asia, are informal conferences on East Asian issues. They have been held with staff from US State, White House, Pentagon and Intelligence officials with Australian counterparts. They provided a mechanism for very frank exchange. That has been broadened out into gatherings advancing the national security and trade agendas. Mostly activity has been of the dimension of my predecessors (though they did better with presidents than me). With the possible exception of the Indonesians and the British, no embassy in my time here uses its residence as opposed to its chancery as much as we do for these purposes.

This representational effort is much enhanced by our cultural and public diplomacy effort. Spaces at the chancery are well used by the cultural effort to display the work of talented Australian artists, photographers and filmmakers. Particularly anticipated is the annual (for a period of a few months) display of Indigenous art and the Anzac exhibition. The latter is often assisted by the Australian War Memorial and the period around Anzac Day heavily engages our American national security counterparts. Spaces at the residence and chancery feature from time to time Australian musical talent. We also host Australians who are performing in venues in Washington. Performances by the Sydney and Melbourne Theatre Companies in my time have been a critical part of our Congressional outreach. More generally, this showcases us having a sophisticated cultural excellence. Figures such as Cate Blanchett, Jacki Weaver and Tommy Emmanuel have been prominent in my time and writers such as Richard Flanagan have featured.

A decade ago then Los Angeles Consul-General, John Olsen, started a celebrity-filled gala under the headline 'G'Day LA'. We showed off talented (mainly cinematic arts and music) Australians for one of the hottest tickets in town. This has now branched out into a 'G'Day USA' rubric. It covers not only the original purpose but now a series of galas, seminars and promotions across the country. The seminars showcase

Australian industry and academia. It is a sophisticated public diplomacy attracting more and more serious American participation. It shows us to be problem-solvers (drought, water and energy) and technologically masterful (niche manufacturing and services). As I will mention below, Australian funds and companies are becoming big players in the US, well beyond what can be usefully managed or value-added by the embassy. What we do achieve is focusing our heavy economic engagement with an Australian brand name. Our public diplomacy section and Austrade take the lead here and the Defence Industry branch is also deeply involved. The chancery and residence further enhance this rounded and capable image with philanthropic activity. We provide space for fundraisers both directly and through prized auction meals prepared by our well-reputed residence chef.

I will not do all of the embassy's activity justice because I will not focus on the activities of the non-defence, foreign affairs and trade agencies. All of them use the residence and chancery actively to further critical elements of the Australian agenda. Treasury is immensely active with its counterpart here. Their representative spends much time in New York and with international agencies like the International Monetary Fund (IMF) and World Bank. The Treasurer's attendance at IMF meetings is a big event here. Likewise our outreach in the education, science, law enforcement and customs areas. Our agricultural representative is to the forefront of battles to get Australian product in. Those fights we have with the Americans are most potent in the agricultural and trade area. Our people are a tough bunch. Immigration also has a significant clientele here. The ambassador is engaged with all agencies. At different points of time they all confront issues that require an ambassador's attention. There simply isn't the space to cover things here.

Aside from consular activities, the heart of an embassy's activity is political reporting. This is essentially the function of DFAT officials here but all agencies contribute. A weekly meeting of division heads ensures sufficient knowledge of each other's priorities across agencies and functions so those reporting know where possibly valuable information might be obtained to add to the comprehensiveness of information being sent home. A critical 'enabler' at the DC embassy is the Congressional branch. A creation of the 1990s, its responsibility is monitoring Congress and, more broadly, American domestic politics. Congress is the coequal branch of government. Its legislation and deliberations impact heavily on Australian interests in the US, the capacities at the heart of American national security policy and pressures on all of the most sensitive aspects of US foreign policy. It is a branch whose intricate relationships with a large array of Congressional staff sees it much under pressure from all agencies to advance legislative causes where appropriate and argument generally. The embassy has its own in-house lobbying firm.

It is information that is on a routine basis the most valuable deliverable to Australia from the alliance. The US–Australia population ratio is roughly 15 to one. When the population of the agencies that drive US foreign, national security, international economic, and intelligence product is calculated, the ratio is more like 50 to one. The Office of the US Trade Representative would be as big as DFAT. Spending on defence in Australia is far exceeded by expenditure on intelligence in the US alone. There is virtually no issue around the globe on which Australian decision-makers would not like an understanding of American knowledge and views. In my pre-briefing before posting the issue pushed first for my attention was nuclear development in Iran. Of particular concern was to discern whether the red lines might be that which could trigger pre-emptive attacks on the capability. A casual glance at the Australian media of the day would not have suggested that would likely be my charge. The consequence of any activity, however, would substantially impact Australian (let alone the globe's) interests. There were not many other sources of serious information on the matter available to us than what could be gleaned from the US.

Australian citizens are better travelled and more globally focused than the average American. Our politicians and foreign agencies are very well-informed. We are probably, pound for pound, more global citizens than any other country. Nothing we do compares with the weight brought to an issue by our US counterparts. The benefit of the longstanding alliance is that we are easily inserted into the US information chain almost as though we are US nationals. For example, when the democratic demonstrations broke out in Cairo's Tahrir Square, the embassy sent 42 cables to Australia in the first week. Deep bonds of acquaintance and friendship existed between Americans inside government, previously in government, in think tanks with what might be described as the deep state in Egypt. No open source reporting, close though it was, on the situation in Cairo got anywhere near the details and nuance available to the US on a moment-by-moment basis. Intelligence failure is always bewailed in Washington. When examined, however, it never shows an absence of information. That is copious. It is always failure to join the dots.

As substantial an example, in its way, as the experience with Cairo was the tsunami and nuclear crisis in Japan. Here we were well-informed but the US adds another dimension. At an early point, the US had noted our public statements on the Japanese coping. I was called in by the administration, concerned that our public statements reflected our state of knowledge. Sat in a corner and permitted to read technically unavailable documents, I was given a picture of very serious difficulties being experienced by those managing the nuclear component of the crisis. My reporting was not welcomed in all circles at home. Fortunately for me, public reporting caught up a couple of days later with what we had been given. In any crisis situation, whether or not the US has human assets receiving critical information, it has a vast array of technical assets available to it. The world is well aware of the fact but not of how good it is. The observable does not indicate of itself intent, but it certainly can tabulate the problem.

One region where we approach American capacity is in the Asia-Pacific. Our information is strongly based on an extensive network of diplomatic resources, business connections, defence activities (our other major military alliance is the Five Power Defence arrangement that includes Malaysia and Singapore), and academic study. On the latter, ANU has the largest collection of Pacific scholars of any university on earth and is represented at the embassy. The US regards our advice to them as a strong quid pro quo for what they provide us. They frequently are over-deferential, not so much on Southeast Asia but on North Asia.

We do have a deep understanding of North Asian, particularly Chinese, affairs. Nothing we have approaches the extensive interpersonal relations of interested American politicians, businessmen and think tankers. We know the questions to ask and have great analytical skills. Americans live with the people they study largely because the people they study want to live with them. I have been taken aback by under-the-radar holidaying by the odd senior Chinese official with the Bush family for example. The way think tankers here quietly expect to drop in on senior Chinese officials, former and present, or dine privately with Japanese prime ministers and ministers is staggering. They think that we do that routinely. We don't, but we don't disabuse them. Members of Congress interested in foreign policy follow a similar path.

Washington is home to over 200 think tanks and like operations. Hanging about in DC private operations is the last administration and the next few. Decision-makers and advisers to the current administration reach out to the private sector every time serious matters are under consideration. Information is king and it is ubiquitous in this town. Global personal networking produces a different style of operation for American decision-makers. Our leaders do it but they tend to come new to it when they take office.

It is easier for Americans because power attracts. Our style is to work through our material, arrive at an Australian position and then seek to engage our foreign interlocutors with the mutually beneficial product of our conclusions. The American method is to envelop the situation with the concentration of a large number of minds and agencies and advance it with senior officials who likely have deep knowledge of the players. One of the factors in the current Secretary of State's deep engagement with the Middle East and Europe is that he knows so many players personally and has known them for a long time. Hillary Clinton's advantage in China was that she was in a similar position. The US is often frustrated. In part that is because there is a high level of expectation that an outcome can be managed. We have the comfort of modest expectations. If you are intimate with the Americans and trusted, and we are, you have access to extraordinary information. Few around the globe feel it is vital to engage us if we are in a quarrel or tangential to the issue. Most want to engage the Americans no matter what. When that is not the case, and the US is just starting to get comfortable in Southeast Asia, their expectation of us is that we can deliver a product to them such as they are capable of delivering to us. On Southeast Asia we make it.

More than in any other Australian embassy our engagement with the US is military. There are over 500 Australian Defence personnel in the US spread across half the states. The majority are embedded in US units or working alongside US equivalents on combined project teams, covering a wide range of US military activity. This includes operational planning and intelligence, capability and development, military education and legal support. Over 100 are in the Washington area. A third are embedded personnel, a third liaison, with the remaining third representative or executive positions. Our intelligence profile is similar. Some have found themselves working on the most sensitive projects, including the US equivalent of our Defence White Papers.

Hawaii is a major centre. We now have 36 staff operating in Pacific Command (PACOM) and rising. They include the Deputy Commanding General of the US Army in the Pacific. PACOM is the go-to point for much of our exercise activity. In Australia in 2013, that involved 21,000 US personnel and 7,000 Australian Defence Force. Our Consul-General in Hawaii is de facto ambassador to PACOM. Of all our consulates, it does the heaviest political reporting.

Thirteen per cent of our defence budget is spent in the US. Defence military and civilian personnel are heavily engaged in managing that, with substantial involvement in acquisition projects, advancing Australian defence industry and deep collaboration on science. Currently, 469 Foreign Military Sales cases are under management with a combined portfolio value of US$18.7 billion. To digress, science is an area of substantial growing collaboration. China is the first or second trading partner of most countries, including the US and ourselves. The US is the primary research partner of most. We punch above our weight. We have the world's 13th-largest economy but we are the eighth-largest research partner of the US. Advancing this is increasingly engaging embassy time.

While Australia's defence decision points are obviously in Australia, they are still advanced in the US. Though Defence in the embassy is largely self-sufficient, the Ambassador is frequently engaged when there is an impasse, with intelligence product, and when an issue involves the broader national security community in Canberra. We are a go-to point when the F-35 program hits snags or when Americans become engaged competitively over buys of earlier generation fighters as interim measures. I have been engaged in frequent discussions on American support for our submarine project. I was delighted to visit Electric Boat in Connecticut and be shown over the USS *Missouri*, a new *Virginia*-class submarine. The young captain in the control room asked me if I recognised it. I said it looked like the equivalent area of a *Collins*-class submarine. 'Yes,' he said, 'it is just like it'. According to him, he thought our submarine had provided a useful test bed for their new class. He had served as an exchange officer on an Australian submarine, which he thought was 'just the best'. The embassy is indispensable in the management of complex projects.

A couple of examples illustrate the importance of an embassy contribution to advancing or resolving key parts of Australian engagement. Afghanistan is managed out of the DFAT political side and Defence. There is a triangular exchange between agencies on the ground in Afghanistan, Canberra and here with major input from our NATO embassy in Brussels. Other European capitals are involved too. Early in my time here we were much involved in the changes in Uruzgan province following and during Dutch withdrawal from an operation they had commanded. US focus was on persuading the Dutch to stay. Ours was on the practical arrangements needed as we assessed the Dutch determination. This produced a little tension, largely managed here. The US wanted Australian command if the Dutch exited. We were prepared to provide it on the civilian side and were prepared to be Military Deputy and provide much of the command personnel on the military side. We wanted to ensure access to American enablers to replace the Dutch. Our judgement was that would best come with an American commander, though we provided the lion's share of the troops. The Americans eventually agreed, though that required a 'full court press' from each leg of the triangle and Brussels. On Afghan matters, I became immensely impressed with my other political colleague, Brendan Nelson, at NATO Headquarters.

We also were involved in the decision to permit the Australian-trained Afghan National Security Forces (ANSF) 4th Brigade to operate outside the confines of Uruzgan. This disturbed some in the political leadership in Australia but was much wanted by the US and the ANSF. Our reporting was heavily involved in the ultimate favourable decision to deploy outside Uruzgan. The key decision-making on American decisions on the build-up and the current withdrawal was done in the NSC in the White House. Here we were treated to considerable knowledge of the various phases of US decision-making well in advance of final determinations. We still are. There have been few surprises for us in the critical decisions there. We were also heavily involved in deliberations over the post-2014 aid package for the ANSF. The US was attempting to obtain US$2 billion from its allies. They hoped for US$100 million a year (over three years) from us. Our starting point was US$50 million. As the Chicago NATO meeting approached the US was anxious for someone to 'bell the cat'. To their relief, the well-advised then Prime Minister Tony Abbott arrived with US$100 million. This and future commitments is a continuing story. The US remains anxious for continued allied support both with the money and with remnant troops. While planning is a Pentagon matter, the decider resides in the White House. Something similar is evolving with Iraq. With the NSC involved, the Ambassador is heavily engaged.

Another example on a defence matter was the ratification of the Defence Trade Cooperation Treaty in 2010. Signed by Bush and Howard in 2007, it had largely lain dormant. This was a task for Congressional branch. Our activity was somewhat controversial here as there was a local preference for Congressional lobbying to be done by administration personnel. It was not a matter that could be left at that. I had to be involved with extensive lobbying of members of both houses on both sides of the aisle. Even more extensive was the work done with relevant staffers, particularly with Republicans and with the Senate Foreign Relations Committee.

The blockage point was a belief that the language in the preamble agreed by the administration usurped the Senate's authority. Senatorial courtesy assigned great weight to the ranking Republican Senator, Richard Lugar, without whose support Chairman Senator Kerry was reluctant to move. Our focus with members of Congress and staff was on advocacy for movement on this point. In some ways lobbying was easier for us than the administration, viewed by some in Congress in a more partisan way. It helped that the treaty's origins were in a Republican Administration.

Acceptability was gradually achieved. High drama started on the day the treaty was to be passed. We had cabled Canberra the night before that the deal was done. We were horrified to receive a call (to Jan Hutton, then head of the Congressional branch) that a 'secret hold' had been placed by a senator on discussion. The staffer explained to Jan that any senator could do this on any item on the Senate agenda, on any day, without a reason given or the senator identified. He promised to get back to us as the issue developed. He phoned later to say that the hold had 'disappeared' (not withdrawn) and the matter went to a successful vote. Good things were said about Australia as it went through. Much of it was around the staunch character of Australia as an ally.

It was a good example of the need to get all our Congressional ducks lined up, advocating our interests with both Democrats and Republicans, with leadership, committees, as well as tangential senators who sometimes signal an interest in particular issues. Even having done that, it is largely left to the Senate gods to determine whether something will be passed or not. We never did get to the bottom of the last blockage. Most likely it was, in issue terms, unrelated. Likely a senator looking to cut a deal on some other piece of business they wanted to progress.

That decision taken in the 1990s to establish a Congressional branch has made us much more effective. Relations with members of Congress is largely a matter for ambassadors. We are the only ones they will see. However, the detailed work of Congress is done by their vastly underpaid (by our standards) staffers. Without them onside, little useful can be achieved even when their employers are willing.

Probably the most important event in my time as Ambassador to this point was the determination by the administration to 'pivot', or what is now known as the American 'rebalance', its priorities to Asia. That was symbolised by the President on his visit to Australia by his announcement of a rotation of a Marine brigade through Darwin. When I arrived I was immediately chastised by the administration for the then government's advocacy of an Asia-Pacific community not unlike the European Union. It was pointed out that no one in Asia supported it and we were talking above ourselves.

We pushed back. We pointed out this was about them, not us. We believed, as Australian governments had always argued since World War II, that the US needed to institutionally embed itself in the Asia-Pacific (or as we prefer, Indo-Pacific) region. The community idea was quietly dropped and American membership of the East Asian summit substituted. Much of the heavy lifting for this within the administration was done by Kurt Campbell (then Assistant Secretary in State for the East Asia and the Pacific) and Tom Donilon (then National Security Advisor, who was particularly focused on the Sino-American relationship).

It came to a head prior to a visit by Secretary of State Clinton to a meeting of the ASEAN Regional Forum. She had prepared the ground by attaching the US to the Malaysian-initiated treaty of Amity and Cooperation. Jeffrey Bader's book *Obama and China's Rise* contains a good chapter (ch. 9) on this from a White House point of view.[4] In mid-2010, Obama presided over a moot among his staff two days before the Secretary was due to leave. On one side was State and the relevant section of NSC. On the other was Treasury, his economic advisers and his schedulers. The economists wanted to focus on APEC. The schedulers thought the President needed another overseas commitment like he needed a hole in the head. We did whatever we

---

4   Jeffrey A. Bader, *Obama and China's Rise: An Insider's Account of America's Asia Strategy*, Brookings Institute Press, Washington DC, 2012.

could to bolster the pro-East Asia Summit (EAS) side of the argument. The President sided with his foreign policy advisers. His agreement was made with the understanding he would need to attend EAS meetings.

As American engagement deepens, all relevant Australian decisions are taken by Australian ministers. Their nuance on features of American engagement, particularly as they bump up against initiatives by China, is vigorously conveyed by those of us engaged in the political section of the embassy here. A week never goes by without cables home reporting facets of American engagement and the results of our own messaging.

The most significant vehicle at the moment for the next phase of American engagement sits with Trade Minister Andrew Robb and our trade negotiators in Canberra: the Trans-Pacific Partnership Treaty (TPP). For myself, the trade section of the embassy and the Congressional branch, the job is to back up the minister and DFAT with advocacy, in Congress in particular. We try to keep track of the detail, conscious of the fact we are not direct players. The minister has developed a significant relationship with his American trade counterpart, Mike Froman.

In DC, the ambassadors of the TPP partners have formed an informal group aimed at engaging collectively and individually members of Congress who, in the end, will determine American membership. We are well served by the presence of New Zealand Ambassador, Mike Moore, once Prime Minister of New Zealand and head of the World Trade Organization. He and I are advantaged in Congress by having once been legislators. We are keenly aware of trade agreement aversion among those in Congress sensitive to constituents who feel US employment has been adversely affected by global free trade arrangements.

We point out to our counterparts that the collapse of the American middle-class relativities over the last 30 years has compromised the ability of domestic consumption to drive American growth. The best chance for American producers to drive local jobs and wealth is for the trade rules in the dominant Asian market to reflect the long-term American advocacy of global free trading arrangements. Congress is only dimly aware of the massive growth of the Asian middle class: now some 580 million (20 per cent of the global middle class), to near 3 billion (or 60 per cent) over the next 15 years. This is critical for the life chances of the next generation of American workers. We have the best lobbying assets among the relevant embassies when combined with our trade branch.

More generally, we are sensitive to the fears of our Asian colleagues that the US rebalance has been sidetracked by events in the Middle East and Europe. Certainly they absorb a substantial amount of Presidential and Secretary of State time (as they do for our Prime Minister and minister, and increasingly, ours in the embassy). But they are a product of the fact that the US is a global power – the unique attribute the US brings to its operation in Asia. It is baggage the US must carry with it. Insofar as there is security of energy supplies tied up in it, Asia has a deep interest in American focus on the Middle East. Asia is now 70 per cent of the Middle East region's oil market, headed to over 90 per cent over the next decade or so. Of all the powers, including China, only the US can affect outcomes that secure the source and sea-lanes. If there is any silver lining to the horror of contemporary events in the Middle East, it is producing a dramatic shift in what was the drift in American public opinion towards isolationism. The international engagement argument is easier now than at any point in my near five years here.

Little of the national security/defence issues have surprised me here. The one surprise on this front has been the discovery that we are much more closely engaged with the US in intelligence and military activity than was the case when I was Defence Minister. What has been a complete surprise has been to see how deep and growing is our economic involvement, a product in particular of the facilitation of investment produced by the free trade agreement negotiated during the time of the Howard Government. I have not been able to produce anything equivalent to the brilliance of my predecessor Michael Thawley's lobby for that agreement, though we will need to for the TPP.

By a large margin, the US is our most important partner in direct and indirect investment. The US investment in us is over US$650 billion, much larger than its investment in China. Ours is AU$430 billion in the US, and, over the last three years, growing faster than investment the other way. That is more than 10 times our investment in China. Indirect investment is very important for us. Though we have the third-largest pool of investment globally, most of it resides in the management of our superannuation funds. The US is a safe haven and easily accessed. Nevertheless, about 10,000 Australian companies do business here, many of them establishing production facilities in the US and outlets. The US gives such Australian companies economy of scale. We have some notables. Westfield is the second-biggest shopping centre owner here. BHP-Billiton and its partners produce 25 per cent of the oil extracted from the Mexican Gulf. It is also the largest foreign investor in the American shale oil and gas revolution. Boral is the biggest brick manufacturer. Lend-Lease manages a large share of American defence housing.

Those are the large stories. The smaller ones are more typical. Australian high-technology manufacturers are accessing the US venture capital industry, the world's largest. We are becoming skilled niche manufacturers. That is particularly noticeable in defence-related product (see the 19 Australian companies directly and indirectly engaged in the manufacture of the F-35). The embassy's public diplomacy, particularly through the 'G'Day USA' campaign, is increasingly engaged with Australian manufacturers and service providers.

This is a very big story but largely ignored in Australia. We are much more focused on our trade and investment relationship with Asia. That is a good thing strategically (and a good selling point for Australia here) and will be ultimately good economically. Investment flows, however, to where it is easily profitable and safely accommodated. It is difficult to see any other country as favourably placed as the US any time in the near future.

These examples give a flavour of operations at our embassy here. They don't remotely tell the whole story. I guess if I totalled the percentage of my activity directly related to them it would be around 10 per cent. However, they usefully illustrate how the embassy now operates. I have to be humble about this. Australian influence in this town fluctuates. We were probably at a peak in the 1950s. There are nearly five times the number of countries represented now in DC than there were then. The leisure that would see a Secretary of State and senior members of Congress dine with us regularly has disappeared. We get a lot from Congress but not with the numbers we got then. Embassies are not the socially attractive institutions they once were. Ambassadors now get very excited when a member of Congress or a senior administration official shows up for an event like a national day. Only the British, Chinese, Israeli, French and some Middle Eastern embassies show greater numbers than us.

On the other hand, demand for our presence in think tanks and peak institutions is growing. There is an insatiable hunger for being talked at in this town. As they follow the American 'rebalance' towards Asia, these bodies crave frank and detailed information. We have a reputation for providing it. This is not only about ourselves but also about others.

I have to be very careful with invitations to discuss regional players. However, we have much to contribute. There is a growing awareness that our governments have been doing some heavy lifting in national security matters. There is an appreciation (as a result of some unwanted activity) that we play a substantial role in the intelligence community. As interest rises again in the broader US public about foreign policy we can only expect these welcome trends to continue.

This has been an essay that has focused on the activities of the Ambassador and embassy from a very functional point of view. That is appropriate because I am a functionary and this embassy is a relationship machine. It does not capture the spirit of the relationship, though this pervades all that we do. The Americans are our polar opposites. We Australians are pragmatic and pessimistic with well-calibrated low expectations. Americans are optimistic and idealistic. The different approaches are probably why we get on. The American approach means most regard us with overwhelming affection even if we are not troublesome enough in a troublesome area to get their undivided attention. A certain amount of foot stamping is necessary.

Our embassy was birthed in the revolutionary cauldron a war induces. Curtin's article of 27 December 1941 in the *Herald* included a revolutionary Australian statement: 'Australia looks to America, free of any pangs as to our traditional links or kinship with the United Kingdom.'[5] This would be of no note now; then it was an overturning of our national identity and by no means bipartisan. The Menzies Government, however, had prepared the ground for the implementation of its practicalities by extracting our representative from the British embassy in the US before Pearl Harbor.

There have been other revolutionary acts and statements of a nature that have redirected the character of Australian polity and society. The Deakin/Fisher governments' determination on an independent Australian war-fighting capability, followed by a separate World War I Australian Army Corps, Calwell's postwar immigration program, Holt's modification of the White Australia Policy (and its subsequent dismantling), the 1970s abandonment of sectarianism in Australian education and the High Court's Mabo judgement can be seen as others. Curtin's was done in extremity and its successful outcome has been an influencing spirit in the

---

5   John Curtin, *Herald*, 27 December 1941.

relationship ever since. Not all of us find this palatable and we are now very good at ensuring we maintain our national character and identity. That is easily seen for good or ill when you come across some of our one million fellow Australians overseas, as I do frequently.

One thing about the Americans is they do pay the price. As commander of our troops, Douglas MacArthur's stature rose in New Guinea and the islands before he cemented his reputation as a great commander in the Philippines with American forces near exclusively. The accompanying Leyte Gulf naval battle saw an 'allied' fleet engage the Japanese because there were Royal Australian Navy ships involved including the heavy cruiser HMAS *Australia*. MacArthur spoke for all Americans though on his first visit to Canberra in March 1942, when he elaborated his nation's military code:

> It embraces the things that are right, and condemns the things that are wrong. Under its banner the freemen of the world are united today. There can be no compromise. We shall win, or we shall die, and to this end I pledge to you the full resources of all the mighty power of my country, and all the blood of my countrymen.[6]

That put things pretty dramatically. Nevertheless, it is still of a piece with the way many Americans in their foreign policy/national security agencies speak to us. To understated Australians it can seem a tad excessive. It is genuinely felt and smart to encourage.

---

6   Gavin Long, *The Six Years War: Australia in the 1939–45 War*, the Australian War Memorial and the Australian Government Publishing Service, Canberra, 1973, p. 182.

Conclusion

David Lowe and David Lee

One of the difficulties for those seeking to identify the attributes most likely to bring success for an Australian diplomat in Washington is the diversity of those who have held the lead position of minister (before 1946) or ambassador. Such diversity and the varied circumstances behind choices suggests that Canberra has not been overly concerned to join with commentators in cultivating a distinctive ideal of what works best for the Australian Government in Washington. Or, at least, that governments have not acted on any ideal they may have. As the chapters in this volume show, for some time Australian governments chose their men in Washington (and it is noteworthy that in 2016 it remains the case that there have as yet been no women in the lead role) with domestic political considerations that were arguably ill-suited to the importance of the post, but common enough in other Western democracies and perhaps even more understandable during the infancy of Australia's professional diplomatic corps. Australian prime ministers have proven willing to institute major changes in Australia's overseas representation, including the Washington post, a disposition that was especially on display during the tenures of Gough Whitlam and his successor Malcolm Fraser.

None of the chapters in this book suggests that they chose poorly, nor do the writers here make a case for superior virtues of either political appointees or professional diplomats over the 75 years examined. Such were the opportunities for different forms of diplomatic building work in the Washington of the 1940s and 1950s that the different attributes Australian representatives brought to their post could be wielded effectively. The first, Richard Casey, has been described as a model diplomat, winning confidences and networking brilliantly with

Washington's policymaking elite in the early 1940s.[1] His successor, former Labor politician Norman Makin, was an abstemious man admired for his integrity, Methodism and cultivation of embassy morale, but who hated the cocktail circuit and was reluctant to engage on key policy issues. And Makin's successor, Percy Spender, former senior politician in the Liberal Party and Australia's most activist Ambassador, loved Washington parties as much as he loved the idea of being a second Australian Minister for External Affairs telling Canberra what to do. In other words, even among three early political appointees, the variability between ambassadors makes it clear that the professional/political line has limitations as a means of distinguishing the characteristics and performances of Australians in Washington. Similarly, during the turbulent years from the mid-1960s to early 1980s, Australia's ambassadors were the cream of the department's professional diplomats, including three former permanent secretaries, Sir James Plimsoll, Alan Renouf and Sir Nicholas Parkinson. Yet, their respective experiences varied hugely, with the consequences of withdrawal from Vietnam, searching questioning of the Australia, New Zealand, United States Security Treaty (ANZUS) and difficult dynamics between the two countries' leaders shifting the ground beneath their feet.

More recently, Kim Beazley, of course, was a former Labor Party leader. Before him were two senior public servants who were trained in External Affairs/Foreign Affairs and Trade: Michael Thawley, AO, and Dennis Richardson, AO. Before them was former Liberal Party leader, Andrew Peacock, AC. This pattern of two department-trained professionals and two former politicians was also reflected in the mix of Australia's ambassadors over the whole 75 years. Of the 20 different Australian Ambassadors to the United States during this time, 10 have been professional appointees, moving to Washington either directly from External Affairs/Department of Foreign Affairs and Trade (DFAT) or from another senior public service post, and 10 have been from beyond the career service: seven former politicians, one judge, one diplomatically experienced public servant, Frederic Eggleston, and one senior public servant, Don Russell, who emerged not from DFAT but Treasury prior

---

1   While we have counted Casey as one of the non-career appointees, on the basis of his having been an elected member of Australian Governments prior to his posting, he could also be said to represent professional diplomats, having served earlier and very successfully in the Foreign Office in London, before a professional Australian diplomatic service existed.

to his becoming principal adviser to Treasurer Paul Keating.[2] The recent appointment of Joe Hockey as Australia's current Ambassador to the US now puts political appointees in a very slight majority.

If there is an evenness in the balance of political/professional Australian appointees to Washington, then both categories have experienced both continuity and profound change in their roles, too. Among the themes to emerge from the 'Witness Seminar'[3] connected to this study was the rise of Congress as a focal point for Australian diplomats, and the relative decline in opportunities for meeting with Washington's most senior members of government. Instead of Percy Spender advancing Australia's interests in the 1950s over one of his semi-regular dinners with US Secretary of State, John Foster Dulles, today Ambassador Hockey might work hard to meet with a Congressional power-broker in relation to legislative measures affecting Australia's interests. Since the 1980s the ease with which ministers in Australian can and do communicate with their counterparts in Washington has also meant that Australian ambassadors are more routinely kept in the loop of exchanges indirectly rather than directly, but this has hardly seen a decline of work for the embassy. One of the more constant themes, as Beazley reminds us, is the importance of the embassy staff building structure alongside the policy foundations of ministers.

Still on the theme of continuity, face-to-face meetings, such an important means by which ambassadors gather information, formally and informally, and convey the views of Australian governments, remain grist to the diplomats' mill, but no guarantee of successful diplomacy. However many meetings in the 1960s Howard Beale and Keith Waller held with the most senior of the American establishment, including President Kennedy, they struggled to firm up a stronger American commitment to contingencies in Southeast Asia that would trigger the operation of the ANZUS Treaty. Some of the most uncomfortable meetings were those experienced by one of Australia's most experienced diplomats, James Plimsoll, who calmly endured the wrath of President Nixon and some of his advisers in the wake of Whitlam's public opposition to the Americans resuming their bombing of the Democratic Republic of Vietnam at the end of 1972, and then Whitlam's subsequent diplomatic recognition of the Democratic Republic.

2   This includes the three Ministers of the Legation between 1940 and 1946, Casey, Owen Dixon, and Frederic Eggleston.
3   See blogs.deakin.edu.au/contemporary-history-studies/witness-seminars/.

The ongoing work around the ANZUS Treaty has, not surprisingly, been a constant focal point for ambassadors, and something of a barometer of the Australia–US relationship more broadly, in the eyes of Australian representatives. Ambassador Parkinson astutely observed at the beginning of the 1980s that Australians were now dealing with a new generation of US leaders without strong memories of World War II and its aftermath, in which the foundations for ANZUS were laid. This made for especially testing times then in the mid-1980s for Ambassadors Cotton and Dalrymple, who helped steer the US Administration through the shock of New Zealand's leaving ANZUS, while preserving the Australia–US component. ANZUS was important in subsequent ambassadorial interventions: indirectly in the case of Michael Cook's facilitating the phone call from George HW Bush to Hawke in 1991 that saw the Australian Government commit armed forces to the Gulf War; and directly in the wake of the 9/11 terrorist attacks in 2001, when Michael Thawley appears to have been influential in encouraging Howard to invoke the ANZUS Treaty as Australia's response.

Parkinson was also alluding to the need for Australian officials to extend their influence beyond the US executive government, a trend we have noted above in relation to the focus on the US Congress, and this also reflected the persistence of thorny trade and tariff issues. Issues of trade and economics were often an irritant in Australia's relations with the US, especially after Australia's acceptance in 1942 of Article VII of the Mutual Aid Agreement. This agreement presaged Australian cooperation with the US in taking concerted action to expand international trade and to eliminate discriminatory treatment in international commerce. Australian policymakers reluctantly accepted the resulting limitations on longstanding imperial preferential arrangements with the United Kingdom. They were not, however, happy with Australia's treatment under the rules of the General Agreement on Tariffs and Trade (GATT) that came into force in 1948. While these rules worked to liberalise trade in manufactured goods, agricultural commodities – by far the majority of Australian exports until the early 1980s – were treated as an exception. This was graphically demonstrated in the early 1950s when the US was granted a waiver without time limit to exempt from GATT disciplines Section 22 of the US Agriculture Adjustment Act, which required the administration to impose quantitative import restrictions whenever agricultural imports interfered with a US farm program.

From the 1950s to the 1970s, Australian governments, and therefore ambassadors and the Australian embassy in Washington, were frequently at odds with the US over its methods of disposal of agricultural products, amounting to dumping in Australian eyes, its restrictions on Australian access to markets like beef and sugar, and its high tariffs on commodities like lead and zinc.

Over the same time period, however, American investment became increasingly important to Australia. North America's share of overseas investment increased from 32.6 per cent in 1959–60 to 42.8 per cent in 1964–65. This trend continued during the mining and resources boom of the second half of the 1960s and 1970s. The benefits of increasing US investment in Australia, however, were accompanied by an increasing public concern about the high level of foreign, and particularly American, ownership and control of Australian mineral resources such as coal and iron ore. On the US side, application of American law with extraterritorial reach to combat Australian mining companies participating in a worldwide uranium cartel involved much work by the Australian Government and its embassy in Washington in protecting the interests of Australian-based enterprises.

Disagreement between Australia and the US over issues of trade and economics reached its high point in the 1980s. The period from 1982 to 1985 was generally marked by a growing crisis in world trade in agriculture, a crisis that the US met by enacting the 1985 US Farm Bill to introduce direct subsidies on US agricultural exports for the first time in history. The Australian embassy, led by Rawdon Dalrymple and Michael Cook, was centrally involved in coordinating Australian opposition to US protectionism in agriculture in the second half of the 1980s and into the 1990s. Australia–US cooperation in the Uruguay Round of the GATT from 1986 to 1993 to reduce agricultural protectionism globally substantially eased friction over trade and economic issues from the mid-1990s onward. Australia–US collaboration of trade and economic issues was enhanced with the establishment of the Australian-led Asia-Pacific Economic Cooperation (APEC) in 1989 and by APEC economic leaders meetings from 1993.

Further steps were taken in the early 2000s to establish a bilateral framework for trade between Australia and the US. In 2005 the Australia–US Free Trade Agreement, negotiated by Prime Minister John Howard and the administration of George W Bush with the extensive involvement of Australia's diplomats in Washington, came into effect. While some have criticised the agreement for the worsening of Australia's trade deficit with the US, others have attributed that decline to the appreciation of the Australian dollar along with the China-inspired resources boom of the first decade of the 2000s. Issues of trade and economics have always been issues at the centre of the work of Australia's ambassadors and the embassy in Washington and are likely to remain so in the future.

Select bibliography

Abella, Alex, *Soldiers of Reason: The RAND Corporation and the Rise of the American Empire*, Harcourt, Orlando, 2008.

Albinski, Henry S, *Australian External Policy under Labor*, University of Queensland Press, Brisbane, 1977.

'Appointment of Ambassador to the United States', *Australian Foreign Affairs Record*, vol. 47, 1976, pp. 95–6.

Australia–United States Ministerial Consultation, *Joint Press Conference at the Conclusion of the AUSMIN Talks with Secretary of State Madeleine K. Albright, Secretary of Defense William Cohen, Australian Minister for Foreign Affairs Alexander Downer, and Australian Minister for Defence Ian McLachlan*, HMAS Watson, Sydney, 31 July 1998, dfat.gov. au/geo/united-states-of-america/ausmin/pages/ausmin-australia-united-states-ministerial-consultations.aspx.

'Australian Ambassador to US Presents Letters of Credence', *Australian Foreign Affairs Record*, vol. 45, March 1974, p. 183.

Ayers, Philip, *Owen Dixon*, Miegunyah Press, Melbourne, 2003.

Bader, Jeffrey A, *Obama and China's Rise: An Insider's Account of America's Asia Strategy*, Brookings Institution Press, Washington DC, 2014.

Baker, James A, 'America in Asia: Emerging Architecture for a Pacific Community', *Foreign Affairs*, vol. 70, no. 5, 1991/92, pp. 1–18.

Baker, James A, III, *The Politics of Diplomacy: Revolution, War and Peace, 1989–1992*, Putnam's Sons, New York, 1995.

Barclay, Glen, 'Australia and North America' in Peter John Boyce and Jim R Angel (eds), *Independence and Alliance: Australia in World Affairs 1976–80*, George Allen & Unwin, North Sydney, 1983.

Barclay, Glen St John, *Friends in High Places: Australian–American Diplomatic Relations since 1945*, Oxford University Press, Melbourne, 1985.

Barwick, Garfield, *A Radical Tory: Reflections and Recollections*, Federation Press, Sydney, 1996.

Beale, Howard, *This Inch of Time: Memoirs of Politics and Diplomacy*, Melbourne University Press, Melbourne, 1977.

Beaumont, Joan, 'The Champagne Trail? Australian Diplomats and the Overseas Mission', in Joan Beaumont, Christopher Waters, David Lowe with Garry Woodard (eds), *Ministers, Mandarins and Diplomats: Australian Foreign Policy Making, 1941–1969*, Melbourne University Press, Melbourne, 2003, pp. 153–85.

Bell, Coral (ed.), *Agenda for the Nineties: Australian Choices in Foreign and Defence Policy*, Longman Cheshire, Melbourne, 1991.

Bell, Coral, *Dependent Ally: A Study in Australian Foreign Policy*, Oxford University Press, Melbourne, 1988.

Bell, Roger, 'Reassessed: Australia's Relationship with the United States', in James Cotton and John Ravenhill (eds), *Seeking Asian Engagement: Australia in World Affairs 1991–95*, Oxford University Press/AIIA, Melbourne, 1997, pp. 207–229.

Bercovitch, Sacvan, *The American Jeremiad*, University of Wisconsin Press, Madison, Wisconsin, 1978.

Berry, Ken, *Cambodia – From Red to Blue: Australia's Initiative for Peace*, Allen & Unwin, Sydney, 1997.

Blewett, Neal, *Cabinet Diary*, Wakefield Press, Adelaide, 1999.

Blewett, Neal, 'No End to History? Thoughts on International Politics and Trade in the 1990s', *Australian Journal of International Affairs*, vol. 48, no. 1, 1994, pp. 25–35.

Bongiorno, Frank, '"British to the Bootstraps?": H.V. Evatt, J.B. Chifley and Australian Policy on Indian Membership of the Commonwealth, 1947–49', *Australian Historical Studies*, vol. 37, no. 125, 2005, pp. 18–39.

Bongiorno, Frank, 'John Beasley and the Postwar World', in Carl Bridge, David Lee and Frank Bongiorno (eds), *The High Commissioners, Australia's Representatives in the United Kingdom, 1910–2010*, Department of Foreign Affairs and Trade, Canberra, 2010, pp. 111–26.

Brett, Judith, *Australian Liberalism and the Moral Middle Class: From Alfred Deakin to John Howard*, Cambridge University Press, Melbourne, 2003.

Brett, Judith, *Robert Menzies' Forgotten People*, Pan Macmillan, Sydney, 1992.

Bridge, Carl (ed.), *A Delicate Mission: The Washington Diaries of R.G. Casey, 1940–42*, National Library of Australia, Canberra, 2008.

Bridge, Carl, 'Relations with the United States', in Carl Bridge and Bernard Attard (eds), *Between Empire and Nation, Australian Scholarly Publishing*, Melbourne, 2000, pp. 142–51.

Bridge, Carl, *William Hughes: Australia*, Haus Histories, London, 2011.

Bridge, Carl, Frank Bongiorno and David Lee (eds), *The High Commissioners: Australia's Representatives in the United Kingdom, 1910–2010*, WHH Publishing, Canberra, 2010.

Buckley, Ken, Barbara Dale and Wayne Reynolds, *Doc Evatt: Patriot, Internationalist, Fighter and Scholar*, Longman Cheshire, Melbourne, 1994.

Burke, Anthony, *Fear of Security: Australia's Invasion Anxiety*, Cambridge University Press, Melbourne, 2008.

Burnett, Alan, *The A-NZ-US Triangle*, Strategic and Defence Studies Centre, Research School of Pacific Studies, Australian National University, Canberra, 1988.

Burns, Kathleen, 'A Stranger in Paradise? A Foreign Correspondent's View of the Press Gallery', Papers on Parliament, no. 23, Australian Parliament House, Canberra, 1994.

Cain, Frank and Frank Farrell, 'Menzies' War on the Communist Party, 1949–1951', in Ann Curthoys and John Merritt (eds), *Society, Communism and Culture: Australia's First Cold War*, vol. 1, George Allen & Unwin, Sydney, 1984, pp. 109–34.

Camilleri, Joseph A, *Australian–American Relations: the Web of Dependence*, Macmillan, Melbourne, 1980.

Caro, Robert A, *The Years of Lyndon Johnson, vol. 2: Means of Ascent*, Random House, New York, 1990.

Casey, Maie, *Tides and Eddies*, Michael Joseph, London, 1966.

Casey, Richard G, *Australian Father and Son*, Collins, London, 1966.

Casey, Richard G, *Personal Experience, 1939–1946*, Constable, London, 1962.

Cawte, Alice, *Atomic Australia*, University of New South Wales Press, Sydney, 1992.

Chauvel, Richard, 'Up the Creek Without a Paddle: Australia, West New Guinea and the "Great and Powerful Friends"', in Frank Cain (ed.), *Menzies in War and Peace*, Allen & Unwin, Sydney, 1997, pp. 55–71.

Clarke, Richard, *Against All Enemies: Inside America's War on Terror*, Simon & Schuster, New York, 2004.

Clinton, Bill, *My Life*, Knopf, New York, 2004.

Coleman, William, Selwyn Cornish and Alf Hagger, *Giblin's Platoon: The Trials and Triumphs of the Economist in Australian Public Life*, ANU E Press, Canberra, 2006.

Cook, Ian, *Liberalism in Australia*, Oxford University Press, Melbourne, 1999.

Cook, Michael, 'The American Alliance and the Shaping of the World', *Quadrant*, vol. 58, no. 4, 2014, pp. 20–23.

Cook, Michael, 'ANZUS and the Monroe Doctrine', *Quadrant*, vol. 57, no. 12, 2013, pp. 20–22.

Cook, Michael, 'Why Australia Fights Other People's Wars', *Quadrant*, vol. 57, no. 9, 2013, pp. 48–54.

Cooper, Andrew F, Richard A Higgott and Kim Richard Nossal, *Relocating Middle Powers: Australia and Canada in a Changing World Order*, Melbourne University Press, Melbourne, 1993.

Cotton, James, 'Australia–America 2006–2010: Waiting for Obama', in James Cotton and John Ravenhill (eds), *Middle Power Dreaming: Australia in World Affairs 2006–2010*, Oxford University Press, Melbourne, 2012.

Cotton, James, *East Timor, Australia and Regional Order: Intervention and its Aftermath in Southeast Asia*, Routledge Curzon, London, 2004.

Cotton, James and John Ravenhill, 'Australia in World Affairs 1996–2000', in James Cotton & John Ravenhill (eds), *The National Interest in a Global Era: Australia in World Affairs 1996–2000*, Oxford University Press/AIIA, Melbourne, 2001.

Craig, Gordon, and Felix Gilbert (eds), *The Diplomats: 1919–1939*, Atheneum, New York, 1963.

Craig, Gordon, and Francis Loewenheim (eds), *The Diplomats, 1939–1979*, Princeton University Press, Princeton, 1994.

Craik, Wendy, 'Trade, Investment and Agricultural Issues', in William T Tow (ed.), *Australian–American Relations: Looking Toward the Next Century*, Macmillan/AIIA, Melbourne, 1998, pp. 206–14.

Crocker, Walter, *Australian Ambassador: International Relations at First Hand*, Melbourne University Press, Melbourne, 1971.

Curran, James, 'Cold War "Love Feast": The First US Presidential Visit to Australia, October 1966', in Joan Beaumont and Matthew Jordan (eds), *Australia and the World: A Festschrift for Neville Meaney*, Sydney University Press, Sydney, 2013, pp. 217–35.

Curran, James, *Unholy Fury: Whitlam and Nixon at War*, Melbourne University Press, Melbourne, 2015.

Davidson, James Wrightman, *Samoa mo Samoa: The Emergence of the Independent State of Western Samoa*, Oxford University Press, Melbourne, 1967.

Day, David (ed.), *Brave New World: Dr. H.V. Evatt and Australian Foreign Policy, 1941–1949*, University of Queensland Press, Brisbane, 1996.

Department of Foreign Affairs and Trade, *The United States–Japan Relationship and its Implications for Australia*, Australian Government Publishing Service, Canberra, 1994.

DFAT White Paper, *In the National Interest: Australia's Foreign and Trade Policy*, Department of Foreign Affairs and Trade, Canberra, 1997.

Doran, Stuart, 'Toeing the Line: Australia's Abandonment of "Traditional" West New Guinea Policy', *The Journal of Pacific History*, vol. 36, no. 1, 2001, pp. 5–18.

Doran, Stuart and David Lee (eds), *Australia and Recognition of the People's Republic of China 1949–72: Document on Australian Foreign Policy*, Department of Foreign Affairs and Trade, Canberra, 2002.

Dorling, Philip (ed.), *Documents on Australian Foreign Policy 1937–49, Volume XI: Indonesia 1947*, Australian Government Publishing Service, Canberra, 1994.

Dorling, Philip and David Lee (eds), *Documents on Australian Foreign Policy 1937–49, Volume XIII: Indonesia 1948*, Australian Government Publishing Service, Canberra, 1996.

Edwards, John, *Keating: The Inside Story*, Penguin Books, Melbourne, 1996.

Edwards, Peter, *Arthur Tange, Last of the Mandarins*, Allen & Unwin, Sydney, 2006.

Edwards, Peter, *Australia and the Vietnam War*, NewSouth Publishing, Sydney, 2014.

Edwards, Peter, *A Nation at War: Australian Politics, Society and Diplomacy During the Vietnam War*, Allen & Unwin and AWM, Sydney, 1997.

Edwards, Peter Geoffrey, *Australia Through American Eyes, 1935–1945: Observations by American Diplomats*, University of Queensland Press, Brisbane, 1979.

Edwards, Peter Geoffrey, *Prime Ministers and Diplomats: The Making of Australian Foreign Policy, 1901–1949*, Oxford University Press/AIIA, Melbourne, 1983.

Edwards, Peter Geoffrey, 'The Origins of the Cold War 1947–1949', in Carl Bridge (ed.), *Munich to Vietnam: Australia's Relations with Britain and the United States since the 1930s*, Melbourne University Press, Melbourne, 1991, pp. 70–86.

Edwards, Peter Geoffrey and Gregory Pemberton, *Crises and Commitments: The Politics and Diplomacy of Australia's Involvement in Southeast Asian Conflicts, 1948–1965*, Allen & Unwin, Sydney, 1992.

Encel, Sol, *Cabinet Government in Australia*, 2nd edn., Melbourne University Press, Melbourne, 1974.

Esthus, Raymond A, *From Enmity to Alliance: U.S.–Australian Relations, 1931–41*, University of Washington Press, Seattle, 1964.

Evans, Gareth, *Cooperating for Peace: The Global Agenda for the 1990s and Beyond*, Allen & Unwin, Sydney, 1993.

Evans, Gareth and Bruce Grant, *Australia's Foreign Relations in the World of the 1990s*, Melbourne University Press, Melbourne, 1991.

Fewster, Alan (ed.), *Trusty and Well-Beloved: A Life of Keith Officer, Australia's First Diplomat*, Miegunyah Press, Melbourne, 2009.

Fousek, John, *To Lead the Free World: American Nationalism and the Cultural Roots of the Cold War*, University of North Carolina Press, Chapel Hill NC, 2000.

Fruhling, Stephan (ed.), *A History of Australian Strategic Policy since 1945*, Defence Publishing Service, Canberra, 2009.

Gaddis, John Lewis, *Strategies of Containment: A Critical Appraisal of Postwar American National Security Policy*, Oxford University Press, New York, 1982.

Garnaut, Ross, *Australia and the Northeast Asian Ascendancy: Report to the Prime Minister and the Minister for Foreign Affairs and Trade*, Australian Government Publishing Service, Canberra, 1989.

Gillies, Donald, *Radical Diplomat: The Life of Archibald Clark Kerr, Lord Inverchapel, 1882–1951*, I.B. Tauris Publishers, London and New York, 1999.

Goldsworthy, David (ed.), *Facing North: A Century of Australian Engagement with Asia, vol. 1 1901 to the 1970s*, Melbourne University Press, Melbourne, 2001.

Goot, Murray & Rodney Tiffen (eds), *Australia's Gulf War*, Melbourne University Press, Melbourne, 1992.

Green, Marshall, *Pacific Encounters, Recollections and Humor*, DACOR-BACON House, Bethesda, Maryland, 1997.

Gray, Geoffrey, Doug Munro and Christine Winter (eds), *Scholars at War: Australasian Social Scientists, 1939–1945*, ANU E Press, Canberra, 2012.

Griffen-Foley, Bridget, "'The Kangaroo is coming into its own": R.G. Casey, Earl Newsom and Public Relations in the 1940s', *Australasian Journal of American Studies*, vol. 23, no. 2, 2004, pp. 1–20.

Gyngell, Allan and Michael Wesley, *Making Australian Foreign Policy*, Cambridge University Press, Cambridge, 2003.

Halberstam, David, *The Best and the Brightest*, Barrie and Jenkins, London, 1972.

Hamilton, Nigel, *The Mantle of Command: FDR at War, 1941–1942*, Houghton Mifflin Harcourt, Boston and New York, 2014.

Harper, Norman, *A Great and Powerful Friend: A Study of Australian–American Relations between 1900 and 1975*, University of Queensland Press, Brisbane, 1987.

Harris, Stuart and James Cotton (eds), *The End of the Cold War in Northeast Asia*, Longman Cheshire, Melbourne, 1991.

Harry, Ralph, *No Man is a Hero: Pioneers of Australian Diplomacy*, Arts Management, Sydney, 1997.

Hasluck, Paul, *The Chance of Politics*, with Nicholas Hasluck (ed.), Text Publishing, Melbourne, 1997.

Hasluck, Paul, *Diplomatic Witness: Australian Foreign Affairs, 1941–1947*, Melbourne University Press, Melbourne, 1980.

Hawke, Bob, *The Hawke Memoirs*, Mandarin Australia, Port Melbourne, 1996.

Hayden, Bill, *Hayden: An Autobiography*, Angus & Robertson, Sydney, 1996.

Hearder, Jeremy, *Jim Plim Ambassador Extraordinaire: A Biography of Sir James Plimsoll*, Connor Court Publishing, Ballarat, 2015.

Hensley, Gerald, *Friendly Fire: Nuclear Politics & the Collapse of ANZUS, 1984–1987*, Auckland University Press, Auckland, 2013.

Herring, George C, *From Colony to Superpower: US Foreign Policy since 1776*, Oxford University Press, New York, 2008.

Hiroyuki, Umetsu, 'Australia's Response to the Indochina Crisis of 1954 Amidst Anglo–American Confrontation', *Australian Journal of Politics and History*, vol. 52, no. 3, 2006, pp. 398–416.

Howard, John, *Commonwealth Parliamentary Debates: House of Representatives*, 39th Parliament, 3 June 1999, Canberra, p. 5990.

Howard, John, *Lazarus Rising: A Personal and Political Autobiography*, HarperCollins, Sydney, 2010.

Hudson, William James, *Casey*, Oxford University Press, Melbourne, 1986.

Hudson, William James (ed.), *Documents on Australian Foreign Policy 1944*, vol. VII, Department of Foreign Affairs and Trade, Canberra, 1988.

Hudson, William James, and Henry James William Stokes (eds), *Documents on Australian Foreign Policy 1937–1949*, vol. VI: July 1942–December 1943, Australian Government Publishing Service, Canberra, 1983.

Hudson, William James, and Wendy Way (eds), *Documents on Australian Foreign Policy 1937–49*, Volume X: July–December 1946, Australian Government Publishing Service, Canberra, 1993.

Hudson, William James, and Wendy Way (eds), *Documents on Australian Foreign Policy 1937–49*, Volume XII: 1947, Australian Government Publishing Service, Canberra, 1995.

Hudson, William James, and Wendy Way (eds), *Documents on Australian Foreign Policy 1945*, vol. VIII, Department of Foreign Affairs and Trade, Canberra, 1989.

Hughes, Adam H, 'Manufacturing Australian Foreign Policy 1950–1966', PhD Thesis, The Australian National University, Canberra, 2012.

Hunt, Michael H, *Ideology and US Foreign Policy*, Yale University Press, New Haven, 1989.

Inboden, William, *Religion and American Foreign Policy 1945–1960: The Soul of Containment*, Cambridge University Press, Cambridge, 2008.

Johnston, George H, *Pacific Partner*, Victor Gollancz, London, 1945.

Kandiah, Michael D (ed.), *The History, Role and Functions of the British High Commission in Canberra*, Foreign & Commonwealth Office, London 2013, retrieved 11 July 2015, issuu.com/fcohistorians/docs/Canberra_witness_seminar/13.

Kay, Robin (ed.), *The Australian–New Zealand Agreement 1944*, Historical Publications Branch: Department of Internal Affairs, Wellington, 1972.

Keating, Paul, *Engagement: Australia Faces the Asia-Pacific*, Pan Macmillan, Sydney, 2000.

Keefer, Edward C, David C Geyer, and Douglas E Selvage (eds), *Soviet–American Relations: The Détente Years 1969–1972*, Department of State Publications 11438, Washington DC, 2007, 15 November 1971–31 December 1971.

Kelly, Paul, *The Hawke Ascendancy*, Angus & Robertson, Sydney, 1984.

Kelly, Paul, *The March of the Patriots: The Struggle for Modern Australia*, Melbourne University Press, Melbourne, 2009.

Kennedy, David M, *Freedom from Fear: The America People in Depression and War, 1929–1945*, Oxford University Press, New York, 1999.

Kennedy, Paul, *The Rise and Fall of the Great Powers: Economic Change and Military Conflict from 1500–2000*, Unwin Hyman, London, 1988.

Kenyon, Don and David Lee, *The Struggle for Trade Liberalisation in Agriculture: Australia and the Cairns Group in the Uruguay Round*, Department of Foreign Affairs, Canberra, 2006.

Kimball, Warren F, *The Juggler: Franklin Roosevelt as Wartime Statesman*, Princeton University Press, Princeton, 1991.

Kimball, Warren F, *The Most Unsordid Act: Lend-Lease 1939–1941*, Johns Hopkins Press, Baltimore, 1969.

Langmore, Diane, *Glittering Surfaces: A Life of Maie Casey*, Allen & Unwin, Sydney, 1997.

Lee, David, 'Cabinet', in Scott Prasser, John Raymond Nethercote and John Warhurst (eds), *The Menzies Era: Reappraisal of Government, Politics and Policy*, Hale and Iremonger, Sydney, 1995, pp. 123–136.

Lee, David, 'The Origins of the Menzies Government's Policy on Indonesia's Confrontation of Malaysia', in Frank Cain (ed.), *Menzies in War and Peace*, Allen & Unwin, Sydney, 1997, pp. 72–98.

Lee, David, *Search for Security: The Political Economy of Australia's Postwar Foreign and Defence Policy*, Allen & Unwin in Association with the Department of International Relations, RSPAS, ANU, Sydney, 1995.

Lee, David, 'Shaw, Sir Patrick (1913–1975)', *Australian Dictionary of Biography* vol. 16, 1940–1980, Melbourne University Press, Carlton, 2002, pp. 220–21.

Lee, David and Moreen Dee, 'Southeast Asian Conflicts', in David Goldsworthy (ed.), *Facing North: A Century of Australian Engagement with Asia, vol. 1, 1901 to the 1970s*, Melbourne University Press, Melbourne, 2001, pp. 270–77.

Long, Gavin, *The Six Years War: Australia in the 1939–45 War*, The Australian War Memorial and the Australian Government Publishing Service, Canberra, 1973.

Lowe, David, 'Australia at the United Nations in th 1950s: The Paradox of Empire', *Australian Journal of International Affairs*, vol. 51, no. 2, 1997, pp. 171–81.

Lowe, David, *Australia Between Empires: The Life of Percy Spender*, Pickering and Chatto, London, 2010.

Lowe, David, 'Makin, Norman John (1889–1982)', Australian Dictionary of Biography, National Centre of Biography, The Australian National University, adb.anu.edu.au/biography/makin-norman-john-14673/text25810.

Lowe, David, 'Mr Spender Goes to Washington: An Australian Ambassador's Vision of Australian-American Relations, 1951–58', *Journal of Imperial and Commonwealth History*, vol. 24, no. 2, 1996, pp. 278–95.

Macintyre, Stuart, *The Poor Relation: A History of Social Sciences in Australia*, Melbourne University Press, Melbourne, 2010.

Mack, Andrew and John Ravenhill (eds), *Pacific Cooperation: Building Economic and Security Regimes in the Asia-Pacific Region*, Allen & Unwin, Sydney, 1994.

Makin, Norman, *The Memoirs of Norman John Oswald Makin*, H and L Makin, Mt Martha, 1982.

Makin, Norman John Oswald, *The Full Light: A Sermon preached at Foundry Methodist Church, Washington, DC, on Laymen's Day February 24, 1951*.

Malik, Mohan, 'Australia and China: Divergence and Convergence of Interests', in James Cotton and John Ravenhill (eds), *The National Interest in a Global Era: Australia in World Affairs 1996–2000*, Oxford University Press/AIIA, Melbourne, 2001, pp. 109–129.

Martin, Allan William with Patsy Hardy, *Robert Menzies: A Life, vol. 2, 1944–1978*, Melbourne University Press, Melbourne, 1999.

McLean, David, 'Australia in the Cold War: A Historiographical Review', *International History Review*, vol. XXIII, no. 2, 2001, pp. 299–321.

McLean, David, 'From British Colony to American Satellite? Australia and the USA during the Cold War', *Australian Journal of Politics and History*, vol. 52, no. 1, 2006, pp. 64–79.

McNamara, Robert S, *In Retrospect: The Tragedy and Lessons of Vietnam*, Vintage Books, New York, 1996.

McQueen, Humphrey, *Gallipoli to Petrov: Arguing with Australian History*, Allen & Unwin, Sydney, 1984.

Meaney, Neville, *The Search For Security in the Pacific, 1901–14*, Sydney University Press, Sydney, 1976.

Megaw, Ruth, 'Australia and the Anglo–American Trade Agreement, 1938', *Journal of Imperial and Commonwealth History*, vol. 3, no. 2, 1975, pp. 191–211.

Megaw, Ruth, 'Undiplomatic Channels: Australian Representation in the United States, 1918–39', *Historical Studies*, vol. 15, no. 60, 1973, pp. 610–30.

Millis, Walter (ed.), *The Forrestal Diaries*, The Viking Press, New York, 1951.

Mills, Charles Wright, *New Men of Power: America's Labor Leaders*, Harcourt, Brace and Co., New York, 1948.

Mills, Charles Wright, *The Power Elite*, Oxford University Press, New York, 1956.

Mills, Charles Wright, *White Collar: The American Middle Classes*, Oxford University Press, New York, 1956.

Ministry of Foreign Affairs of Japan, *The Japan–US Joint Declaration on Security- Alliance for the 21st Century*, 17 April 1996, www.mofa.go.jp/region/n-america/us/security/security.html.

Nixon, Richard M, *RN: The Memoirs of Richard Nixon*, Arrow Books, London, 1979.

Nossal, Kim Richard, 'Middle Power Diplomacy in the Changing Asia-Pacific Order: Australia and Canada Compared', in Richard Leaver and James L Richardson (eds), *The Post-Cold War Order: Diagnoses and Prognoses*, Allen & Unwin, Sydney, 1993, pp. 210–23.

Osmund, Warren G, *Frederic Eggleston: An Intellectual in Australian Politics*, George Allen & Unwin, Sydney, 1985.

Parkin, Russell and David Lee, *Great White Fleet to Coral Sea: Naval Strategy and the Development of Australian–United States Relations, 1900–1945*, Department of Foreign Affairs and Trade, Canberra, 2008.

Parliament of Australia, 'Don Russell: The Role of Executive Government in Australia', Papers on Parliament, no. 41, Canberra, December 2003, www.aph.gov.au/senate/~/~/link.aspx?_id=0C347E23897C4885BB8B 5E5875D21141&_z=z.

Pemberton, Gregory, *All The Way: Australia's Road to Vietnam*, Allen & Unwin, Sydney, 1987.

Pemberton, Gregory J, 'Australia and the United States', in Peter John Boyce and Jim R Angel (eds), *Diplomacy in the Marketplace: Australia in World Affairs, vol.7, 1981–90*, Longman Cheshire, Melbourne, 1992.

Pemberton, Gregory J, 'Australia, the United States and the Indo-China Crisis of 1954', *Diplomatic History*, vol. 13, no. 1, 1989, pp. 45–66.

Penders, Christiaan Lambert Maria, *The West New Guinea Debate: Dutch Decolonisation and Indonesia, 1945–1962*, University of Hawaii Press, Honolulu, 2002.

Porter, Robert, *Paul Hasluck: A Political Biography*, University of Western Australia Press, Perth, 1993.

Powaski, Ronal E, *Return to Armageddon: the United States and the Nuclear Arms Race 1981–1999*, Oxford University Press, New York, 2000.

Renouf, Alan, *The Champagne Trail: Experiences of a Diplomat*, Sun Books, Melbourne, 1980.

Renouf, Alan, *Let Justice Be Done: The Foreign Policy of Dr. H.V. Evatt*, University of Queensland Press, St Lucia, 1983.

Reynolds, David, *The Creation of the Anglo–American Alliance*, Europa, London, 1981.

Reynolds, Wayne, *Australia's Bid for the Atomic Bomb*, Melbourne University Press, Melbourne, 2000.

Robertson, John, *Australia at War 1939–1945*, Heinemann, Melbourne, 1981.

Russell, Don, 'Economic and Business Aspects: An Australian Perspective', in Jeffrey D McCausland, Douglas T Stuart, William T Tow and Michael Wesley (eds), *The Other Special Relationship: the United States and Australia at the Start of the 21st Century*, Army War College, Strategic Studies Institute, Carlisle, Pennsylvania, 2007, pp. 215–41.

Satake, Tomohiko, 'The Origins of Trilateralism? The US–Japan–Australia Security Relations in the 1990s', *International Relations of the Asia-Pacific*, vol. 11, no. 1, 2011, pp. 84–114.

Schedvin, Boris, *Emissaries of Trade: A History of the Australian Trade Commissioner Service*, Austrade and the Australian Department of Foreign Affairs and Trade, Commonwealth Government of Australia, Canberra, 2008.

Schlesinger, Arthur, Jr, 'The Measure of Diplomacy: What makes a Strategy grand?', *Foreign Affairs*, vol. 73, no. 4, 1994.

Sherwood, Jessica Holden, *Wealth, Whiteness and the Matrix of Privilege: The View from the Country Club*, Lexington Books, Lanham, 2012.

Smith, Gary, Dave Cox and Scott Burchill (eds), *Australia in the World: An Introduction to Australia's Foreign Relations*, Oxford University Press, Melbourne, 1996.

Spender, Jean, *Ambassador's Wife*, Angus and Robertson, Sydney, 1968.

'South Viet-Nam: Australian recognition', *Australian Foreign Affairs Record*, vol. 46, May 1975, p. 296.

Starr, Graeme, *Carrick: Principles, Politics and Policy*, Connor Court Publishing, Ballarat, Victoria, 2012.

Stubbs, John, *Hayden*, William Heinemann Australia, Port Melbourne, 1989.

Subritzky, John, *Confronting Sukarno: British, American, Australian and New Zealand Diplomacy in the Malaysian–Indonesian Confrontation, 1961–65*, St Martins Press, New York, 1997.

Tate, Audrey, *Fair Comment: A Life of Pat Jarrett, 1911–1990*, Melbourne University Press, Melbourne, 1996.

Terrill, Ross, *The Australians: In Search of an Identity*, Simon and Schuster, London, 1987.

Thorne, Christopher, *Allies of a Kind: The United States, Britain and the War Against Japan, 1941–1945*, Hamilton, London, 1978.

Toohey, Brian and William Pinwill, *Oyster: The Story of the Australian Secret Intelligence Service*, Heinemann, Melbourne, 1989.

Tow, William T, and Leisa Hay, 'Australia, the United States and a "China Growing Strong": Managing Conflict Avoidance', *Australian Journal of International Affairs*, vol. 55, no. 1, 2001, pp. 37–54.

Trood, Russell, 'The Australian–American Alliance: Beyond Demystification', in William Tow, Russell Trood and Toshiya Hoshino (eds), *Bilateralism in a Multilateral Era*, Japan Institute of International Affairs/Centre for the Study of Australia–Asia Relations, Tokyo, 1997, pp. 132–48.

United States Department of State, *Foreign Relations of the United States, 1946. The Near East and Africa*. Volume VII, US Government Printing Office, digital.library.wisc.edu/1711.dl/FRUS.FRUS1946v07.

United States Department of State, *Foreign Relations of the United States, 1947. The Far East*, Volume VI, US Government Printing Office, digital.library.wisc.edu/1711.dl/FRUS.FRUS1947v06.

United States Department of State, *Foreign Relations of the United States, 1948. The Far East and Australasia*, Volume VI, US Government Printing Office, digital.library.wisc.edu/1711.dl/FRUS.FRUS1948v06.

United States Department of State, *Foreign Relations of the United States, 1950. East Asia and the Pacific*, Volume VI, US Government Printing Office, digital.library.wisc.edu/1711.dl/FRUS.FRUS1950v06.

United States Department of State, *Foreign Relations of the United States, 1950. Korea* Volume VII, US Government Printing Office, digital.library.wisc.edu/1711.dl/FRUS.FRUS1950v07.

'Visit of Mr Whitlam to the United States', *Australian Foreign Affairs Record*, vol. 46, May 1975, p. 264.

Viviani, Nancy, 'Of Voices, Visions and Texts', in Greg Fry (ed.), *Australia's Regional Security*, Allen & Unwin, Sydney, 1991, pp. 22–31.

Waller, Keith, *A Diplomatic Life, Some Memories*, Centre for the Study of Australia–Asia Relations: Griffith University, 1990.

Waters, Christopher, '"Against the Tide": Australian Government Attitudes to Decolonisation in the South Pacific, 1962–1972', *The Journal of Pacific History*, vol. 48, no. 2, 2013, pp. 194–208.

Waters, Christopher, *The Empire Fractures: Anglo–Australian Conflict in the 1940s*, Australian Scholarly Publishing, Melbourne, 1995.

Watt, Alan, 'Australia and the Ambassadorial Issue', *Australian Quarterly*, vol. 36, no. 4, 1964, pp. 11–18.

Watt, Alan, *Australian Diplomat: Memoirs of Sir Alan Watt*, Angus and Robertson in association with The Australian Institute of International Affairs, Sydney, 1972.

Welfield, John, 'Australia's Relations with Japan and the Korean Peninsula', in Peter John Boyce and Jim R Angel, *Diplomacy in the Marketplace: Australia in World Affairs, vol. 7, 1981–90*, Longman Cheshire, Melbourne, 1992, pp. 253–68.

Weller, Patrick, *Cabinet Government in Australia, 1901–2006*, University of New South Wales Press, Sydney, 2007.

Whitlam, Edward Gough, 'Senior Diplomatic Appointments', *Current Notes*, vol. 44, September 1973, pp. 622–4.

Whitlam, Edward Gough, *The Whitlam Government*, Penguin, Melbourne, 1985.

Whitlam, Gough, *Abiding Interests*, University of Queensland Press, Brisbane, 1997.

Wiseman, Geoffrey, 'Australia and New Zealand: A Review of Their Contributions to Asia–Pacific Security', in Thomas Bruce Millar and James Walter (eds), *Asian-Pacific Security After the Cold War*, Allen & Unwin, Sydney, 1993, pp. 101–23.

Woodard, Garry, *Asian Alternatives: Australia's Vietnam Decision and Lessons on Going to War*, Melbourne University Press, Melbourne, 2004.

Woodard, Garry, 'Best Practice in Australian Foreign Policy: "Konfrontasi" (1963–66)', *Australian Journal of Political Science*, vol. 33, no. 1, 1998, pp. 83–93.

Woodward, Bob and Carl Bernstein, *The Final Days*, Simon and Schuster, New York, 1976.

Woolcott, Richard, *The Hot Seat: Reflections in Diplomacy from Stalin's Death to the Bali Bombings*, HarperCollins Publishers, Sydney, 2003.

Contributors

The Hon Kim Christian Beazley AC is President of the Australian Institute of International Affairs, Distinguished Fellow at the Australian Strategic Policy Institute, Senior Fellow at the Perth US Asia Centre and Board Member of the Australian American Leadership Dialogue. He was Australian Ambassador to the United States from 2010 to 2016. Having been elected to the federal Parliament in 1980, he was Special Minister of State (1983–84), Minister for Aviation (1983–84), Minister for Defence (1984–90), Vice-President of the Executive Council (1988–92), Minister for Transport and Communication (1990–91), Minister for Finance (1991), Minister for Employment, Education and Training (1991–93) and Minister for Finance (1993–96). He was Leader of the Opposition (1996–2001 and 2005–06). His publications include *The Politics of Intrusion: The Super Powers in the Indian Ocean* (1979).

Frank Bongiorno is Professor in History at The Australian National University and co-edited, with Carl Bridge and David Lee, *The High Commissioners: Australia's Representatives in the United Kingdom 1910–2010* (2010) for which he wrote the chapter on John Beasley. He has published on Australian foreign policy in the *Australian Journal of Politics and History*, *Australian Historical Studies* and *Irish Historical Studies* and is author or co-author of four books, including *The Eighties: The Decade that Transformed Australia* (2015). He has also edited the Australian Historical Association's journal, *History Australia*.

Carl Bridge FRHS is Professor of Australian Studies, King's College London. He taught in the History departments at Flinders and the University of New England before his appointment to his current position in 1997. He has held visiting fellowships at Churchill College and Clare Hall, Cambridge, the National Library of Australia, and the Australian Prime Ministers Centre, Canberra. His current research falls into four areas: the history of Australian diplomacy and defence; war and society in 20th-century Australia; Australian historiography; and the history of the British world. Among his many publications are as editor of *A Delicate Mission: the Wartime Diaries of R. G. Casey 1940–42* (2008) and as co-editor of *The High Commissioners: Australia's Representatives in the United Kingdom 1910–2010* (2010).

James Cotton FAIIA is Emeritus Professor of Politics, University of New South Wales, Australian Defence Force Academy. He was a Procter Fellow at Princeton University, and studied at the Beijing Language Institute. He was Australia Scholar at the Woodrow Wilson Center for International Scholars, Washington DC, 2009, and Harold White Fellow, National Library, 2013. Between 1997 and 2003, James Cotton was a foundation member of the Foreign Minister Alexander Downer's Advisory Council. He is a Fellow of the Royal Asiatic Society (London) and of the Australian Institute of International Affairs. His most recent books are *Middle Power Dreaming: Australia in World Affairs 2006–2010* (with John Ravenhill) (2012); *Australia and the United Nations* (2012) (with David Lee); and *The Australian School of International Relations* (2013). His current project is a work in the *Documents on Australian Foreign Policy* series covering the period 1920–36.

Peter Edwards AM FAIIA is an Adjunct Professor at Deakin University and has published extensively on the history of Australia's national security policies. His most recent book is *Australia and the Vietnam War* (2014). As the Official Historian of Australia's involvement in Southeast Asian conflicts 1948–75 (Malaya, Borneo and Vietnam), he was general editor of the nine-volume Official History and author of the volumes dealing with strategy and diplomacy, *Crises and Commitments* (1992) and *A Nation at War* (1997). He is also the author of *Arthur Tange: Last of the Mandarins* (2006), *Permanent Friends? Historical Reflections on the Australian-American Alliance* (2005), and *Prime Ministers and Diplomats* (1983); the editor of *Defence Policy-Making* (2008) and *Australia Through American Eyes* (1977); and one of the founding editors of the series of *Documents on Australian Foreign Policy*.

Jeremy Hearder is a graduate of the University of Melbourne and Stanford University. He spent 38 years in the Department of Foreign Affairs and Trade, which included serving overseas in Vientiane, Dar Es Salaam, Bangkok, Nairobi, Brussels, Harare (as High Commissioner), Suva (as High Commissioner), Chicago (as Consul General) and Wellington. Afterwards he became a part-time consultant in the department, and is the author of *Jim Plim: A Biography of Sir James Plimsoll* (2015).

Matthew Jordan is a senior historian in the Department of Foreign Affairs and Trade. He is the author of *A Spirit of True Learning: The Jubilee History of the University of New England* (2004) and co-editor with Joan Beaumont of *Australia and the World: A Festschrift for Neville Meaney* (2013). He is currently editing volumes on Australia and Southern Africa and preparing a major study of Australia and the White Australia Policy.

David Lee is Director of the Historical Publications and Research Unit of the Department of Foreign Affairs and Trade and General Editor of the *Documents on Australian Foreign Policy* series. He is co-author with Russell Parkin of *Great White Fleet to Coral Sea: Naval Strategy and the Development of Australia-United States Relations, 1900–1945* (2008) and author of *Stanley Melbourne Bruce: Australian Internationalist* (2010) and *The Second Rush: Mining and the Transformation of Australia* (2016).

David Lowe FASSA is Chair in Contemporary History, Deakin University. He is a co-founder of the Australian Policy and History network and a member of the Australian Department of Foreign Affairs and Trade Editorial Advisory Board, advising the Australian Foreign Minister with respect to the *Documents on Australian Foreign Policy* series. He has published on Australia's involvement in wars, including the Cold War, and on aspects of Australia's overseas policies after the Second World War. He has authored or co-authored four books: *Menzies and the Great World Struggle: Australia's Cold War 1948–1954* (1999); *Ministers, Mandarins and Diplomats: Australian Foreign Policy Making 1941–1969* (with Joan Beaumont, Chris Waters and Garry Woodard) (2003); *Australian Between Empires: the Life of Percy Spender* (2010); and, *Remembering the Cold War* (with Tony Joel) (2013).

Christopher Waters is an Associate Professor in Australian and international history at Deakin University. He has published widely on Australian international history, Australia's relationship with the United Kingdom and the decolonisation of the European Empires. He is the author of *The Empire Fractures: Anglo-Australian Conflict in the 1940s* (1995); joint editor *of Evatt to Evans: The Labor Tradition in Australian Foreign Policy* (1997); co-author with Joan Beaumont and David Lowe of *Ministers, Mandarins and Diplomats: Australian Foreign Policy Making 1941–1969* (2003); and author of *Australia and Appeasement: Imperial Foreign Policy and the Origins of the World War II* (2012).

Index

www.ingramcontent.com/pod-product-compliance
Lightning Source LLC
Chambersburg PA
CBHW050809270326
41926CB00036B/4597